Borderlands of Blindness

Disability in Society

Ronald J. Berger, series editor

Borderlands
of Blindness

Beth Omansky

LYNNE
RIENNER
PUBLISHERS

BOULDER
LONDON

Published in the United States of America in 2011 by
Lynne Rienner Publishers, Inc.
1800 30th Street, Boulder, Colorado 80301
www.rienner.com

and in the United Kingdom by
Lynne Rienner Publishers, Inc.
3 Henrietta Street, Covent Garden, London WC2E 8LU

Library of Congress Cataloging-in-Publication Data
Omansky, Beth.
   Borderlands of blindness / Beth Omansky.
      p. cm. — (Disability in society)
   Includes bibliographical references and index.
   ISBN 978-1-58826-780-1 (hardcover : alk. paper)
1. Disability studies. 2. Blind. I. Title.
   HV1593.O43 2011
   305.9'081—dc22
                                              2010041199

British Cataloguing in Publication Data
A Cataloguing in Publication record for this book
is available from the British Library.

Printed and bound in the United States of America

⊗   The paper used in this publication meets the requirements
       of the American National Standard for Permanence of
       Paper for Printed Library Materials Z39.48-1992.

5 4 3 2 1

To my father, Sid—
May his memory be a blessing

Contents

Part 4   Conclusion

Acknowledgments

I am blessed to have comrades, friends, teachers, and helpers who encourage, support, challenge, teach, entertain, prod, assist, mentor, listen, laugh, and cry with me—people who care about the research and about me. I am grateful to all who assisted me along the way; to you who inspire me to do the work; to you who live in the borderland between sightedness and blindness; and to you who have, by choice or by necessity, moved to a permanent territory.

I thank Karen Rosenblum for introducing me to social constructionism, which is the foundation of this work—for being an ally, a teacher, coauthor, and friend—and Roger Wilkins for being an astute and encouraging mentor, and for teaching me his three rules of writing. I am grateful to all my volunteer readers for the most precious gift they could give of themselves—time. Relationships with readers are unique, requiring trust, skill, patience, reliability, and compatibility with those to whom they read. When those relationships work, they are priceless.

I am thankful for Judith Beyer, Joanne Mikell, "Tucson" Bob Thomas, Nathan Say, Stephanie Bailey, Sandi Riley, and Jeff Alpert for all the reasons they already know. I am grateful to Mike Oliver for paving the way for the rest of us, for welcoming me into disability studies, and for treating me like a peer. I am deeply indebted to him both personally and professionally, and I keep his model of integrity and steadfastness in mind as I pursue my own work. I am especially grateful to Mark Sherry, my colleague and friend, for helping me craft the conceptual framework of the study, for challenging me to examine "more complex" ideas in new ways, and for encouraging me to persevere on days when I thought the task at hand was impossible. He is a true scholar, ally, friend, and comrade.

I appreciate my editor at Lynne Rienner Publishers, Andrew Berzanskis, for believing in the work, for understanding my intent, for gently suggesting ways to improve the construction of the book. Thank you to Sonia Smith and Shena Redmond, also at Lynne Rienner Publishers, for their expert attention to detail.

I treasure the memory of my friend and advocacy partner, Michael Malinowski, who died while advocating for the cause.

To my true companion, Moses, I am grateful for everything.

Most of all, I want to thank the research participants—Larry, Catherine, and J. R.—for their openness and sincerity; for their keen observations; for being patient with the length of the project; and for their shared stories, which will make a difference to those who either identify with or learn from their lived experience.

A section of the chapter on language previously appeared in an earlier form in the *New Zealand Journal of Disability Studies*, 2006, vol. 12, pp. 203–207. Portions of the discussions of the history of and statistics about blindness previously appeared in the *Encyclopedia of Disability 1* (Thousand Oaks, CA: Sage, 2006), pp. 185–193. Portions of the participants' stories appeared in a different form in my chapter "Not Blind Enough" in Karen Rosenblum and Toni-Michelle C. Travis, eds., *The Meaning of Difference: American Constructions of Race, Sex and Gender, Social Class and Sexual Orientation* (New York: McGraw-Hill, 2003), pp. 326–332.

1

Introduction

It is no measure of health to be well adjusted to a
profoundly sick society.
                                    —Krishnamurti

We placed a hand on the shoulder in front of us and were led
single file down a dark hallway. When the floor's angle suddenly
shifted, changing in texture as well, I was thrown off balance, physically and emotionally. We had entered the Portland Blind Cafe, an
event promoted as "a mind bending/heart opening experience
where the audience will dine and enjoy a concert in the pitch
dark"—where we would "discuss issues related to visual impairment, celebrate and explore spatial awareness, indulge in unencumbered music listening (without distraction of visual conditioning)."

I felt a little panicked and wondered whatever possessed me to
voluntarily plunge myself into total darkness. People around me
laughed nervously or murmured similar sentiments.

"I don't want to do this."

"Can we turn around now?"

"I'm not so sure about this."

"Where are we?"

We stopped. Apparently there was a "logjam" at the front of our
line. This gave me a chance to get a more solid footing and take a
couple of deep breaths.

Finally, blind wait staff guided us to our tables in the main dining area. At the same moment my hand traced the corner of my
table, I heard my friend Emily's voice disappearing away into the
darkness. Alarmed, I felt like we were falling off opposite sides of a
raft. I called out, "Emily! We're getting separated," and to the
waiter, "She's my friend. You're separating us. Don't do that!" The

1

waiter responded with great calm, and somehow managed to arrange us next to each other. Now we knew the shape of our table but we still didn't know anything about the larger space. Big auditorium? Small room? How many tables? Where were we in relation to everything else?

We awkwardly located utensils, paper plates, and covered glasses of water with straws. We passed around the family-style bowls of chilled quinoa with broccoli and chopped ginger, and bite-size fresh melon chunks with red onions. We were hesitant at first, but it didn't take long for us to adopt verbal strategies and physical cues with our new tablemates. The person across from Emily said, "Here is a bowl of . . . maybe couscous? Not sure." Emily spooned some on her plate, then leaned in toward me, saying, "Here's the bowl," I scooped a portion onto my plate, not knowing if I had too little or too much because I didn't know the size of the spoon head. I gently elbowed the woman to my left and held the bowl until I could feel she had a good grasp on it. A tablemate announced she found a sticky vegetable roll already resting on her plate, so I ran my left hand across my plate to find mine, and tentatively picked it up with my right. The roll started to unravel but I managed to secure it with my fingers, albeit a bit sloppily. More to myself than to anyone else, I said, "I found mine! But it's falling apart. Ooops. . . ."

The mutual discovery of the sticky rolls bonded us somehow, and we introduced ourselves all around. I relaxed; I could handle the pure blackness for the next two and a half hours.

"Are you guys doing all right? Need anything?" The waiters moved noiselessly and flawlessly through the dark space, their disembodied voices surprising us with each kind query. There is no way I could have moved around that room without bumping into tables, chairs, people, or knocking things over. I couldn't tell if the wait staff carried trays or brought items one or two at a time. However they did it, I was impressed by their ability to navigate in the total dark.

Our new custom of passing bowls, describing their contents, and elbowing neighbors to pass again continued easily until, as often happens at family-style meals, all the bowls inadvertently ended up resting in front of one person. We were full.

A woman seated across from me remarked, "I'm getting comfortable not seeing. I notice I keep closing my eyes. I don't know why since it doesn't matter." Others agreed. Someone else said, "I'm doing okay without my eyesight right now, but then again, I haven't tried moving around."

Another voice from somewhere else in the room began speaking. He said his name was Gerry, and that he came from Boulder, Colorado, just for this event. He said he has plastic eyes, and has never had sight. Gerry told us how he became a coffee roaster and café owner. Two more blind people shared their stories, another recited poetry, and an acoustic string group performed music that perfectly fit the ambience—dark, moody, and nurturing all at once.

When they were done, and the wait staff had served us individual bowls of dark chocolate mousse with plump, fresh blueberries folded throughout, I seized the opportunity to ask my tablemates the question that had been gnawing at me all evening.

"Is anyone at the table blind?"

"No," they each responded.

"I am," I said. I had dropped the blindness bomb.

"Can you see anything?"

"Yes. I am legally blind."

Everyone fell silent. That I was legally blind, yet retained some vision—unlike the "blind" experience of total darkness that we were sharing—took a moment to process. Then, the questions spilled out.

"What does that mean?"

"Would you be able to see my face?"

"What is being here like for you?"

"I am as much a stranger to the darkness as you all. This event is not how I experience blindness."

"What can't you see?"

"I don't know. I can't see it."

We all laughed. By then, the couple to the left of me excused themselves and left. Emily and I felt our way to their vacated chairs to be closer to a couple of women to continue our conversation about their filmmaking, about blindness, about borderlands, about identities.

In retrospect, I enjoyed the food, company, poetry, and the music. But the evening left me wondering: what did participants learn about blindness? It heartened me to find people interested in trying out blindness. But I wondered if sitting in the dark for two hours teaches a sighted person as much about blindness as, perhaps, playing a game of Monopoly teaches you about the experience of being Donald Trump. Which is not to dismiss the experience completely; the event did acquaint sighted people with a few aspects of blindness and I hope that it will pique further interest—but it lacks a social context, does not present skills acquisition, and cannot provide experience over time. Specifically, an event like this offers no knowledge about institutionalized oppression; barriers in the built environment, including technology, signage, and inaccessible public transit; or joblessness due to employer prejudice about what blind people can or cannot do.

In any case, total darkness is not my lived experience as a legally blind person nor is it that of the majority of blind people since most have residual, usable vision. I just didn't want the sighted guests to leave with an incorrect idea—a stereotype—about what the lived experience of blindness is. And even more, I hoped I wasn't an inadvertent party to a "freak show"—a circus-like spectacle of human oddity on display for others' curiosity and amusement (Adams 2001; Bogden 1988).

(Here, I should note that I contacted the event organizers afterward. They were very responsive to my concerns and are exploring ways to appropriately enhance the educational value of future Blind Cafe events.)

This book is my chance to present a more complete understanding of the diverse lived experience of blindness. Usually, books and other media representations of blindness portray the phenomenon as a world of complete darkness, like what we encountered at the Blind Cafe. A false binary of sightedness/blindness pervades every aspect of society, including medicine, education, the workplace, the built environment, religion, and personal attitudes and beliefs. This book explores the most common lived experience of blindness—an unfixed borderland within which legally blind participants describe a richer, deeper, more confounding existence than society typically apprehends.

Throughout recorded history, the eyes and the sense of sight—of looking and seeing, of vision and blindness—have been a fascination for artists and scientists alike. Writings about blindness as symbolic of human traits and action, or as a sign of divine intervention, are found across many cultures and societies and date back to ancient times.

Totally blind people fall into a discrete stereotyped classification of blindness as darkness, which, in many ways, is comforting to sighted people because they do not have to guess what the blind person can or cannot see. However, when interacting with legal blindness, sighted people often try to relieve their own dubiety by pressing borderland blind people to choose one side or the other—usually pushing them into the socially preferred land of the sighted—a land in which they experience egregious inequality. Gloria Anzaldúa (1987, p. 3) describes "borderland" as "a vague and undetermined place created by the emotional residue of an unnatural boundary." Such is the case with "legal blindness."

Blind people are treated differently *because* of their blindness—they face environmental, economic, social, attitudinal, and educational barriers. This may be particularly problematic for legally blind people whose families, friends, and potential employers are most likely confused about what a legally blind person can actually see or not see. Because legal blindness is abundantly ambiguous, the sighted might fail to apprehend how legally blind people make sense of the physical world; what is more, they feel tentative about how to treat blind people or even to trust that those who claim the legally and medically constructed identity of legal blindness are, in fact, blind. Unlike totally blind people, borderland blind people are often accused of fraud because they act too sighted. John Hull (1990, pp. 67–69) describes this social phenomenon in a journal entry titled, "You Bastard! You're Not Blind!" Hull tells of a passerby repeatedly yelling at him, insisting that he was not *really* blind.

People who fit the criteria of the medically constructed category of *legal blindness* have idiosyncratic phenomenological and sociocultural experiences that are vastly different from those of either sighted or totally blind people. Borderland blind people are subjected to pressures that totally blind people do not endure; they are pushed and pulled back and forth across the border between sightedness and blindness, resulting in disallowance of citizenship in both lands, which leaves them in a state of what American pacifist civil rights leader, Bayard Rustin, aptly called "social dislocation" (D'Emilio 2004).

Borderland blind people are vulnerable to attempted regulation by disquieted but well-meaning acquaintances, friends, and family, who yearn for their loved one to be "normal." In reaction, borderland blind people might internally monitor and regulate their own behavior or else succumb to external pressures as they try to "pass"—to be perceived by others as sighted, even during times when they clearly reside on the blind side of the pale. The dynamics of such interactions press everyone concerned into denial (French 1993).

Uncomfortable with the contradictions of "border" behavior, a companion requested that Larry, a legally blind participant in this study, refrain from reading the newspaper in restaurants with his guide dog at his side because it would "confuse" sighted restaurant-goers and give them false impressions of what blindness is. Perhaps she was afraid observers would disbelieve Larry's claim of blindness, and by association, this might reflect on her own character.

While totally blind people have no choice about hiding their blindness, legally blind people can make situational decisions about when to "pass" and when to "come out in order to have their environmental access, material, and psycho-emotional needs met at all levels—societal, interpersonal, and personal" (Omansky Gordon and Rosenblum 2001). Thus, legally blind people experience the borderland in both their external and internal existence. In casual conversation with several of my acquaintances who became totally blind from degenerative eye diseases, some mentioned that total blindness is easier for them in some regard because things are more definite, they do not experience the ambiguities of societal misunderstanding, and they no longer feel pressure to assimilate into the sighted world.

Legally blind people experience social pressure to be "sighted," to explain their eye condition to passersby, to answer the same questions over and over again about what they can or cannot see, or even to defend their "blindness" identity. When people mistakenly believe that to be blind one must see only blackness, they think legally blind people fraudulently claim to be blind. Legally blind people often see well enough to witness onlookers staring at them when they use a white cane, guide dog, or low vision aids. On top of ongoing societal pressures, legally blind people may use low vision aids such as magnifiers, computers with screen magnification, sunglasses designed to help lessen the pain often caused by photophobia (intolerance to light associated with some eye diseases), and eyeglasses that require the user to hold objects one or two inches from the face. Chronic neck and back pain and extreme eye fatigue are common side effects of the use of these aids, as well as the ongoing physical stress of straining to see during activities of daily living. Such persistent social pressures and body pain are physically and emotionally draining.

Legally blind people face choices about trading their personal privacy for access to the material world. Both sighted and totally blind people often misunderstand and misrepresent legally blind people because of preconceived expectations that they can do more or less than is actually physically possible. This may be especially problematic for people living with progressively degenerative eye diseases in their relationships with family, friends, and employers. Some people experience conditions, such as multiple sclerosis, that create transient blindness, or eye diseases that create wildly fluctuating vision from day to day, in different lighting situations, or during different seasons when the relationship between shadow and light shifts. Therefore, they are eligible for services or social privileges one day and not the next, which results in them having to confront "border guards" on both sides of the fence between blindness and sightedness.

Unlike totally blind people, legally blind people grapple with institutional regulations that deny them some social privileges, yet they still fail to qualify for blindness services or benefits. For example, someone who is denied a driver's license based on failing the Department of Motor Vehicle's vision test may then be turned down for disability discounts on public transportation by their local public transit authority because the two agencies have conflicting policies about legal blindness (Gregory 2004; Omansky Gordon and Rosenblum 2001). Making one's way through barriers and roadblocks in the borderland can be extraordinarily difficult and troublesome.

What is more, legally blind people often fall through the cracks of educational institution policy by not receiving accommodations and training that are unquestioningly offered to totally blind people, such as braille instruction, orientation and mobility training, access technology, or information and referral to blindness resources. Strained by limited financial and human resources, agencies for the blind are directed to serve the most "severely disabled"; hence, totally blind people receive services, while legally blind people are categorized as less severely disabled and then placed at the bottom of service provision waiting lists.

Nowadays, blindness is framed as a major public health problem, which is addressed by health, economic, and charitable organizations, and by governments at international, national, state, and local levels. Modern medicine has constructed specific definitions of blindness and visual impairment in which to arrange data collection, research findings, and public policy.

Purpose of the Book

This book examines the experience of legal blindness in a unique way, cross-fertilizing the best elements of an American cultural studies approach with a British social model of disability. Lumping legally blind and totally blind people into the same studies harms medical model–based blindness research in that it tends to ignore these critical differences. Moreover, such positivistic research typically designs survey instruments that assume in advance what is important to know about blindness and blind people; hence, researchers maintain unequal power relations over their subjects and may miss central aspects of the blindness experience. As evidenced by a lack of research designed to learn what legally blind people want to say about themselves, medical model research has failed to express interest in these matters, and so legally blind people's stories have mostly gone untold (with the exception of blindness memoirs as a genre).

As one means of redress, in this study I used emancipatory disability research principles and postmodern theories to analyze the stories, and thus I sought to maintain equal power relations between the researcher and the researched. In this research monograph, participants told their stories in their own words, they chose what was important for us to know about them, and they maintained control over their stories throughout the research and writing processes.

I am interested in how society treats blind people and what meaning blind people make of such treatment. Furthermore, with this disability studies research I strayed from orthodox disability studies research in that I wanted to learn and record the embodied experience of legal blindness as well as issues of blindness identity formation. Using postmodern methods of analysis, these aspects were not framed within a medical model, even though they are related to impairment; instead, they were analyzed within a social model of disability.

In Chapters 2–4, I set the scene for the study by laying out my methodology, and the participants introduce themselves. The next few chapters take up the issue of ocularcentrism in a political economy: Chapter 5 on education, Chapter 6 on the perils of rehabilitation, and Chapter 7 on work. The next section addresses social life outside, inside, and across borders: Chapter 8 on social constructions of blindness, Chapter 9 on being blind from the inside out, and Chapter 10 on identity. Finally, I share my thoughts on inter-sections along the border in Chapter 11, and in Chapter 12, the participants conclude the study by sharing their own continuing experiences.

Intersections of Postmodernism, Social Constructionism, and Disability Studies

Over the past twenty-five years, the emergence of disability studies as a distinct and respected academic discipline has been remarkable in its growth and its influence on academia worldwide. In this sec-tion, I trace some of these developments and argue that both post-modernism and social constructionism laid the foundation upon which disability studies is building its discourse of difference.

The nature and attributions of postmodernism, social construc-tionism, and disability studies demonstrate many intersections, including rejection of traditional science, and "a questioning of the modern idea of progress, official forms of knowledge, expertise and 'paper qualifications'" (Ross 1988, p. xiv; Luke 1989c; Melucci 1990, all cited in Rosenau 1992).

Concerning blindness, some scholars apply postmodern princi-ples by rejecting the medical model, deconstructing blindness, and reconceptualizing it as a "natural" bodily experience whose negative aspects are socially constructed. As Moshe Barasch (2001, p. 3) points out, blindness is as natural a phenomenon as sight:

> Blindness itself is, of course, a natural condition. . . . (It goes with-out saying that the rapidly changing developments in the medical treatment of blindness are not part of the condition itself.) . . . Our understanding of blindness, our views concerning its "mean-ing," are matters of culture.

It is important to note, however, that while the etiology of vision loss manifests as "natural"—a condition that is the result of biolog-ical processes—"blindness" and "sight" are culturally constructed in similar subjective ways that "sex," "race," and "gender" are; such categorization presumes a nature/culture binary, which is itself an interpretive cultural distinction.

Characteristics of Postmodernism and Social Constructionism

Postmodernism

Postmodernism, a twentieth-century political, art, and literary theory advanced by the social sciences, posits: "Instead of single sets of values or political loyalties [as modernism asserts], there is a wide variety of groups and classes, aims and ideologies" (Bothamley 1993, p. 424).

Postmodern social scientists have shifted their reliance on goals, choices, behaviors, and attitudes (Potter and Wetherell 1987), instead, directing attention to

> what has been taken for granted, what has been neglected, regions of resistance, the forgotten, the irrational, the insignificant, the repressed, the borderline, the classical, the sacred, the traditional, the eccentric, the sublimated, the subjugated, the rejected, the non-essential, the marginal, the peripheral, the excluded, the tenuous, the silenced, the accidental, the dispersed, the disqualified, the deferred, the disjointed. (Rosenau 1992, p. 8)

Postmodern social scientists problematize the idea that "evidence" is an empirically valid concept; therefore they prefer alternatives to such traditional scientific methods when conducting and reporting research. Rosenau (1992) asserts that modernists search for elemental aspects of whatever they examine, detail relationships between these elements, and draw generalizations. In contrast to modernism, postmodernists prefer indeterminacy and diversity, and they honor difference, looking for "complexity rather than simplification" (Rosenau 1992, p. 8). Unlike modernists, they are not particularly interested in either causality or repeatable experiments. Postmodernism's "confidence in emotion" (Rosenau 1992, p. 8) is highly congruent with the aims and goals of life story research and disability studies.

In *Researching Life Stories: Method, Theory, and Analyses in a Biographical Age*, Goodley et al. (2004) assert that "expert discourses are being challenged by exposing their narrative construction" (p. ix). Disability studies as a discipline scrutinizes how medical narratives of impairment and disability are socially constructed through examination, diagnosis, treatment, and prognosis.

Social Constructionism

According to Gonzales, Biever, and Gardner (1994), social constructionist theory

1. Views meanings and understandings of the world as developed through social interaction;
2. States that those constructions of meaning are derived from the social context;
3. Places knowledge of the world—reality—within the process of social interchange;
4. Emphasizes the social nature of understanding, with knowledge of the self and emotional experience also evolving from such interchanges;
5. Views language as the primary vehicle for the transmission of such meanings and understandings;
6. Views actions and behaviors as secondary vehicles of social interaction, since some language or unspoken understanding has to precede the initiation of most meaningful acts;
7. Considers the social origins of taken-for-granted assumptions about psychological processes, which can differ markedly from one culture to another; and
8. Recognizes that historical contexts can play a significant role in how our interactional experience is constructed.

Social constructionist analysis can therefore be aptly applied to the experience of legal blindness for several reasons. First, "legal blindness" is a socially (medically, legally, and attitudinally) constructed category of impairment. Second, society perceives legal blindness as pathology rather than difference. Third, blindness is culturally constructed across time and geography, having different meanings in different ages and cultures. Lastly, linguistic constructions, such as metaphor and medical and legal terminology, help define and express how society thinks about blindness.

Conversely, medicine takes an essentialist approach to blindness, since it thinks of blindness solely as a physiological condition with its locus in the eyeballs and relevant neuronal paths to the brain. Medicine perceives blindness as an *essential* experience directly relational to ocular dysfunction. Rosenblum and Travis

(2003, p. 3) explain differences between essentialism and social constructionism:

> While the essentialist presumes an external world with distinct categories existing independent of observation, the constructionist argues that reality cannot be separated from the way that a culture makes sense of it. From the constructionist perspective, *social processes* determine that one set of differences is more important than another. . . . The constructionist assumes that "essential" similarities are conferred and created rather than intrinsic to the phenomenon. . . . The way that a society identifies its members tells us more about the society than about the individual so classified.

The essentialism/constructionism debate is a key feature used in feminist theory to examine sex, gender, and sexual orientation, and several disability studies scholars have utilized this earlier work to help make sense of social constructions of impairment, disablement, and disability. However, blindness scholars, including feminist disability studies scholars, have rarely applied social constructionist theory to examine sexuality and blindness. This is a significant gap in the literature and does nothing to dispel societal stereotypes of blind people as asexual. White (2003) relies on an interdisciplinary approach that utilizes queer and feminist theory, disability studies, and blindness literature to examine the social construction of blindness as a heterosexual experience. He critiques the social construction of heterosexuality in sex education for young blind people, inquiring into dominant beliefs that construct sexuality as a visual process and how this frames young blind people as sexually underdeveloped. He writes, "Blind people are in a sense queer, in that heterosexuality, at least in its institutionalized forms, presumes a sighted subject" (White 2003, p. 134). Hence, blind children are presumed to fall into two statuses—heterosexual and sighted—either of which may be relevant (or not) to each individual. As will be discussed in Chapter 5, blindness education has been, and is still, dominated by sighted values, by sighted people.

One cannot get a complete story of blindness without examining its phenomenological aspects based upon features of *embodiment*. For the most part, disability studies has chosen to reject essentialism, opting instead to concentrate on social, material, and cultural factors. While I used social constructionism as a primary method of analysis, I simultaneously challenged the binary of essentialism/social constructionism because impairment, disablement, and disability are complex and do not all fit into either stance. The experience of impairment is integral to understanding the lived experience of blindness; therefore, I departed from the orthodoxy of traditional disability studies, which fails to address directly how impairment has significant effects on the everyday lives of blind people.

Bridging the Gap

While ideas are not always disparate along geographical boundaries, the US model of disability studies is characterized largely by attention to cultural constructions of disability and an exploration of phenomenology, whereas the British model, with its Marxist orientation, emphasizes materialist factors and draws a clear line between *impairment* and *disability*. The British social model has been criticized for its lack of attention to phenomenology (Hughes and Paterson 1999) and for its underestimation of the importance of culture in the processes of disablement (Shakespeare 1994; Riddell and Watson 2003). Conversely, American works have been criticized for a lack of a materialist perspective (Barnes 1999a). However, noted British scholars Tom Shakespeare (1994), Carol Thomas (1999), and the late Mairian Corker (aka Mairian Scott-Hill) and Sally French (1999) found fault with strictly materialist disability studies for its inattention to cultural factors. Shakespeare (1994) writes:

> If the social model analysis seeks to ignore, rather than explore, the individual experiences of impairment (be it blindness, short stature or whatever), then it is unsurprising that it should also gloss over cultural representation of impairment, because to do otherwise would be to potentially undermine the [materialist] argument. (pp. 283–284)

This book attempts to bridge the American and British paradigms by exploring the concomitance of both material *and* sociocultural factors in the disablement of blind people.

Reconceptualizing Impairment, Disablement, and Disability

Disability studies literature generally concentrates *either* on impairment or disability, but not both. The distinctions between impairment and disability are perplexing because many times authors use these terms interchangeably. Such conceptual obfuscation can cause confusion and linguistic chaos; it is problematic to grasp theoretical concepts when key terms such as *disability* and *impairment* are used in inconsistent or ambiguous ways. Of course, much of this indistinctness can be attributed to the complex forces that create master statuses; thus, disability language is reflective of larger social questions about the meaning of the lived experience of impairment, disability, and disablement. Words are often carefully chosen to represent particular theoretical or political stances.

In what is frequently considered the seminal book in disability studies, *The Politics of Disablement*, Oliver (1990) coined the term *disablement* to describe disabling social processes, but in subsequent works, he opted to use *disability* instead. This type of word-switching causes confusion both within and outside of the organized disability community. Ongoing discussions, dissent, and confusion occur within the disability community about what terminology to use to describe and interpret various aspects of the disability experience.

Language Confusion and Lack of Consensus

One way disabled people pay a high price for indecision and inconsistency is that we fail to understand each other because we use terms interchangeably that have opposite meanings. For example, how do we know what a person means when they call an *impairment* a *disability* or use both words interchangeably? Is the person discussing a biologically based condition or a social barrier? Moreover, because the disability community doesn't agree about how to say what we mean when we describe our individual and social conditions, the nondisabled community becomes befuddled about what to say to disabled people, and so may distance themselves to avoid discomfort.

While language cannot solely account for the historical legacy of discrimination and segregation disabled people have experienced for many generations in many societies, it may, indeed, contribute to lack of interaction between disabled and nondisabled people. This may be especially true for nondisabled people exposed to "disability etiquette" who find the language issue daunting in interpersonal exchanges with disabled people.

Sorting It Out

Impairment is most often understood to mean the physical, cognitive, emotional, or sensory condition within the person as diagnosed by medical professionals. *Disability* is used to describe social, economic, political, and cultural processes that produce oppression and stigma experienced by people with impairments. *Impairment* is located inside the person, while *disability* is externally situated. British activists and scholars sometimes use *disablement* to describe what people in other countries more often identify as *disability*. But *impairment* and *disability* are most commonly used, which makes for uneven linguistic parallels.

Simply, *impairment* and *disablement* were created out of the same suffix, *ment*, which is defined by *The American Heritage Dictionary of the English Language* as "1. Action; process: 2. Result of an action or process; and 3. Means, instrument, or agent of an action or process" (Pickett 2002). *Disablement*, marked by the suffix *ment*, more accurately depicts the highly active social, medical, and cultural processes commonly discussed in disability studies than does the more passive term *disability*. By using this terminology, *impairment* would retain its current reference to the internal causality, symptomology, effects, and prognoses of physical, cognitive, psychological, or sensory conditions. *Disablement* would refer to the external forces that are imposed on people with impairments. *Disability* would then refer to the result of *disablement*, to describe otherness; social, cultural, political, and economic oppression; exclusion; institutionalization; hate crimes; abuse; and so forth. In this context, *disability* would then be interpreted as an identity that the disabled person may choose to claim, to resist, or to accept, claim, and then resist or challenge.

By using *impairment* and *disablement*, disability studies scholars and disability activists and advocates could more precisely draw parallels and contrasts between the two experiences. Disability could also be understood in similar ways within both the medical and social model communities, which might assist communication efforts between the two often-opposing fields. Furthermore, this usage could help bridge the divide between those who choose "person first" language (as in *people with disabilities*) and those who prefer *disabled person*. Since *disability* would mean more than *impairment* alone, both groups would be less likely to feel offended by either phrase.

As I make these suggestions, I remain aware that impairment, disability, and disablement are, to some degree, socially constructed, and that they are not necessarily binaries. Constructing these categories helps us make sense of the world around us and our relationship to and with it. Society creates constructs to clarify impairment and disability. People with impairments use these categories to form personal and social identities, and to make sense of their relationship to conflicting societal interpretations of the space where disabled people reside between their own condition and experience and what society tells them about that condition or experience.

Definitions of Blindness

The US Bureau of the Census (1996) defines blindness simply as unable to see regular size newsprint, while most other US agencies have adopted the medical profession's three constructed categories of visual impairment, which are used to determine eligibility for services and financial compensation. They are as follows:

1. *Totally blind.*
2. *Legally blind.* Visual acuity is 20/200 or less in the best corrected eye (this means that what a fully sighted person sees from 200 feet away, a person with 20/200 vision sees from 20 feet away) and/or visual field is 20 degrees or less.
3. *Partially sighted.* Visual acuity is 20/70 in the best-corrected eye or visual field is 20 degrees or less.

The World Health Organization's "International Statistical Classification of Diseases, and Related Health Problems" (ICD), defines *blindness* as visual acuity of "less than 3/60 (0.05) or corresponding visual field loss in the better eye with best possible correction (visual impairment categories 3, 4 and 5 in ICD-10). This corresponds to loss of walk-about vision." *Low vision* is classified as visual acuity of "less than 6/18 (0.3) but equal to or better than 3/60 (0.05) in the better eye with best possible correction (visual impairment categories 1 and 2 in ICD-10)."

For the purpose of this study, I use "blind" to describe both legal blindness and total blindness, which will help keep the language unencumbered from several discrete medically and legally constructed categories. Even though I use "visually impaired," "legally blind," and "totally blind" to describe biological (embodied) conditions, I remain fully aware that such categories are cultural constructions, and my use of them in no way implies that I accept or endorse them as "truth." Most often, these categories are created to soothe the discomfort of ambiguity that societal institutions experience when confronted with difference.

Conclusion

This chapter introduced the reader to the role society plays in the creation of legal blindness and began to describe some problems arising from false notions about what it means to be legally blind as opposed to being fully sighted or totally blind. The concept of the "borderland" of blindness was introduced, wherein those labeled "legally blind" are pressed to choose one territory or another and so do not fit as equal citizens anywhere.

Next, the chapter introduced theoretical concepts undergirding the research, such as postmodernism and social constructionism, which are employed within the overarching social model of disability, initially created by the Disabled People's Movement in the United Kingdom and developed by the academic discipline of disability studies in the United States and elsewhere. Finally, language and medical definitions of sight and vision were offered.

PART 1

Exploring Borderlands

2

An Insider Approach

This existential phenomenological case study is constituted of a small collection of life stories gathered through unstructured, open-ended interviews. This style of data collection allowed as much space as possible for participants to express their authority about their own lived experience. Bertaux (1981, p. 39) asserts: "A good interview, and even more so, a good life story is one in which the interviewee *takes over the control of the interview situation* and talks freely" (emphasis in the original). Bertaux's opinion is especially significant for emancipatory projects because traditional disability research ignored the whole person, concentrating instead on medical aspects as if disabled people have been considered nothing more than specimens of impairment. As an "insider" researcher, I chose to include my personal story with accompanying sociological analysis.

The case study approach shares common goals with both emancipatory disability research principles and phenomenological inquiry. A case study is an inquiry that investigates a contemporary phenomenon within its real-life context. It is especially useful when the boundaries between phenomenon and context are not clearly evident (Myers 1997; Yin 2002), and this study explores the relationship between the person and the society in which the participant lives. I sought to learn if and how public perceptions of blindness are discrepant from the authentic lived experience. Most important, during the entire research process, I remained open to participants' priorities, observations, perceptions, opinions, and meanings about their lived experience; therefore, my research adjusted accordingly over time. Such reflexivity is an indispensable component in staying true to both emancipatory and phenomenological research methodologies. As one means of being reflexive, my own insider experiences as a legally blind person demanded that I learn more about myself—how I think and feel about my life story, my relationship with society, religious and spiritual beliefs, disability identity, and, of course, my personal relationship with legal blindness.

Use of life story data collection is especially appropriate considering this study's emancipatory principles because it provides an optimal setting for participants and researcher alike to deeply explore the blindness experience. Rather than employing a horizontal approach in which the researcher seeks generalization through a large number of research participants, this study worked vertically in order to mine rich, detailed data about how each of four participants experiences their own life in the borderland called legal blindness. Bogdan (1998, p. ix) writes: "Research is often more than an intellectual journey; it can be an emotional odyssey in which you confront who you are and what you carry with you as a member of your culture."

Life Story Research Methods

Life story research is reflective and interpretative in that participants relate their lives retrospectively not as isolated fact, but within contextual sociocultural influences (Goodley et al. 2004). Fact-finding is not the research goal here, because life story research understands that "facts" are shaped and reshaped by memory, time, and personal interpretation. Hence, the weight of the research design relies upon the participants' own expert memories, perceptions, and interpretations of their own experiences within their particular sociocultural contexts (Ochberg 1994; Wallace 1994; Oplatka 2001). Another beneficial feature of life story research is that participants are not acted upon by the researcher, as is the case with traditional positivistic disability research. Life stories can be told in a way that is more plausible (Goodley et al. 2004), meaning research participants may come to understand their personal experience within a broader social context, and so may genuinely be inspired to rewrite their narratives within a more empowering frame wherein they "incorporate reconstructed past, perceived present and anticipated future" (McAdams 1996, p. 307). Moreover, such narrative-based research has the potential to inform about both individual and collective experience (Goodley et al. 2004). This method has the advantage of examining a person's life holistically; that is to say, the story unfurls multiple layers of personal and public phenomena. Bringing together the work of Bruner (1986) with Marshall and Rossman (1989), Oplatka (2001) asserts that these entities are "in a state of mutual simultaneous shaping, so that it is impossible to distinguish one element and study its nature without taking into account its linkage to the other elements consisting of the phenomenon." Accordingly, the research may expose and challenge negative sociocultural and material factors that impact particular group identities—those who are labeled legally blind. Two of the participants in this study are female, two male, and all four white, although they do represent more than one ethnicity and socioeconomic status. Gender and class were considered, but for obvious reasons, race as a category of oppression was not (although some may argue that "Jewish" is a racial category). These life stories were constructed within an environment of racial privilege, but bear in mind this did not foretell material advantage, as illustrated by their own stories.

Storytelling has a long-standing, dignified tradition of conveying history and lore from one generation to the next and across cultures around the world. Goodley et al. (2004, p. ix) argue that ideas about identity are "linked into projects by which people write their own lives in varying conditions of alienation and empowerment." Not surprisingly, in this research, participants told stories about isolation, oppression, resistance to medical and social constructs, success, defeat, achievement, humor, resilience, and keen understandings of the relationship between society and legal blindness.

Like the stories themselves, methodological processes in emancipatory disability research are simultaneously simple and complex. The collaborative process between researcher and participant and the unstructured interview design provided space and time for people to tell their stories as they desired. The participants decided what was important to know about them and were offered full editorial control over how their final stories were presented.

As they related their interpretative intertextual relationship of internal and social experiences, the life story method may have both reflected and shaped participants' self-identities. As a small example, participants were encouraged to choose a name to be used in this study. Only one chose a pseudonym (not particularly to protect anonymity, but because he plans to write his own book). One chose her birth name, stating, "I feel it's good for me. I think it's kind of good publicity to have myself out there." Another chose to use his real name, stating, "I don't give a damn what they think." Their decisions are congruent with the assertion by Rosenblum and Travis (2003) that naming oneself is an act of self-empowerment and of declaring a group identity.

Stories are not fixed in the moment of time they were initially experienced; they are narratives that change shape through the storyteller's understandings and order of importance, and, they may be adapted to the storyteller's audience "with an intent, often implicit, to convince self and others of a particular plot or present ordering of experience rendered sensible within a particular culture" (Cohler and Cole 1994, p. 6).

This point is pertinent to insider research because the participants in this project, for instance, were amenable to revealing themselves more intimately with a researcher with a shared master status ("master status" is a sociology term used to describe a quality either achieved by an individual or assigned to a person by society that is perceived by others as the dominant quality in a person). To illustrate this point, in the course of the interviews, both Catherine and Larry made unsolicited comments that they would not have participated in this study if the researcher were sighted.

This study's potential contribution to blindness research as a whole and its significance to participants will be described in the next section, including an examination of some positive features of insider research, such as the "naming" example cited earlier. It will also assess reflexivity as well as potential pitfalls during the practical application of insider research.

An Insider Stance

While it is not necessary to be disabled in order to do genuinely emancipatory research (Barnes 1992, 2004), being a disabled insider has its own merits (and drawbacks), which have the potential to advance emancipatory principles. In concert with prior calls to consider disability research as part of ongoing endeavors by disabled people to combat oppression (Oliver 1992; Linton 1998; Barnes 2004), and because of my intrinsic interest in a topic that profoundly imposed itself upon my own place in society, I set out to learn what other legally blind people experience, and what meanings they ascribe to living in a socially constructed borderland between sightedness and blindness. Here I begin with an overall discussion about the aims, merits, and pitfalls of insider research, and then move on to relate how these factors—such as *countertransference* (a term usually applied to psychotherapy that occurs when the therapist's repressed feelings emerge in response to a client's problems, situations, or emotions [Corey 2000]) and relationship boundary-setting—played out during the research process.

Research about groups that are the targets of social stigma has traditionally been designed to learn about a dominant group's attitude toward the stigmatized group where the dominant group is the "object" and the stigmatized group becomes the "subject" (Oyserman and Swim 2001). The dominant group retains the power and importance. In this conventional paradigm, the research either covertly or overtly assumes that those who are in the stigmatized group passively internalize the social meanings ascribed to their status—that group members fail to exercise agency (Duckitt 1992; Oyserman and Swim 2001). Insider research, on the other hand, challenges such careless assumptions, asserting instead that those who are members of stigmatized groups actively try to build a "buffering life space" (Oyserman and Swim 2001). The authors also note that one of the most important aims of insider research is to examine "a stereotyped or stigmatized ingroup's responses, experiences, and beliefs and the paradox of being both an active constructor of one's everyday reality and an involuntary target of negative attitudes, behaviors, and beliefs that shape this reality" (Oyserman and Swim 2001).

It is necessary to understand from the outset that positioning "insiders" and "outsiders" as a binary would be misleading as it would imply that outsider research is "objective and detached" with insider research characterized as "immersed and subjective" (Sherry 2002, p. 141). Moreover, according to Naples (1997), such a false separation fails to acknowledge that research is an interactive process. She writes: "'Outsiderness' and 'insiderness' are not fixed or static positions, rather they are ever-shifting and permeable social locations that are differentially experienced and expressed" (p. 71).

No two people share *all* identities with anyone else; for that reason, no researcher can be either a complete "insider" or "outsider." Race; class; sex; gender; sexual orientation; age; religion; geography; physical, cognitive, or sensory conditions; social opportunity; level of education; family of origin; and individual personality traits are some variables that add flavor and color and make each individual unique. Notwithstanding, having some master statuses in common with research participants affords researchers an entrée into the community of interest that others might not have. Some barriers to communication might be easily broken through (or absent altogether) due to similar phenomenological experiences, group identity, or "indigenous knowledge" (Naples 1997). Some examples of indigenous knowledge might be acquisition of orientation and mobility skills, knowledge of braille, or use of acronyms related to the blindness community, as well as knowing what it feels like to be objects of societal treatment related to membership in a stigmatized group—in this case, legal blindness.

Shared knowledge about what it is to be legally blind in a dominant sighted society can engender trust and rapport more quickly than could be attained by an outsider. Although Sherry (2002) warns against making sweeping assumptions that having a shared identity is an automatic ticket into the inner workings of participants' lives, he concedes that, as a brain injury survivor, he held some social and cultural capital in his research with other brain injury survivors. Citing Mitchell (1998), Sherry (2002, p. 141) asserts that "being perceived as an 'insider' is fundamental in terms of emotional attachment, objectivity, trust, access and rapport."

Reflexivity

Reflexive engagement is an especially critical component of both emancipatory and insider research as it helps sustain integrity of the interactions between researcher and participants, and assists the researcher in maintaining a rigorously honest relationship with self. Hertz (1997, p. vii) explains: "Reflexivity implies a shift in our understanding of data and its collection—something that is accomplished through detachment, internal dialogue, and constant (and intensive) scrutiny of 'what I know' and 'how I know it.'"

Being an insider myself, I am aware of how I know what I know about my own lived experience of legal blindness. Yet this in no way means that I could presume participants might react the way I do in the face of similar phenomenological and social experiences. In order to avoid the pitfall of assumption, I called upon my past training as a counselor, which taught me to be a good listener, to give space and time to participants to tell their stories, including what meaning *they* made of their lived experience, while reflexively revealing myself when and where appropriate. Discernment, self-awareness, and timing are requisite to making sound decisions about if, when, and how much to self-disclose during interviews. Again, I called upon my counselor training to guide my decisions, keeping in mind that insider research contains an element of researcher self-disclosure that helps build trust and bonding with regard to common experiences associated with legal blindness.

A Rogerian Approach to the Interview Phase

As an experienced counselor, I felt comfortable and confident with my interviewing skills. Much of my education and training was grounded in Rogerian therapy, so I felt qualified to take such an approach to create an ambience of genuineness, empathy, support, active listening, and unconditional positive regard in my interactions with participants. Values set forth in Rogerian therapy are so well accepted that this person-centered approach has gone beyond the psychotherapy profession, for which it was originally intended, into such activities as conflict resolution, corporate team building, theology and education training, and human and social science research.

A person-centered Rogerian philosophy and the researcher's way of being seeks to establish genuine relationships built upon respect and a belief that clients—or in this instance, participants—and not therapists or researchers are the experts about their own lives. Answers to problems or issues are inside their stories, inside themselves, although sometimes they may need allies to assist them in accomplishing self-awareness and to experience self-encouragement.

The process is nondirective, which is a fundamental factor in emancipatory research wherein participants are invited to tell researchers what they want researchers to know about their lives. Additionally, a Rogerian stance on the part of the researcher requires self-reflection, a central component of both insider and emancipatory research. Like other postmodern paradigms, Rogerian research is skeptical toward the notion of objectivity. It is nonprescriptive and is perceived more as a stance than a fixed set of tools. Existential philosophy grounds a Rogerian stance, given that it emphasizes freedom and responsibility; therefore, it well befits both emancipatory and existential phenomenological research. Mearns and McLeod (1984, pp. 371–372) write:

> There are . . . strong themes running in parallel through the work of both phenomenological researchers and writers on counseling, therapy and groups [which may also employ a strong existential influence]; the primacy of experiencing; respect for the beliefs and values of others; an emphasis on relationship and process factors; and a search for authenticity.

For all those reasons, I maintain that Rogerian principles and interview tools are entirely harmonious with emancipatory disability research, and actually enhance the aims of life story research and existential phenomenology as well. I used Rogerian skills to meet participants in their situation, establish rapport, and build trust through active listening, accurate reflection of fact and feeling, probing without leading, and providing emotional support through empathic responses. As an insider—a member of the group I researched—I found it easy to establish both genuineness and empathy because we, as legally blind people, have had shared experiences in many life areas. Nonetheless, it was important for me as an insider researcher to be vigilantly self-reflective, to ensure empathy did not descend into countertransference. It was important to keep in mind that when a participant related a painful experience, it was up to me to be a supportive listener without donning my "counselor hat" or revealing my own emotions in such a way that I could have influenced how participants related their experiences. Reflexive detachment can temper feelings of countertransference. During the research, I remained attentive about not crossing the line between effective Rogerian-style interviewing (reflecting accurately, paraphrasing, nonthreatening probing, etc.) and doing actual counseling, which was absolutely not my role during this project.

Application of Emancipatory Principles

Emancipatory disability research emerged out of the social model of disability in the 1990s and was quickly embraced by British disability researchers (Mercer 2004). It is important to note that while engagement with emancipatory disability research most certainly does not promise immediate emancipation for any party or institution involved, its goals are highly congruent with the aims and goals of the disability movement. Oliver (1992) explains that the emancipatory paradigm, as the name implies, is about the facilitating of a politics of the possible by confronting social oppression at whatever levels it occurs. According to Fry (1983, p. 4),

> the experience of oppressed people is that the living of one's life is confined and shaped by forces and barriers which are not accidental or occasional and hence avoidable, but are systematically related to each other in such a way as to catch one between and among them and restrict or penalise motion in any direction.

Emancipatory research works to discover how such social restrictions have affected disabled people and it also "changes the social relations of research production" (Oliver 1992, p. 111).

Emancipatory disability research does not deny its political nature. As Moore, Beazley, and Maelzer (1998, p. 12) observe, "Research design moulds research findings." Barnes (1996) argues that researchers cannot be independent in researching oppression: control is placed in the hands of the researched and reciprocity, gain, and self-empowerment characterize the model. Emancipatory research "has much in common with feminist, anti-racist and anti-imperialist research ethics. The key features of this model include a redefinition of the social relations of research production, a rebuttal of positivist and interpretative claims to objectivity, and assertions about the political position of the researcher" (Stone and Priestley 1996).

Emancipatory disability research must not be perceived as a set of technical procedures to be precisely and methodically followed (Oliver 1992, p. 102; Watson 2004, p. 105). Moore, Beazley, and Maelzer (1998, p. 14) write: "Other than the need for critical reflection, and for unswerving commitment to making human rights issues explicit, we cannot pin-point what the essential ingredients of good disability research are." Emancipatory research can be practiced in qualitative, quantitative, or mixed method designs. There is no prescription for conducting emancipatory disability research. Rather, this praxis seeks to record the lives of disabled people and uses various methodologies to do so. Watson (2004) calls for ongoing discussion among disability researchers. This study contributes to this dialogue among researchers by testing the use of existential phenomenology as a method guided by the ethical principles of emancipatory research as an ethical guideline for this study (Priestley 1997, p. 91):

1. The adoption of a social model of disability as the ontological and epistemological basis for research production;
2. The surrender of falsely premised claims to objectivity through an overt political commitment to the struggles of disabled people for self-emancipation;
3. The willingness only to undertake research where it will be of some practical benefit to the self-empowerment of disabled people and/ or the removal of disabling barriers. (This principle does not promise emancipation of disabled people; it promises *only* a "willingness" on the part of the researcher to believe in self-emancipation for disabled people);
4. The devolution of control over research production to ensure full accountability to disabled people and their organisations;
5. The ability to give voice to the personal whilst endeavouring to collectivise the commonality of disabling experiences and barriers; and
6. The willingness to adopt a plurality of methods for data collection and analysis in response to the changing needs of disabled people.

In practical terms, Sherry (2002, p. 150) outlined specific strategies that support the objectives of emancipatory research, including a commitment to the population he researched; gaining the trust of his participants; "being open and honest about [his] intentions in the research and its aim to break down barriers that disable"; establishing "clear boundaries which identified what was and what was not part of the research"; and engaging the participants in each step of the data analysis and write-up process, including the account of their words and manuscript drafts. I remained vigilant with regard to these ideals and methods throughout the research, analysis, and writing process.

While I did not expect that each participant would achieve a profound sense of self-emancipation, some did find it liberating to have their story accurately related from their point of view, knowing full well that they were accorded respect and unconditional positive regard, and that their stories could contribute to the collective history of all blind people. The collaborative nature of this process is a step in the direction of self-emancipation.

During initial explanations of the research design, I invited each participant to decide as we went along how many interviews they needed to tell their story, and that it would be up to them to tell me when they were done. Catherine was satisfied with the telling of her story after three interviews, and then, a few months later, requested another interview to talk about how the "bourgeoisie" at her art college treated her because of her blindness. As it turned out, we did not have that interview, but we did have one more eleven months after the initial interview. J. R. told his story in four interviews. Larry asked for eleven interviews altogether. Because Larry began orientation and mobility training the week after our initial interview, he was keen to relate his experiences and adventures as well as share new insights about being legally blind in a sighted society. Of the four participants, Larry had most recently become blind. Through these interviews, we chronicled a story of blindness identity formation and development, of new phenomenological experiences with a white cane and then with a guide dog, and of a variety of societal reactions to him throughout these experiences.

The next section examines both modern and postmodern research values, leading into my rationale for choosing particular ways to approach the data analysis. It was my desire at the outset not to take the defensive posture often used by qualitative researchers in reaction to hegemonic positivistic paradigms, and originally I had not intended to discuss positivism at all. Nevertheless, I finally decided to touch on aspects of positivism so as not to sweep the issue under the rug. This in no way implies that I feel any need to explain myself to positivistic researchers who may be skeptical about the worthiness of qualitative research; it means only that I wish to provide a brief historical background. I argue that the models and methods I have chosen are, at the least, of equal value as modern quantitative methods in the social sciences, and for the purposes of this study are, indeed, superior to such traditional methods as surveys and controlled experiments, for example.

Trustworthiness and Quality

Emancipatory disability research grew out of the idea that traditional social research models are disempowering. Mercer (2004) explains:

> Emancipatory disability research was not only allied to the social model, it also adopted a radical critique of traditional "scientific" research claims such as its impartiality and objective processes for validating knowledge. (p. 118)

Traditional positivistic researchers have dominated all disciplines, and their concepts of *validity* and *reliability* have long been used to police the social sciences by setting up a binary between "valid" or "invalid" research based on whether particular methodologies are deemed worthwhile (Aguinaldo 2004) (note that unworthy research is labeled with the same word, *invalid*, that is historically linked to physically impaired people). Although deterministic quantitative research considers *validity* and *reliability* two quintessential measures of an efficacious research praxis, many qualitative researchers find them irrelevant, antithetical, and inapplicable to the aims and goals of their core methodology. Many qualitative researchers believe it is important to resist reacting to positivism, and refuse to engage in defensive rebuttal; consequently, they fail to address the issues altogether (Aguinaldo 2004). Instead, one trend has been to reframe the discourse by substituting *validity* and *reliability* with values of *trustworthine*ss (Lincoln and Guba 1985), which is also cast as credibility, genuineness, quality, subjectivity, reflexivity, and issues related to interpretation and presentation to be key determinants of methodologically successful research (Morrow

2005). But these values come with their own complex set of problems because they mirror positivistic power positions by constructing yet another binary that determines what constitutes good or bad research praxes, and so replicates the very methods they seek to resist (Scheurich 1996; Aguinaldo 2004). However well-intended such shifts in language are, they remain in danger of exercising what Aguinaldo (2004) calls "de/legitimation of social knowledge, research practice, and experiential possibilities." He confronts the issue of "validity" by reframing the traditional positivistic question, "Is this research valid?" as a more postmodern qualitative, "What is this research 'valid' for?" He explains:

> Implicit within this reformulation are the ideas that (a) validity is not a determination (i.e., "is valid" versus "is not valid"), but the process of interrogation and, (b) this interrogation necessitates multiple and sometimes contradictory readings of the functions any particular research representation (whether the research findings or the research project as a whole) can serve. (Aguinaldo 2004)

This central question speaks directly to the values of emancipatory disability research. Although Aguinaldo's creative reconceptualization of validity was both compelling and tempting, and despite the risk of perpetrating what Foucault conceived of as a "regime of truth" (Lather 1993), in the end, I chose to take a stand against using traditional positivistic terminology and adopted more unmistakably qualitative language—*trustworthiness, quality,* and *fidelity.* I kept such obvious (and more likely not so obvious) shortcomings of these concepts (discussed previously) in mind and braved the risks for the sake of avoiding potential breakdowns in reflexive apparatuses, as well as to serve Aguinaldo's goal of an ongoing "process of interrogation."

From the outset of the study, I informed and updated the participants about my intentions, aims, goals, and processes and continually reiterated that they had control over how much they wished to be involved at every stage. I maintained confidentiality and anonymity between each participant. This was especially sensitive as two of the participants were acquainted with each other, and I did not know if either of them had disclosed to the other that they were engaged in this study. None of us mentioned this connection at any time during the research. At one point, Larry expressed a desire to meet the other participants; I told him that when the study was complete I would ask the others if they were interested in such a meeting as well, and, if so, I would arrange it.

Not only is *trustworthiness* a value in qualitative research in general, it is an essential component of an emancipatory paradigm with its commitment to equal power relations between researcher and researched. Again, thanks to my Rogerian training and work, I felt quite comfortable establishing an atmosphere of authentic mutuality. I already sensed how to gauge appropriate times and spaces to self-disclose or when to just listen, reflect, and support, all the while providing a principled environment for participants to tell their stories. On the other hand, in my dual role as participant and researcher, I felt that some self-disclosure on my part was not merely appropriate but essential. I gauged when and how much to disclose as we went along in the interviews, always keeping in mind that I was there to collect *their* stories, not to co-opt their time talking about myself. If a participant related an anecdote, observation, or expression of emotion about either a societal or a phenomenological aspect of blindness that was quite similar to my own experiences, then I would briefly self-disclose in the moment or after the interview session.

With regard to *fidelity* in qualitative research, Moss (2004) reported that she remained reflective and reflexive in her education research with Spanish-speaking students and with Amish culture in education by keeping in mind that doing research with oppressed minorities is political in nature. She held a deep sense of responsibility to her participants because she recognized and understood that *fidelity* (trustworthiness) emerged through understanding participants' struggles as well as perceiving the "researcher as a co-struggler for cultural-political identity" (Moss 2004, p. 367). Because I was researching members of an oppressed minority that has historically been objectified, used, and abused by traditional research using a medical model; because I too am a member of this group; and because I hold a deep belief that all human beings deserve respect, I felt a great sense of responsibility to earn and keep the participants' trust in me and in the research process. While I perceive blind people to be an oppressed minority group, two participants did not particularly perceive blindness as either a social construction or political matter. None of them had heard of the social model of disability. J. R. had engaged in advocacy efforts, but not as part of a group. He belongs to the National Federation of the Blind, but "stays out of the politics." Perhaps because his blindness was a relatively new phenomenon, Larry was in the early stages of blindness identity development, and his contacts with other blind people were largely through medical model institutions such as an eye clinic at a local hospital that sponsored an exhibit of the work of blind artists. However, Catherine understood the socioeconomic and political nature of the blindness experience and had formed many opinions about it long before our interviews commenced. She had already correlated her knowledge of women's studies issues to her experience of being blind in a sighted society.

The next section chronicles how the participants and I coped with the data coding, which was an arduous and fairly impossible task for four busy blind people to tackle. Access and time issues caused me to adjust my original plan for data coding and analysis.

Data Coding and Analysis Methods

As Morrow (2005) asserts, some qualities such as ample amounts of and immersion in the data are "indispensable" to *all* research para-digms. Staying true to emancipatory intentions, I planned from the outset to involve participants in every phase of the research includ-ing working collaboratively with each participant to code their respective transcripts; each of them agreed at the start of the study to engage actively in this (and every other) project task. Knowing firsthand how frustrating it can be for legally blind (and other print-disabled) people to be denied alternative formats, I explicitly stated that I would make all materials available according to their access needs. However, I had not anticipated that our preferred formats might conflict with each other's, which resulted in barriers that, at times, felt almost insurmountable. The initial plan was to use the Microsoft Word tool "track changes" to insert coding comments. As the process developed, I discovered that each one of us used either different access technologies or no computer at all. We tried print versions; each participant requested different font styles and sizes, ranging from 14-point to 20-point type.

On one occasion, Larry came to my home so we could code his first transcript. After almost two hours, we had completed only 10 pages of data coding, and we both experienced painful eye strain, which lasted for more than one day. Quickly, it became evident that this system would not work. We then printed out a 20-point font copy for Larry to work from at home. We worked together over the phone three times, he with his print copy and me on the computer. This turned out to be an extremely time-consuming process, completing 8–10 pages per 90 minute session, which was minuscule considering we had over 1,000 pages of data from our eleven interviews. What is more, this method also caused both of us severe eye strain.

After much thought, I approached Larry with the following suggestion: I would go through the transcripts myself and build his story in his own words, which I would then take back to him for comments, edits, and suggestions. I reiterated that I wanted to stay true to emancipatory intent, and that I wanted to make sure this method did not make Larry feel less in control of his story. He stated that he felt we had acted egalitarian throughout, and that he trusted both the procedure and me.

During the last few weeks of the research process, J. R. and Catherine carefully combed through sections pertinent to their own stories. I invited them to disagree with my analysis, and told them I would include their comments alongside mine; however, they were in accord with the analyses. Even though this part of the research process required more work than if I had done traditional methods wherein I would have full control of the write-up, I found working with them most satisfying. First, their approval of their stories and the analysis provided validity of the research. Second, I was happy to have their input so that their stories were presented as they wished them to be. Finally, doing this last bit of work with them provided an opportunity for emotional closure, which I think was beneficial, especially considering we had worked together for well over a year.

Conclusion

This chapter outlined the methodology of this study, including life story methods, insider research values and techniques, such as reflexivity, self-disclosure, and some experiences of the actual research praxis. Positivist research is briefly discussed to help create an appreciation for the merits of qualitative, emancipatory research. Due to the nature of the methodologies employed in the research, I did not seek to generalize beyond the scope of the individuals' own lives. Rather, the study identified some of the experiences that blind people have had and provided alternative ways of understanding blindness. The detailed attention given to each participant is considered one strength of the process, leading to a closer, more intimate, and more accurate portrayal of the particular experiences of the participants. For the same reason I do not personally claim to speak for other blind people, neither do I put the participants' stories forward as generalizable experiences. We also learn about some of the specific challenges of working with a borderland population whose individuals' phenomenological requirements are varied, unique, and sometimes at odds with each other's access needs.

3

Prejudice and Poverty

This chapter investigates how blindness is traditionally understood within the hegemony of vision and sight. Using Jay's (1993) ideas about *ocularcentrism,* I demonstrate how society places vision as the most ontologically and epistemologically valued of the five corporeal senses. I discuss how the medical model constructs and perpetuates ocularcentrism in social and materialist practices in school, rehabilitation, and work settings. This is significant in that ocularcentric education and employment practices believe that vision is the superior of all senses, which makes for a faulty paradigm within which legally blind people are inherently perceived as less than whole. No matter how much education or rehabilitation they receive, blind people can never catch up; they can never truly achieve the ocularcentric goal of *normalization,* a condition judged in comparison to sighted people.

Understanding Ocularcentrism

Ocularcentrism describes an implicit set of attitudinally generated social practices that privilege vision and debase blindness (Jay 1993). Within conventional ocularcentrism, "the subject is invariably either in the role of a dominating observer or in the role of an observable object, submissive before the gaze of power" (Levin 1993, p. 4). So it is for ophthalmology patients when their eyes become objects of a potent medical gaze under which blindness is perceived only within definitional confines of disease or damage relative to healthy sight-generating eyes.

Ocularcentrism is a term coined by historian Martin Jay around 1992. David Levin, whose work is consistent with that of Jay (1993), describes ocularcentrism as "a vision-generated, vision-centered interpretation of knowledge, truth, and reality" (1993, p. 5). According to Levin, the sighted majority privileges vision as "the corporeal sense which is primary and predominant, at least in the conduct of our everyday lives" (p. 2). The problem arises when vision is cast as not merely predominant, but superior, to other ways of knowing the physical world. Sociocultural beliefs and mores devalue those who learn the world around them through other than visual modes of perception. Levin asks, "Can it be demonstrated that, beginning with the ancient Greeks, our Western culture has been dominated by an ocularcentric paradigm, a vision-generated, vision-centered interpretation of knowledge, truth, and reality?" (p. 2). One answer to Levin's question is Arendt's (1978, pp. 110–111) assertion that conceptual language can trace its ocularcentric roots all the way back to ancient Greek philosophers:

> From the very onset, in formal philosophy, thinking has been thought of in terms of seeing. . . . The predominance of sight is so deeply imbedded in Greek speech, and therefore in our conceptual language, that we seldom find any consideration bestowed on it, as though it belonged among things too obvious to be noticed.

Parallels can be drawn between the ideology of ocularcentrism and other forms of sociocultural oppression, such as racism. For example:

> Whites are the non-defined definers of others. They name but they are not themselves named; their dominance is reflected in their ability to impose names on others, but themselves remain invisible. (Frankenberg 1993 in Omansky Gordon and Rosenblum 2001)

In the same way that whites have dominated US society and so do not have to be self-conscious about their social status in ways racial and ethnic minorities do, sighted people do not have to think about being sighted. Through imposition of ocularcentric values on blindness and blind people, sighted people retain the power to define categories of visual impairment, to describe how blind people need to act in order to be successfully blind people—that is, to act as sighted as possible—and then, to position blind people in a no-win situation by devaluing the status of blindness and, thus, stigmatizing blind people.

While Michalko (1998, 1999, 2002) does not specifically use the term *ocularcentrism*, he does base a tremendous amount of his work on these ideas. Sight is deemed "normal"—the standard by which blind people are measured as "lacking." Michalko (1999) describes this ocularcentric perception of blindness as "lack"—of "something missing": he explains that the language used to describe the condition of "losing sight"—of vision "going" or "being gone" demonstrates that "there is a problem built into the word [blind] itself" (p. 25). He asserts that "the ways in which blindness is spoken about renders blindness a source of negative representation" (Michalko 1999, p. 45).

Blindness represents darkness, fear, and powerlessness in the weakest sense of the word. Levin (1993) supports this history in his extensive study of twentieth-century philosophers, including Martin Heidegger, Michel Foucault, and Jacques Derrida, who argued the thought and culture of modernity not only continued the historical privileging of sight but allowed its worst tendencies to dominate. Jay (1993) writes:

> In addition to the ocular permeation of language, there exists a wealth of what might be called visually imbued cultural and social practices, which may vary from culture to culture and epoch to epoch. Sometimes these can be construed in grandiose terms, such as a massive shift from oral culture to a "chirographic" one based on writing and then a typographic one in which the visual bias of the intermediate stage is even more firmly entrenched. (p. 2)

For example, when the Gutenberg press was invented in the fifteenth century and print became readily available, roving blind bards and balladeers were no longer needed to relay current events through story, poetry, and song across the countryside. Consequently, either they found themselves out of work or they resorted to becoming street musicians (Ross 1951). White (2003, pp. 133–134) notes that the "written word is a technology developed by and for the sighted, through which the blind are spoken *about* but rarely *to*." These days, reliance on visual media such as television, film, print, and computer technology, in particular, reinforces ocular-centric notions about sight being the superior sense. Ocular-centrism is exacerbated by the difficulties blind people face with regard to accessing media sources because the locus of the "problem" is placed on individual blind people instead of where it belongs—on issues of access and universal design. Even the term "assistive technology" is a misnomer because it implies that the problem lies within the individual rather than as an issue of inaccessibility built into systems usually designed by and for the sighted.

Because blind people were excluded from employment opportunities, they resorted to begging, and blind beggars became objects of interest to both the public and art communities. Blind beggars were treated with derision and suspicion and sometimes perceived as "fraudulent" (much like homeless people are currently characterized) (Barasch 2001, p. 96). Moreover, an idea grew that characterized blind persons as suffering grave, incurable illness. Moved by this belief, Louis XIV of France established asylums for both blind people and those with leprosy, according to Barasch (2001, p. 144), who asserts these institutions served a dual purpose: to both render care to as well as wield control over these two populations.

Later, attitudes toward blind people shifted during the Italian Renaissance when blindness became a metaphor for overcoming difficult times; darkness was conceptualized as a channel to unobstructed spiritual meditation. Barasch (2001, p. 134) writes: "From the Cloud of Unknowing by an anonymous late-fourteenth-century author to the Dark Night of the Soul by St. John of the Cross, conditions obscuring vision—the night or the clouds—are perceived as a precondition for true contemplation." In the seventeenth century, stereotypes of the blind beggar and the sinner combined to make a doubly difficult image for blind people (Barasch 2001). Historically, metaphors about illness and impairment have been (and still are) understood to be harmlessly metaphorical; they have not been scrutinized as ocularcentric social constructions reflective of deeper social meanings, that is, until the advent of disability studies.

Materialism and Disability

Especially in the United States, a largely ignored theoretical approach to blindness is materialism. Oliver (2009) explains:

> Within this worldview, the production of the category disability is no different from the production of motor cars or hamburgers. Each has an industry, whether it be the car, fast food or human service industry. Each industry has a workforce that has a vested interest in producing their product in particular ways and in exerting as much control over the process of production as possible. The production of disability therefore is nothing more or less than a set of activities specifically geared towards producing a good—the category disability—supported by a range of political actions, which create the conditions to allow these productive activities to take place, and underpinned by a discourse that gives legitimacy to the whole enterprise. (p. 90)

Although a materialist approach was widely advanced by disability scholars such as Oliver (1990, 2009), Barnes and Mercer (1997, 2004), Priestley (1997), and Thomas (1999), it is a relatively underexplored perspective within US disability studies or anywhere with regard to blindness. Oliver (1990) argues that material factors are fundamental to understanding the social model of disability. In this regard, it is important to note that blind people experience economic oppression and social isolation in even larger percentages than other disabled people do, including higher unemployment and underemployment rates, and lack of access to basic print information, Internet technology, and accessible transportation. Potential employers, community development and urban planners, mainstream technocrats, rehabilitation agencies, and retailers alike tend to balk at the financial cost of environmental barrier removal and universal design, leaving blind people stranded in or altogether shut out of the workplace and therefore exiled from a consumer economy. Additionally, government agencies, nonprofit charities, and for-profit businesses employ tens of thousands of sighted workers engaged in maintaining institutionalized oppression of blind people. Sheltered workshops—segregated places of employment, usually funded and managed by government agencies for disabled people, most often for blind people, people with developmental disabilities, or multiple impairments—abound across the United States and elsewhere. Rehabilitation agencies often place clients in business settings at minimum wage or less as part of a trial work period, which can last a year or longer. Rehabilitation agencies sometimes consign clients to prepackaged programs that do not match either the clients' interests or career goals, because these programs are easier for the agencies than having to do education and outreach to potential employers. Failure to examine these factors as influences in blind people's lives is a failure to mine a deep and rich source of research data.

Ocularcentrism and the Medical Model

The medical model of impairment and disability is particularly important with regard to obtaining an official diagnosis because medical, social, and human service providers function as gatekeepers. They rely upon diagnosis to decide who has a right to monetary compensation, social services, and avenues to employment training and placement. These gatekeepers have the power to make or break a disabled person's well being, sometimes even the ability to obtain basic sustenance—food, clothing, shelter.

Examples of the medical model of impairment and disability can be found whenever one types in "blindness" on any Internet search engine. Typical search results concern disease, rehabilitation and counseling services, product catalogs, information about blindness prevention, medical research, and blindness "etiquette" information designed for sighted people to learn how to interact with blind people. A sparse sprinkling of information will appear about organizations *of* the blind, initiated and controlled by blind people themselves, that are consumer and rights oriented. More common, however (and better funded), are associations *for* the blind, which have deep historical roots in the medical model and are usually administered by sighted people. These mostly charity-based organizations promote blindness prevention media campaigns, information about specific eye diseases and related services and product information, and reports of medical research aimed at prevention and cure. Generally, neither type of blindness organization conducts independent social or medical research.

Actual protocol decisionmaking and research work in these cases is left to medical and educational establishments. Medical institutions typically devote their energies to prevention, diagnosis, treatment, and cure. On the other hand, educational institutions tend to address matters of adaptation, accommodation, and rehabilitative training, with the ultimate goal of *normalization* of blind people. This goal advances transformative practices in order to regulate the person by regulating the body. As Foucault (1979, p. 25) argues, "It is always the body that is at issue—the body and its forces, their utility and docility, their distribution and their submission."

Medicine, Poverty, and Public Policy

The most common causes of blindness vary according to geographic location, socioeconomic status, and age. Largely preventable and treatable bacterial diseases such as onchocerciasis, otherwise known as river blindness, and trachoma are leading causes of blindness in the developing world. Many international health-promoting organizations, such as the Carter Center and the Fred Hollows Foundation sponsor blindness prevention programs. They work in rural, poverty-ridden communities to improve hygiene education, sanitation conditions, and access to health care. The US Center for Disease Control (CDC) reports that many causes of blindness occur before birth although some conditions clear up over time. Older children (between three and ten years old) have more vision impairments than do children younger than three years old. Nearly two-thirds of visually impaired children also have at least one other impairment. This may, in part, be due to the fact that some diseases have visual impairment as secondary effects. Diabetes, glaucoma, and cataracts are the most common causes of blindness among adults in Western nations. Moreover, because people are living longer than did earlier generations, age-related macular degeneration is more prevalent.

The World Health Organization (2004) estimates there are about 45 million blind or visually impaired people around the world, with nine of ten cases occurring in developing nations. There is a strong link between poverty and blindness. Of the more than 1.4 million blind children around the world, more than 80 percent live in developing countries. Approximately 85 percent of cases are preventable, but adequate financial commitment to prevention and treatment programs, healthier agricultural practices, and more attention paid to nutritional deficits are needed (World Bank 1994). The level of ophthalmic health care is shaped by each country's political system. For example, countries that were part of the USSR are currently grappling with shifting its socialist (free) health care to nongovernment-subsidized health-care systems (e.g., private health insurance); hence, health care, including ophthalmic care, is in transition and not always adequate (Kocur and Resnikoff 2002). In the United States, there are approximately 20 million visually impaired people (National Center for Health Statistics 2006). In the United States, approximately 1 million people over the age of forty are blind (US National Eye Institute 2001). One problem with gathering accurate data is that people who begin to lose their vision as part of the aging process often do not register for social or rehabilitation services (Royal National Institute for the Blind 2003). Additionally, different countries have different data collection methods, which hinders accurate estimates of total numbers of blind and visually impaired people.

Employment figures as well as prospects for future employment of blind and visually impaired people are dismal in every country around the globe. Public policy toward blindness is measured in terms of economics—cost-benefit ratios. Statistics about the cost of blindness prevention, treatment, and rehabilitation are analyzed in comparison with productivity levels to determine if governments are making good capital investments. Blindness and blind people are characterized as "financial burdens." No other socioeconomic group in the United States has more unemployment than that of blind people (American Foundation for the Blind 2001).

In 2004, the US National Center for Policy Research for Women and Families published the first statistical data about legally blind people (US Bureau of the Census 1996, National Health Interview Survey [NHIS] 1994–1995). NHIS surveyed 779 legally blind adults representing 993,766 noninstitutionalized adults ages eighteen and older nationwide. This report revealed that "blind adults who live alone are more likely to live in poverty than the general population" (Zuckerman 2004).

Conclusion

A deep form of societal prejudice known as ocularcentrism privileges sight and vision and relegates blind people to second-class citizenship. Ocularcentrism has profound repercussions on the everyday lives of blind people. This chapter traced the lineage of ocularcentrism in history and the media and demonstrated the severe effects hegemonic public policy practices have on this population's basic human rights.

4

Living Stories:
In Their Own Words

Life story social science research most often examines specific circumstances of people's lives. In the data analysis process, portions of their stories not directly related to the specific research interests fall into danger of being glossed over or discarded altogether. Consequently, researchers expropriate valuable information that the reader could (and should) be privy to and, just as important (if not more), that the researched wanted to be told. I contend that such aspects of the researched are wholly interesting for their own sake and further present a more holistic portrayal of the participant's background and personal beliefs. Bertaux (1981) asserts that "a good interview, and even more so, a good life story is one in which the interviewee *takes over the control of the interview situation* and talks freely" (p. 39). Bertaux's opinion is especially significant for emancipatory projects because traditional disability research ignored the whole person, concentrating instead on medical aspects as if disabled people are nothing more than specimens of impairment. Moreover, this may be the first time their voices are not only heard, but highly valued as the most indispensable part of the research.

The portraits in this chapter are presented without interference of analysis by the researcher. During the initial chapter planning, I thought that this would be a completely natural and logical way to support emancipatory life story ethics because it created a venue wherein the participants would take center stage and could, on their own terms, welcome readers into their thoughts, feelings, and experiences. After a search of a dissertation database and queries to disability studies colleagues engaged in emancipatory life story research around the world, I posit that in combination with data analysis sections, this style of presentation in a formal emancipatory study is unusual and perhaps even original.

Overview of Life Story Research Styles

Generally speaking, life story research designs either present the stories without analysis or, conversely, use analysis throughout the entire write-up. The lack of analysis in some classic, transformative life-history research projects (e.g., by William Isaac Thomas and Florian Znaniecki, Clifford Shaw, Edwin Sutherland, Oscar Lewis, and Leo W. Simmons) supports my choice to present this chapter content sans analysis. Bertaux (1981) believes that the nonanalytical projects cited above contributed to social science's increased understanding of sociostructural relations in the stories themselves and actually made "analysis irrelevant" because the stories "stand by themselves" (p. 39). Obviously, this thesis goes beyond just the telling of the stories; but this chapter is dedicated to the tradition from which Bertaux was inspired to conduct life story research as well as assess its value to social science. Bertaux credits one book in particular that used the participants' stories as powerful evidence on their own, without needing analysis to make the points clear. He writes about

> the enlightening experience of reading Oscar Lewis's *The Children of Sanchez* in 1964. What was so new and stimulating about this book was the kind of emotions that its reading induced. Looking back now, it becomes clear that in comparison with all other books available, this one was quite unique. It was neither a work of fiction nor a work of social science. It did not fit into any of the established categories and yet it struck me as the kind of book I would have liked to read more often. It was human all the way through; not through the medium of the writer's own humanism, but straightforwardly so. (1981, p. 173)

It is in this spirit that this chapter has been crafted out of the participants' own words, wherein they show us their personhood without interference of my impressions or interpretations of them.

Basically, the participants wrote this chapter, while I merely assumed the role of editor. Their comments were selected from the entire body of interview transcripts and are not necessarily in order of time; rather the quotations are organized according to subject matter. I was careful to maintain the integrity of their personalities; further, as part of the emancipatory process, participants were offered the final say in exactly how their words were presented. The chapter is organized according to which person came to the study first—Larry, Catherine, J. R., and finally, me. I wrote my story after all the other data had been collected, not for any particular reason other than that I was more interested in conducting the interviews while the participants were available and enthused, knowing that my story was on hand to me anytime.

Larry

Oh, yeah, one of my big names is Sigmund cuz I'm constantly internalizing and reflecting and psychoanalyzing my, you know, my hangnail, you know. Like, oh my, I wonder what that's about. Where's that deep-seated phenomena from? When I'm painting I'm not thinking about anything except just what I'm doing. It's like an opiate. It really is.

I was born in upstate New York and we were there because my father was in a defense plant during World War II. I was really lucky because the street that I lived on, umm, it was like a United Nations. It was really cool because, like, one block behind my house, they were either all Irish, and then one block to the other side they were all German or Italian or they were Jews from Europe, and, my, my street that I lived on was like the crease in the pants. Okay. Across the street was, was, was a family called the Franks, and I used to play with their grandson, Steve. And, Mrs. Frank, or Grandma Frank, which we all called her; she had the tattoo on her arm from the concentration camp. And as a little kid, I, I became exposed to, and . . . to this day, I can't stand bullies. Okay? And, Hitler was a son of a bitch.

I have an older brother and a younger brother. I'm the middle in the birth order. And, . . . I'm glad I'm in the middle because I can handle my own insanity. I don't think I could handle either one of theirs. It was very difficult growing up.

I never, I never was really given—or if I picked it up, it was frowned upon—crayons. Childhood was . . . it was a difficult childhood in terms of, like today, today there's this openness between parent and child, and back then, it wasn't the same. Everybody has these specific roles, and, um, you didn't cross certain lines in those relationships. And, I spent a long time getting a closure with my father who is dead because, you know, he never said to me, "Put less glue on the model airplane" that I was making. And, in a way, that's what I needed. I needed someone like a father to take a little bit more interest in what I was doing. He was a pretty good provider when it came to putting food on the table, and things like that. And, I remember him saying, "You know, I can almost afford anything that we would ever want. We just can't afford to waste things."

There was emotional, psychological, and physical abuse on [my father's] part. I didn't feel safe. In fact, it got to the point where, uh, I stopped doing things with my friends when I was in, like, oh, like 8th grade, when I was still . . . because I had a kid brother, and, uh, I would play with him because, when I played with him, I knew that I was protecting him from my old man.

The problems I had with my mom, [she] never had the ability to protect me . . . from the bully. So, you say, like, "Okay, Dad. You gave it a shot, and you had a small bag of tools to do it with, and you did the best you could, so I love you, anyway." You despise the things that the person did wrong. You cherish the things the person did right. But you always try to love the person . . . because they might not have had a choice in what they did for you to despise. And if you practice loving the person over the act, then perhaps when it's your turn, you, too, will be loved.

To my kids, especially my sons, I'm not only their father. I'm their best friend. And, they, they, I mean my kids, one's 31 and one's 27. And, we can walk through a restaurant with a gazillion people, and they'll stand there in front of everybody, and give me a hug and a kiss, and say, "Thanks, Dad."

Um, the way I was really lucky was that I had a biological mother, but then I refer to these two other women as my nurturing mothers. My mother, I don't talk to my mom at all. Not that she would understand me, cuz she is like in a nursing home. She never really knew how to nurture. Um, so her sister and her sister-in-law took over the task of nurturing. I don't know what they did with my other brothers, but with me, they nurtured the bejeesus out of me. I have closure with both my parents.

I worked since I've been . . . I painted my first house, uh, as my own business, when I was 13 years old. And, you know, I worked illegally in a machine shop . . . cuz you had to be 16 to work. I was 14.

[When] I was through college and I was through teaching, and I said, "I gotta do something," so I picked up my father's old camera, and I would go out and I would take photographs with that. And, then I would develop them, and then I started to do some painting. Uh, and, at times I might be disappointed, but my disappointment is because. . . . Let me just say this. When I stopped trying to be perfect, I got better. But you know like old habits are hard to kill off. And one of my mottos is mediocrity is easy; good things take time.

[After college] I was teaching at that time, junior high school. Yeah, sex, drugs, and rock 'n' roll—I was teaching Health. I love teaching. It was, it really was the coolest thing I ever did. Well, I started to teach because of two things. The kids were number one. Don't go into teaching if your summer vacations or the chance to become an administrator is your number one priority. The reason you teach is because you care for kids. If you don't care for kids, then get the fuck out of the business—in plain English. You know?

Where my head is at. . . . To me, happiness is equal to reality divided by expectations. My humor is a clarifier for me. The most important thing I need is to stay grounded.

There are people that, um [pauses]. There are people in this world that you know that if they think you did something wrong you would second guess what you did because you know them well enough to love and trust them that if they thought you did something wrong you might've done it. And then there are other people, if they said you did something wrong you'd say, "Oh why don't you go out and stuff your face or something?" The thing is on . . . you know, like there are certain values, uh, I would die for, and honesty and loyalty are right up there. So, when I meet a person who is honest and loyal and truthful to me, that's a gift I don't ever want to disappoint. The thing is . . . when I look back in life, I really don't give a shit what people think of me. The important thing to me is what I think of other people. And let's face it; living life with your eyes closed is worse than being blind. It really is.

But in my life I've encountered a small number of people that their opinion of me was very, very important. If I was in a room with a thousand people, and these thousand people said, "You made a mistake," I'd say, "Fuck you." Whereas, if one of this small group of people said, "Hey, Larry, like, you wanna reconsider this?" I would say, "I might have made a mistake," because of the respect I had for them.

I wanted to learn how to play a musical instrument, but that wasn't for me to do. I wanted to play, I wanted to play the guitar. I still do. [A friend] fell in love with one of my pieces of art, and, um, I told him. I said, "I want to give you that piece of art," and he said, "I can't take it because I'm not giving you anything in return." And, I said, "Oh, yes, you are. I already know what I want." I said, "I want you to teach me to see the music." So he's going to teach me how to play guitar.

I have artwork done, and this guy that does my matting is really a great young man. And I'll give him a five dollar tip, and not that I can afford it, but I give it to him as an appreciation for his craft. And he comes up to me and he says, "You know Larry you don't have to do this." And I say to him, I said, "That's the reason why I'm doing it," because if I had to do it I probably wouldn't.

It would really be cool to be able to come up with word definitions. Do you realize how powerful you could be if you came up with words and definitions for words? If the whole world depended on you for the definitions of words, you got a mass of control. So, it's all these, it's all this—I'm going to say something here—it's like everybody wants to get this social and industrial erection, you know, that excludes other people. And, what the hell for? I don't understand it. You know. So since I don't understand it . . . it has to be bullshit so I don't pay any attention to it. You just don't argue for the sake of arguing. You argue because it's of a value to you. And I always told my kids. I said, "Listen," I said, "you'd be better off thinking about what I'm asking you to do and really, like, don't argue. Just don't think about [arguing]. And if you feel that it deserves an argument or a discussion come back and we'll talk about it." I said, "But remember, the less you come back [pauses] the more I'm willing to listen because you've thought about it, and what you're coming back for must really be important to you."

Catherine

I have lots of identities, um, um . . . I'm finally not so secretive about having them converge. Being self-aware is being open to learning and that's a really positive thing. I think my family life is where a lot of things haven't converged. I have not really told the rest of my family [except for my father] that I'm bisexual. I hide the polyamory thing. I hide the bisexual thing. I hide the content of some of [my] work . . . stuff that, anything that would have to deal with any sort of problems with having violence in the home as a child.

My neighborhood is a strongly ethnically mixed neighborhood. Predominantly it's a poor neighborhood which is going through a lot of gentrification right now. A light rail line has been recently put in, and, um, is growing far, I would say, far more liberal. And, a seriously gallery-oriented art community is growing up the streets about a mile and a half above me on the same street—just this little section is still very poor. There's like more churches in this area of Portland than there is probably per block in most of the entire state.

My next-door neighbors are homosexual. My across the street neighbors are homosexual. And the neighbors over here are directly um, from where I'm sitting, are um, they sell drugs. So it's like we have a section where it's kind of a safe pocket I feel like because it's predominantly homosexual and so I feel protected in my neighborhood, well if you ignore the meth to the left, whereas when I was living in southeast; everybody's really homophobic and it was really scary. I would see things on people's bumpers that were just horrible. Whereas there was a lot of racist people; it seemed you'd see people's tattoos that were racist. . . . Like there's a large section of like Vietnamese, Korean . . . located near to here. It's just, it's really nice to have a good influence of many cultures and not like stuck in a pocket of white Middle America.

I'd rather be here in a poor community. People watch out for people in the neighborhood. There may be a lot of crime but people do watch out for each other. That's something that is rare.

I have one sister who is sixteen years my elder. So that would make her. . . . My dad, you know, says that's . . . his pretty daughter, and I'm the smart daughter, the studious daughter, you know. Um, my mother, she's mentally sick, and she has a lot of disabilities like as far as she was, she had an eating disorder where she overate all the time, and she became obese and diabetic and had massive strokes. . . . But when things got very exacerbated, then my mother would be violent. So she was a handful . . . especially with the mood swings. And, my father was getting, ah, his kidneys were failing at that point in my life around 11 through 13. And he got onto dialysis; I think when I was 14 or 15. I think it was um, yeah, those were hard years.

I started cooking. And like eighth grade I started to help with doing bills a little . . . balancing the money that was from rental houses. I'd help negotiate a rental contract. Like a little girl trying to negotiate a rental contract. It's pretty funny. [Laughs] I was good. And, I've always had a bust and always had hips so I looked like I was 16 at 13, 16 or 18. [Laughs] I was like the jail bait. It was really bad. Um, and you know like I used to always have to be aware of how I looked, how I acted. It was like always had to be an adult; always had to be put together. Now I'm like I have to be young. I have to be giggly and I'm more like I've got to get this back—fun: Exactly. This is my time!

I ended up moving out . . . out of my parents' house at 15. I moved in with a friend of mine and her family. And I took care of the mother's long-term boyfriend's daughter who had um, I think ADHD, and since I had been taking care of our house for . . . ever since I was like 9 years old, it was a breeze.

I can talk in-depth with my father about things. I love him! He's like one of my favorite people. I told him, "You don't need to be close to anybody that I'm dating unless you really like them. It's not your job. We're not training anybody to be your son-in-law."

I was thinking about getting married. I was thinking about having children, and I knew I wanted to have children. I knew I wanted to have children when I was young. It was like . . . I reckon I couldn't be able to do this when I get older. Like there's no way. I've got a career. I'm not going to give up a career for my children. I'm going to build a career with my children so I wanted to start young.

Yeah, you know I was with the guy for four and a half years. [Breaking up with him] was the most freeing experience. The relationship had been dead for like six, seven months so it was like good news over because it was; I was like picking out wedding dresses and starting to cry. . . . [Laughs] Like I don't want to do this. And you know what? I saved my friendship with my best friend by not marrying him.

I think I will never marry [pause] because what marriage means to me—what adultery really means to me is being unfaithful and sexuality is not synonymous with being unfaithful. I can't commit adultery. And marriage in the Catholic Church with being [pause] monogamous and it's also synonymous with being faithful, with living in the same place, with procreation—things that I kind of don't want to be a part of. We'll cross that bridge when it comes cuz I don't know what that's going to look like.

This is my first place that I've ever had by myself. I love it! It makes it easier to do things. I can leave dishes in the sink when I want to—yeah! So, it's really nice during finals.

I'm not terribly too private about a lot of things but like [pause] I'll be very open about sexuality with you. [I have experimented with] BDSM (bondage/domination/ sadomasochism). I didn't really know about it until I started studying it because I wanted to find the place where—because what I wanted to study in feminism (we could go on our own tangent) was, "How do women sexually oppress other women?" Wow! This is a great subject. Because there's a scene. People throw sex parties where—it's called a sex party but at more BDSM parties people usually don't have sex at the parties. They just practice whatever they do that they like. And foreplay— that's all they do if they want. So I feel a lot more comfortable with being intimate with someone, without having sex, for the environment fosters that sort of thing. More play is ok there if that's what you'd want to do.

I am such a good girl. I like, I'm not kidding. Every time I get on the Max I pay my fare. I'm, I am seriously like super paranoid to follow all the rules you know. It's just that there's rules I think are made to be broken. You know it's like [high pitched tone and reduced speed of speech], just do it once, you know?

And then there's like little stupid taboos that I think are kind of dumb and, oh, like polyamory like not dating one person at a time. [Polyamory is when you have] many partners. So it's like you don't specifically have one person you're with. I messed around with polyamory pretty much ever since I was sexually active. I knew how I wanted to do things. . . . It was the book and community I was not aware of. Found the book (*The Ethical Slut*) and then I was like, "Well, where the hell's the community?"

Polyamorous communities tend to foster emotional responsibility. . . . Those that are not responsible for their own emotions [pause] tend to not have so many lovers. So, the nice thing about polyamory for me is that I really have to evaluate what I want all the time, and I either get it or I don't. I make mistakes with it. I have [laughs].

I should also say the wonderful thing about polyamory is it's something I would not force on anyone because it is a very hard lifestyle because you must be conscious about being honest [pause] and brutally honest sometimes. There are some people who are very monogamous and the partner is polyandrous. Honesty and reassurances are the key. Faithfulness is not synonymous, by any means, with monogamy. Every freedom has responsibility. Being free to date multiple people, you have to be responsible to your own emotions. You can't have everything in the world—that's just how it is. I'm completely aware that [polyamorous relationships are] ephemeral, and that's something that's nice. And, I've become more aware that my own family is ephemeral, and if I don't like them, they're gone.

All sexuality is alternative. We're all self-taught; at the same time, we're not. But when it comes to the actual mechanics of our love life, we're all self-taught. There's no two ways about it.

Seeing all my artwork—me being an artist—is all autobiographical. I'm already out there in like a very vulnerable naked form. Now that I know this is going to be my lifestyle, and that I'm proud of who I am, and that's a good thing. . . .

And I wouldn't say that I'm good at interacting with human nature, but I'm pretty good at predicting it. Not that I don't keep from eating my own foot. Um [laughs], like, "Hi, how's it going? Let me tell you how much I hate that hat." I [laughs]. It's like, I; if I could just say what's on my mind without any other consideration. It's like I realize it's wrong, I realize it's dumb. I realize I should shut up, but it's like I don't. I know a lot of people have these kinds of problems, but I just feel kind of you know [pause]. Especially when I'm like advocating for them, people just kind of be nice to one another.

J. R.

I'm an inventor. I just got my first patent from the US Patent Office. I am a civil engineer. I am working on writing a couple of books, too. I designed it and built [my] house.

My bachelor's was in civil engineering. My master's was engineering majoring in urban transportation engineering and minor in structural engineering, and undeclared minor in economics. During my junior, at the end of my sophomore year I recognized my junior year academically was going to be difficult enough that I didn't have the time to take ROTC. Yeah, and, ah . . . we did lose 40 people out of our; out of the civil engineering class that year. I mean I wasn't one of 'em, so [laughs]. But the trouble is engineering is taught by theorists. You have to understand the theory and apply the principles of the theory to individual problems to build solutions. If you're a person that learns by rote memorization, which most of grade school is taught, and part of high school, you won't make it in engineering. You're expected to take and solve problems, based upon the principles of a theory.

Well, I grew up in this town. I only lived about five blocks away . . . over here. Yeah. I mean, you know I know a lot of people that live around here.

Because I couldn't hear well enough to talk like everyone else . . . I went to, in first grade, speech therapy. I had a speech therapist and, I would say, "no it's chimney not chimily. And it's ambulance, ambulance not ambuance." There were a lot of other words I had problems with. Those two just kept hammering them. My sister would tell people I spoke Chinese and she could interpret because she could understand what I was trying to say. That, or sometimes, sometimes she wanted to interpret differently than what I was saying.

When I was like three years old, she was like four and a half; we'd gone out in the backyard. My dad had a pile of bricks he'd collected. He eventually built a barbecue out of it. My sister, being a little lazier, says oh . . . to just throw 'em [laughs] and she's just throwing 'em back. Oh, she hit me in the back of the head with one. So, I ran up to the house and I had blood coming out the back of my head. And [pauses] I tell my mother what; you know I'm a little bit hysterical what happened. And, my sister comes up there. She said, "Oh he fell and hit his head." So she kept herself out of trouble.

Well she got a lot of favors that um were maybe a little bit inappropriate. She wanted something, she got it. I got a birthday card for her one time. She thought it was very appropriate. It said, happy birthday to the person who gave her family character. In fact, you open it up; in fact you were the family character. She was a little clown all the time.

In first grade my mother was a school secretary, and we went, my sister and I went to a private school. So after school we were given a ride back up to her school, and then we'd come home with her. And we had about an hour to kill up there. My sister ended up on their swimming team. And, I went down to the gym and found a rowing machine I could row. I was a first grader but [alters voice to a grated tone], "Ha! You don't mess with me" [laughs].

Apparently my grandparents lived four houses away from us and they had a pool table in the basement. I spent a lot of time over there because my dad's business was over there in the basement. He was in business with his father, a French perfume business. They made; they manufactured French perfume there. . . . They made, they manufactured French perfume in the basement.

And so I go over there. You know, wash 'em, shake 'em off [the perfume bottles], take all the water out and set 'em upside down to drain out and dry. So I did that [sighs] and then when I wasn't doing that right around the next room was a pool table. So, I went out and played pool. Well, and my mother's school had a pool table down there. I remember the eighth grade . . . I'd go down there; these eighth grade boys figured they were goin' to hustle me real well. I was in the first grade, but I could hustle them [laughs].

After I got my master's degree, I went on active duty. I went to a transportation officer's course, and graduated fourth in my class. There was a reserve officer's school. I was in that for a while and then I had a [pauses] a company commander came over from the unit. . . . It was a transportation unit, and he was looking for transportation officers. So I happened to be a transportation officer. He talked me into transferring to his unit, which I did.

So [pauses] it was a different kind of unit than you'd expect. And, it was a group of stevedores that were . . . that had come in to run a terminal, load and unload a ship. Load and unload ships. Or load 'em. Or load and unload um, unload um landing craft on the beach. Another fun thing we got to do every once in a while. Just south of North Island in San Diego Bay out there's a Navy amphib. Working out of the amphib vehicle . . . working on the ocean side of the spit there. And they'd bring in, they had a Navy ship out, a couple of miles out, and they'd bring in these landing craft. And they'd dummy; it was dummy cargo. It was a pallet with maybe three 55-gallon drums filled with sand on it, strapped to it. The trouble is they wouldn't let our people work on the ship. They wanted Navy guys to work on the ships. It was more an Army/Navy type squabble. I got to be; I got to be supply officer, safety officer, and platoon leader.

[I am a] captain, Army Reserve retired yeah. But I mean if they, if they showed at my door and said, "Hi. You didn't show up for your . . . or you were ordered for active duty." I'd say, "Yeah. You really want me?" I'd reach around the corner and grab a white cane [laughs].

[After the tumor behind my eye was mostly removed it affected my] sense of smell. You know, for a while I was married and lived [outside the city]. I went to; one day my wife and I went out to the [store]. And the parking lot there was right next to a field that had; they were growing cabbage in that year. And they; when they cut the cabbage they cut the main head and they just left the outer leaves. They hadn't ploughed them under so they were just rotting. And that breeze just blowing in over that field; my wife got out of the car; she just [groaned loudly], "That's a terrible smell!" And I went [deep inhalation], "Smells like good clean country air to me."

My wife then she went down and filed for divorce. But, ah, yeah I found out later she'd take our ATM card. She'd go down to the ATM machine; she'd take out $200 which was maximum you could take out of there and she'd take it across the street to her bank and deposit it. She was, she was robbing me blind. And ah, until one day I went in, one Saturday into; one Sunday to use the ATM machine for myself to get some money to pay. Because I got. After, you know after the, the [pauses]. After she left I got a car pool driver and I wanted to get some money to pay him. And no she hadn't left yet. I wanted some money anyway out of the ATM machine, and I went there Sunday and put the card in and it says "request denied." And I said, "What the heck." And she tried to tell me, "Oh it's probably your card's bad." Monday I called the credit union, and I asked them what's going on. They said, "Oh, well, the way the system works is you have a limit of $200 per day. And it considers Saturday and Sunday to be one business day." And so—you learn something new every day when you talk to me.

One day, so I was at work and I said, "I've got to figure out a way of getting to and from work." And so I had a friend, so I called him up and I asked him if there was any chance that he might be able to give me a ride to and from work for awhile. So he gave me a ride to and from work for awhile. And [then] I talked to somebody in personnel and they said, "yeah." They gave me a name now, I don't remember but . . . they gave me his number; I could call him up. "Sure!" He said, "No problem!" So next morning he pulls in my driveway with his Mercedes and picks me up [laughs]. And he wouldn't allow me to pay him anything. I don't know if he enjoyed my company, but . . . he was a pleasant change over Old Yeller.

You know, I was in Scouts. I gotta go to a meeting tonight. I'm . . . a committee member. I hate to tell ya, but it looks like they took the outing out of scouting. They had the camp. My dad's gone camping there when he was in Scouts. We went camping there when I was in Scouts. Like, we'd go out once a month. Maybe we'd go out one week in a month we'd go out there. And because it was close, it was easy to get to; and they sold it to raise money for something. And the um [pauses]. So now if the kids want to go camping they've gotta go on maybe a three-hour drive each way.

Beth

I was born in Boston, but I don't remember that much about living there because we moved away when I was seven. We spent our summers on Cape Cod, eight miles into the woods from any town. It was really primitive—no hot running water, no shower or bathtub. Several men, including my dad, built the cottage out of used barn wood and the fireplace bricks came from an old bakery oven. We bathed and washed our hair in the lake. We would put dishtowels at the edge of the lake shore, cover them with sand, and wait for a school of minnows to come up. We'd pull the towel up and, there ya go, we had caught the bait for anyone who wanted to fish for sunfish and perch. A couple of the dads were professional amateur photographers, so our lives were well-documented, and I treasure these old black-and-white photos.

Things at home were pretty rough. My mother was mentally ill. She could be very charming and fun-loving, and also manipulative, unpredictable, and violent. This caused a constant low-level tension in the house, and we did whatever we had to do to keep her happy. My dad was a really gentle, funny, simple, old-fashioned guy—so different from my mother. He didn't have a clue about how to deal with her. Looking back on this, I can only imagine how hard all that was on him.

So, yeah, there were lots of mixed messages. Over the years since she died I've come to understand she probably couldn't help herself. She was not all bad—she was ill.

When I was seven, we moved to Tucson, Arizona, which was a small town back then—only 52,000 people. The culture was just coming out of Old West days, so it was very cowboy, Indian, and Mexican. A lot of things about that part of the desert Southwest are harsh—cactus everywhere, unrelenting heat and sunshine for more months than not, and it is said that there is something poisonous under every rock. It was really a pretty strange place to grow up, but it was a great lesson in survival and adaptability. Anyway, the smell of wet creosote after a rainfall is unforgettable—one of the best fragrances I've ever known. And you can't beat the golden orange and red sunsets anywhere.

There were tent revivals coming through Tucson every year. As a Jewish kid, I was sometimes urged by my classmates to accept Jesus into my life. This got pretty intense during high school. I felt like an outsider because the pressure for everyone to be Christian was always part of the backdrop, reminding me that I was in the minority. We got unexcused absences on our report cards when we were out for the Jewish High Holy Days.

I didn't learn about the Holocaust until Adolph Eichmann was captured in Argentina in 1961. His trial made the front page for months. But, our family and friends still didn't talk about it. It was just too awful, I guess. I began collecting the local newspaper articles about him with the horrifying pictures of mounds of decaying bodies bulldozed into ditches, and of the ovens and of walking skeleton people. I kept these articles in a manila folder hidden in the back of my closet. I thought there was something wrong with me because of this morbid fascination. I'd stare at those unbelievable photos and I'd try to picture my friends and myself in those piles. I thought about how their lives must have been like ours before they were sent off to concentration camps. I just couldn't believe it happened to my people. I couldn't process that hatred and sickness. I've heard that all Jews who are currently alive are in some way survivors of the Holocaust. That is in no way meant to trivialize the experience of the actual survivors whose experiences we could never really comprehend, but it did explain the psychological impact it had on my generation. And, it also explained one of the reasons I felt different than most people I knew. Then when I got into disability studies and started learning the history of disabled people in the Holocaust, this shook me up all over again. I'm glad this history is finally being told.

My high school was almost three-fourths Mexican American, a little Chinese, and one-fourth middle- and upper-middle-class white. I hung out at the Jewish Community Center where our friendships and romances were found and lost and found again. The Center was a sanctuary away from my home. I think I lived to go there. I could be myself and I was loved and accepted there. Some of our friendships have lasted throughout our lives.

During 1961, my junior year in high school, our speech teacher turned me on to the works of Norman Thomas, who ran for US president, I think five times, on the Socialist Party ticket. I loved his passion for social and economic justice. That same year, my high school sweetheart and I went to see Martin Luther King, Jr., speak at the university auditorium. . . . This was the first time we had heard of a civil rights movement. That changed my life. And then just a few months later—my senior year in high school—Bob Dylan's first album was released, and I was hooked. I still am. I have almost all his albums, and have seen him in concert a lot. At the same time, I got into the "Beat" poets—like Lawrence Ferlinghetti and Allen Ginsburg. These guys all changed me forever. But then again, so did Hitler.

I met the man who I would marry when I was nineteen. He is my first cousin by marriage, not by blood. I think it was sort of a modern-day arranged marriage—pretty much doomed from the get-go. I had two kids by the time I was twenty-three. I mostly was a stay-at-home mom—a "homemaker," which is what we did back then. I did volunteer work in my community,

and even got a letter of commendation from the mayor.
Through that work, the Urban Program Division manager of
the City of Tucson invited me to work for them paid part-time
in their annexation program. I loved that job. I was proud to
contribute to my community.

About a year after I went on the city payroll, my husband
took a job in San Diego. Even though I was leaving a job and
friends I loved, and even though we didn't know a soul in San
Diego, I was happy to leave Tucson.

Nine months after we moved I volunteered part-time for
the Democratic Party. I met a group of young Social Democrats
in the labor movement, which was totally thrilling because I had
no idea the party of Norman Thomas still existed and that there
were other people my age who believed as I did. I joined
Frontlash, which was a youth organization of Social Democrats
dedicated to voter registration and voter education of the newly
enfranchised 18-year-old voters. We went wherever we thought
working-class young people went, and we walked every precinct
in San Diego County. We went to theaters, concerts, factory
gates, beaches. We even formed a temporary alliance with a
motorcycle gang. They walked the beaches with us, registering
voters. ABC News ran a national story on us. We were that
good. For a few months, I also organized and ran one of the
presidential candidate's San Diego campaign and won election as
a delegate to the National Democratic Convention. I was high
on politics but things were not going so well at home, and we
ended up separating about a year later.

I wasn't a very good wife. He wasn't such a good husband,
either. Let's just leave it at that. I tried my best to be a good
mom even though I was scared a lot of the time because I didn't
want to screw my kids up. I was very immature and naïve and
was just plain uncomfortable in my own skin—as though I was
living someone else's life, not my own.

The gap between my politics and my husband's got bigger.
Well, could you have a worse match than an oil company junior
executive married to a labor person working on a "Tax Big Oil"
initiative? I think not. That about sums the basic problem up
right there—our basic values and views about what's important
in life were too different.

I've had the good fortune to travel a lot to many countries—
England, Ireland, Hong Kong, Singapore, the Philippines,
Japan, Indonesia, and to Israel twice. I hope to live in Ireland for

a year or two sometime. My spirit feels at home there. Don't know why. . . .

I've made a lot of mistakes in my life, but I don't dwell on them—just learn from them and move on. Regrets are useless. I'm a happy, optimistic person. I read somewhere that dogs approach each day with "Yahoo!" attitudes. I learned from that. So, every morning, I wake up next to my little dog, pick him up, and as our six legs hit the carpet, I say, "Moses! We got another day! Yahoo!" Even on days when I don't feel like saying it, I do.

Conclusion

In summary, this chapter stands on its own as a location for each participant to offer the reader an intimate, uninterrupted version of their life. As to the point of writing a chapter in this style, such a format has rarely, if ever, been employed in an emancipatory life story study that also provided data analysis in subsequent chapters. I provided a brief overview of some existing literature about life story research, which supported my rationale for the design of this chapter.

As was demonstrated with this technique, disability researchers using a life story design might do well not to omit a goodly portion of their participants' data, even if the material is not immediately recognized as being relevant to the research questions and aims. By paying close attention to what the participants told us about their life philosophies and experiences, which added color and texture to each person's story, readers could come to know them beyond the lived experience of blindness.

PART 2

Borderlands in a Political Economy

5

Education

In the United States, some blind people continue to live in segregated residential schools. Blind children have had conspicuously similar histories to other minority groups, such as the "Stolen Generation" of Aboriginal children in Australia and Native American Indians who were systematically taken from their homes and segregated from their families and the general public (Lomawaima 1995; Conference of Education Systems Chief Executive Officers 2000; Gitter 2001). All these children were derided for practicing what came naturally to them. For instance, after replacing Native American students' moccasins, school workers then devalued them for walking uncomfortably in Western-style shoes; curricula pursued "correct physical posture, proper ways of moving and of exercising and correct details of dress" (Gitter 2001, p. 198). In parallel, blind children are discouraged from using blindisms such as rocking, eye-rubbing, and/or awkwardly shuffling (Kleege 1999), and they are told not to hunch over their desks even though they must do so in order to see print books or to write and take tests.

Another sad commonality among Aboriginal, Native American, and blind children was that their school curricula emphasized the domestic arts, which fairly well ensured a life of dependence with little chance for successful gainful employment or self-sufficient living. This exclusion from mainstream education, oppression of natural blind behaviors, and its consequences forms the substance of this chapter.

Historical Background

The first school for the blind was founded by Valentin Haüy in 1784 (Rubin and Roessler 1995; Koester 1976; Ross 1951; Lowenfeld 1973). Haüy was inspired to found his school after watching a group of blind men staring blankly ahead as they performed mummery—holding musical instruments, producing a cacophony of sound, as they pretended to be symphonic musicians—at a Paris street fair (Kuusisto 1998). The irony of what he saw expressed here caught his attention and prompted his response. Haüy recruited a blind beggar, Francis LeSeur, off the streets of Paris and made him his assistant and first student. Together they developed an embossed type system for tactile reading as well as a system for teaching math to blind students (Ross 1951). Unfortunately, Haüy was replaced as head of the school he founded by Sebastien Guillie, and Haüy's humanitarian attitude toward blindness education left with him. Guillie believed "blind people are 'immodest, inhuman, selfish, irritable, vindictive, implacable, irreligious, and ungrateful'" (Ross 1951, p. 114). Guillie reversed many of Haüy's educational and social advances.

Education of the blind took a dramatic turn in the 1830s when a young blind student, Louis Braille, invented the braille alphabet. Braille said he could explain how his alphabet works, "but that only the blind could know what it really meant" (Ross 1951, p. 132). Ross writes, "The world of letters opened up for them through their fingertips" (p. 132). Braille was not immediately accepted by schools in Europe because sighted administrators thought they, not the blind, knew what was best for blind students and were reluctant to convert from embossed type to a new format.

In the United States, the first school for the blind was founded in Baltimore, Maryland, in 1812. In 1832, the Massachusetts Asylum for the Blind opened and later changed its name to Perkins Institute (Shapiro 1993). Samuel Gridley Howe, founder of the Massachusetts Asylum, was intent on shifting the European emphasis on arts and crafts training of the blind toward academics. He observed that European students who completed their education at the blind school were ill-equipped to support themselves. Howe regarded the European schools as "beacons to warn rather than light to guide." According to Gitter (2001), Howe characterized Haüy's French school in this way:

> At first glance, Howe wrote, he . . . [thought] the school presented a "delightful spectacle" of "smiling faces" gleaming with "awakened intellect." Deeper investigation revealed to him, that "a spirit of illiberality, of mysticism, amounting almost to charlatanism" pervaded the establishment. The students were trained for mere intellectual display. (p. 34)

It is a shame that both the French blind school and the Massachusetts Asylum for the Blind exploited their students by using them as poster children—putting them on public display for fundraising purposes. These exhibitions were precursors to modern-day fundraising efforts such as the telethon. It is difficult to understand how being a spectacle, a curiosity put forward for public comment, could engender the self-respect Howe hoped his students would attain. Even though Howe felt comfortable in the company of his blind students, he characterized their blindisms (body movements, arm swinging, neck positions, etc.) as "disagreeable habits," and tried to "cure" the students of these natural mannerisms (Gitter 2001). Howe created many innovations for blindness education, especially the concept of individualized education plans that took into account students' backgrounds, interests, talents, and goals. He fostered concepts of self-respect, self-reliance, and citizenship (Rubin and Roessler 1995; Ross 1951). Howe's theories of blindness education were lost in the modern rehabilitation system until around twenty years ago when disabled people and their advocates demanded participation in their own education and training plans.

During the nineteenth century, German schools for the blind were linked to the state. Ross (1951) reports that the work was paternalistic, and once students completed their industrial training, they were given supplies, placed in jobs, and finally, a local official was assigned responsibility for their well being. This model of blindness education is known as the Saxon model and is the foundation for such current institutions as sheltered workshops, where disabled people toil for minimum wage or less, do tediously repetitive factory labor, and find themselves doomed to dead-end jobs.

The Saxon model has left a deep, sorrowful scar on society and on blind people alike. Oftentimes, state blindness rehabilitation agencies consider workers in sheltered workshops "successfully rehabilitated" and close their cases, which creates a new roadblock for blind people who need to obtain additional services or equipment. I pick up this thread in the next section about rehabilitation where I discuss how these practices continue to plague blind people in pursuit of education and training.

Early schools for the blind left a mixed legacy. They encouraged education for blind children in an era when education was not mandatory—not even for the nondisabled. Teachers, students, administrators, and advocates fashioned practical methods of access to reading, math, and geography. On the down side, many children became institutionalized by these residential schools, and, even though they had homes and families, they stayed on throughout their lives. Graduates who tried to sustain themselves in the general population typically found a job market closed to them because of perceptions they were unable.

At the present time, many residential schools serve both deaf and blind children. Ironically, deaf people and blind people find communication with each other difficult, if not impossible because blind people cannot see sign language, and deaf people may require light on the speaker's face in order to read lips, which can be physically painful for legally blind people. Evidently, educators, who are usually trained within a medical model of impairment and disability, think it is a good idea to lump children with sensory impairments together, despite the obvious access mismatch.

Since the passage of the US Individuals with Disabilities Education Act, Part B in 1975 (amended in 1997), which applies to blind and visually impaired students, blind children have legal rights to an education within the "least restrictive environment." The 1997 amendments stress the rights of parents to participate in major decisions about their children's education. Schools are required to offer educational materials in braille, and orientation and mobility training. The Department of Education decided to include orientation and mobility in the 1997 amendments as an example of "related services" because they are "reflecting an awareness that a blind or visually impaired individual's ability to learn braille and move around independently is closely linked to the individual's self esteem" (US Department of Education 1995). This memorandum is a typical example of the medical model of disability's influence on education; it emphasizes the needs of the individual rather than addressing environmental access. The assumption that blind people suffer low self-esteem emanates from a gestalt of ocularcentrism that constructs blindness as bad and sight as good and sometimes uses "evidence" to support the notion that blind people necessarily feel loss, shame, sadness, bitterness, and so on. However, "low self-esteem" is a psychosocial device used to make sense of people's experiences; thus, when ocularcentrism projects its own depressing perceptions onto blind people, it cannot help but presume that blind people feel bad about themselves.

Some current debates in blindness education revolve around whether it is better to retain segregated education or have children mainstreamed into public schools with nondisabled students. A moderate compromise that is popular in the United States is to have itinerant blindness teachers who (paid by the public school district) travel to mainstream schools and take blind students into "resource rooms" for teaching blindness skills during a portion of the school day. A team approach is used that includes mainstream teachers, itinerant teachers, parents, social workers, access technology instructors, and rehabilitation agency counselors. Nonetheless, the law is unclear about student involvement in the planning sessions.

What to Do with This Child:
The Dilemma of Legal Blindness in Public Education

From the origination of modern Western asylums for the blind to the present, education has been directly linked to what was considered "rehabilitation"—preparation for employment—which, in reality, fairly well amounted to doing menial craftwork in sheltered workshops for a pittance with no hope for a better future. For the most part, education of the blind was, and still is, built upon ocularcentric misperceptions that blind people's abilities and potential success are limited *because* they are *deficient* in sight.

While the goals of blindness education have improved on paper, confusion still exists about where and how to fit borderland blind children into curricula designed for either sighted or totally blind students. Because Larry and J. R. became blind in adulthood they experienced public school as sighted children; thus, the majority of findings presented here relate largely to Catherine and me, with comments made by Larry or J. R. included where relevant.

The model of ocularcentrism as "a vision-generated, vision-centered interpretation of knowledge, truth, and reality" (Levin 1993, p. 5) is especially critical in school settings given that the whole point of education is to garner knowledge. School is, in fact, an institution where one goes to learn "truth and reality." We are taught to trust school and to place ourselves and our futures at the feet of educators so they can mold young minds and help shape their moral and ethical values. School is a seat of incalculable power and authority.

Customarily, students who are diagnosed as legally blind are deprived of educational opportunities because schools fail to pre- pare themselves to serve those who do not fit into a medically con- structed binary of sightedness/blindness, which assumes blindness means total lack of sight and vision (Michalko 1998). Sighted pro- fessionals put themselves forward as experts about how to cope with blindness. Their goal is to make blind people as "normal" (sighted) as possible. Such was my experience:

> Initially, my parents were advised by my eye doctor to turn lights on where I was reading my schoolbooks even though I found a dim setting more soothing to the eyes. And the doctor also said to correct me whenever they saw me holding books close to my face and whenever I tilted my head, which was my way of seeing around the blind areas in my vision. I was supposed to look "nor- mal" even though my vision was not "normal." It was like Fer- nando from *Saturday Night Live* whose catchphrase was, "It's bet- ter to look good than to feel good." I learned not to squint at the blackboard even though it helped block out the sun streaming in the windows of my classrooms.

This account is consistent with Kleege's (1999) observation about how blind people are taught not to act out "blindisms"—postures and movements that come naturally to blind people but are socially unacceptable among the sighted majority.

The School Years: Where Do "Inbetweeners" Belong?

Catherine's and my stories uncover subthemes of power relations and authority confusion when mainstream educational institutions bump up against the borderland of legal blindness. Our stories as what Catherine calls "inbetweeners" bring to life some of the complexities being debated about inclusive versus segregated education for disabled children. While I thought I could have done better at the state school for deaf and blind children in my hometown instead of the public high school I did attend, Catherine has very different ideas about the value of a segregated education. She believes that children who are raised in blindness education are less self-sufficient, less motivated, and somewhat lacking in both social and personal daily living skills. She bases her opinion on observations during rehabilitation events that brought her together with young people raised in segregated blindness education. Catherine said:

> Blind people are taught to be careful about the type of lifestyle that they lead so that it's easy and smooth and simple as possible. So if they want to choose something a little more challenging, a little harder. . . . So it's like you know it's like [pause]. I don't know many blind people that would even go so ambitious about life to make their own decisions and not follow the pattern . . . [they're] kind of discouraged by the people that they're trying to look up to for help.

Catherine's description evokes an image of blindness educators encasing their students in a cocoon of the safety and security of sameness. Whether borderland blind people are cocooned within segregated settings or left out in the borderland, the result appears to be the same, that is, they are surrounded by walls that separate them from everyone else.

Catherine and I shared the same experience with our parents' dilemma about where we should be placed for a proper education. Catherine recalls:

> One of the hard things is the way that your parents treat you
> because you're not quite there. But you're almost there. So it's like
> you're put into a normal like school . . . and then you're sheltered
> a lot more. They don't really know how to take it.

Catherine is glad that she was educated in public schools and
believes this helped her to know both sides: "cuz I think I would not
be as good a person as I am if I had been born blinder and had gone
to blind school and done everything I was 'supposed to do.'"

Since I was not privy to conversations between eye doctors,
educators, and my parents, I do not know exactly what transpired in
discussions about where to place me:

> My parents wanted me to be as "normal" as possible, and so they
> decided to keep me in the regular public school system. They
> believed this would serve my overall development better than
> attending school with other blind children only.

My parents had accepted ocularcentric beliefs that blindness is an
abnormal ontology inferior to sighted ways. However noble their
hopes for me were (and I have no doubt they deeply wanted the best
for me), an accessible education wherein I could learn blindness
skills was traded off for the appearance of normality. What is "normal" is what is "sighted," according to sighted professionals whose
aspiration is to fashion borderland blind people in their own image.

Catherine believes sighted educators sometimes misinformed
her about best practice in the real world:

> seems that's what . . . the number one thing when you're being
> trained how to get around in the world, that's like the number one
> thing . . . it's like, please just ask and be out there you know. Don't
> be afraid to ask for what you need. And that sounds easy but you
> know I find that a lot of the people that say that are the sighted
> people that are teaching me how to be blind.

Larry relates a similar sentiment that highlights sighted professionals'
embedded commitment to ocularcentrism, "Sighted people make up
everything. That's why things are so fucked up." During another
interview, Larry resists and challenges ocularcentric perceptions:

It's like people that see, okay, meeting people that are blind and you know it's like almost humorous in a way that they know better than blind people which maybe they feel they do, right, but don't tell me you hate the spinach if you never tasted it.

Educators and rehabilitation workers who frequently partner with each other to produce Individualized Education Plans use their power to normalize the students by teaching them sighted ways. As Levin (1993) points out, "The subject is invariably either in the role of a dominating observer or in the role of an observable object, submissive before the gaze of power" (p. 4). Students most frequently find themselves in the latter situation before the gaze of adults who, however well-intended, want what *they* think is best for blind people—which is not to act "blind." Michalko (1998) relates a story of a blind girl whose perceptions about where a pole ended and the sky began were correct to her but were challenged by a teacher. *Ocularcentrists* insist that the perceptions of the blind must be incorrect because they are different from their own way of knowing the world through sight and vision. This attitude pervades public school curricula.

When Sighted Educators Fail School

Catherine and I both relate stories that highlight common experiences as we made our way through public education's acclimation to the needs presented by legal blindness. Doctors, teachers, and administrators *determine* which disability-related services will be prescribed for each child. However, oftentimes, blind children and their parents or guardians are not considered integral players in the decisionmaking process.

Conventionally, parents of children with impairments are expected to perceive and accept the medical and educational team to be the experts. Unless educated or otherwise equipped to find a way around the systems through advocacy strategies and resistance to the hegemony of the medical model, parents merely defer to the will of medicine's ocularcentrism. This was certainly my experience as my parents acquiesced to the demands of teachers and doctors. As one consequence of the hegemony of ocularcentrism in school policy matters, schools continue to demonstrate severe functional limitations that constrict students' possibilities for accomplishment.

Public education tends to accept medicine's idea that blindness is a tragic deficit and that blind people cannot achieve much. Therefore, schools do not provide an education that could, under a more positive model, prepare blind people to achieve as much as anyone else. The school fails. When the education system lacks faith in blind students' potential, the system's investment in the education of blind children becomes proportionate to its low expectations; these negative attitudes create a self-fulfilling prophecy, because the child leaves school with an inferior education.

On top of these problems, when public schools do commit to providing an appropriate education for the blind, the system prepares itself only for those who are totally blind. The specific needs of borderland blind students are repeatedly glossed over or wholly ignored because curricula are developed and implemented for either the sighted or for the totally blind, but not for "inbetweeners." Borderland blind children end up with no curriculum to fit their access needs, which often culminates in their being misplaced in classrooms designed for the sighted. Then, to fit into sighted classrooms, borderland blind students are covertly or overtly pressured to "act" sighted. Catherine explains one of the personal costs of such deficits in the educational system: "My other cousins turned out Harvard and I'm sitting here at PNCA [Pacific Northwest College of Art], not only am I blind, I'm not good enough in that sense."

To Braille or Not to Braille? That Is the Question

Another subtheme unique to the legal blindness borderland is the issue of if, and/or when, to teach braille. How do people decide whether they even need or want to learn this print alternative? This decisionmaking process is likely to be influenced by an ocular-centric reluctance to help borderland blind people cross over into the land of the blind, where hopes and dreams are nearly absent. Institutional decisions are made case by case. In 1997, the Individuals with Disabilities Education Act (IDEA) amendments mandated braille training for all legally blind children unless evaluations by professionals determine otherwise. Unlike my experience of not receiving any blindness skills training, Catherine received some training from a vision specialist—a woman whom she remembers fondly. At first, Catherine did not learn to read print, but she did learn to pretend she could in order to fit in with her sighted peers. She said:

> It took me a long time to learn how to read because no one would give me braille. Because I wasn't totally blind. . . . Everybody wants to be accepted, especially as children you want to be very accepted so you pretend to read. You pretend to do this, you pretend to do that. You need help. You need some help.

Social institutions, including education, pressure borderland blind people to remain on the sighted side of the border. One technique is to encourage them to use residual vision rather than resort to braille, which is considered by ocularcentrics to be of lesser value than print. Catherine and her vision specialist discussed whether braille or print would serve her best in the long run. The specialist was concerned that braille might inhibit Catherine's reading level progress. So, she taught Catherine grade-one braille, which, while slow-going and somewhat limiting, gave her the rudiments of a print alternative. Once she learned elementary-level braille, the vision specialist moved Catherine back into print; therefore, her vision specialist made it possible for Catherine to access information on *both* sides of the border.

My eye disease was degenerative, thus, not as severe at onset as what unfolded later on in life, so the need for braille in the future was indeterminate. I acquired my eye disease in middle school, several decades before Catherine's birth, at a time when borderland blind students in mainstream schools received no blindness skills training at all, so the question of whether to learn braille or not was never considered. Although my eye disease was diagnosed during middle-school years, it was not until high school that any possibility of accommodations was addressed. Like Catherine, there were personal costs for these administrative decisions. For example, the only thing I was given to help me with vision loss was a conspicuously cumbersome large-print typing textbook; and I was the only freshman allowed to take a typing class. I recall that

> I felt out of place in that class because the book was so big and noticeable and because everyone else was juniors and seniors. I was different, my book was different, and my sight was different and I

was keenly conscious of all that. So, it was not just the school that didn't know what to do with me; I didn't know what to do with me either. One year someone got the bright idea that I should read to a totally blind boy in my school. That was weird—not the reading, just that I had to do it. I think I only did that a couple of times. I've never figured out exactly why they wanted me to do that.

Catherine's term for legally blind people—"inbetweeners"— certainly captures the essence of the borderland where educators do not know what, where, when, or how to teach borderland blind children. Sometimes children are not taught skills that could be very useful as they try to cross the borderland into the majority society. For example, Catherine observed:

> I know somebody who's—especially blind men that don't dress nice. It's like, honey, someone needs to help you out more. [Laughs] It's like; especially like their in-between area, you know. It is like the between areas people just don't ask enough or no one feels like they need to help them out enough.

While dress is certainly an ocularcentric value, blind people must make themselves presentable according to ocularcentric rules. Totally blind children are taught to limit their color choices and to label their clothes, but borderland blind children who are put through the mainstream are left to fend for themselves with regard to fashion decisions.

During Catherine's attendance in art college, she did not receive access accommodations but was expected to perform the same tasks as her sighted peers, which is a common subtheme found in this study. She related an anecdote about an art assignment that challenged her vision, as well as the feelings that emerged as a result:

> Yeah, so sometimes it's like if you stare at it long enough it'll pop out. Um [pause] just really (finally . . . ?) like (. . . ?) when I was trying to draw a damn seed because your drawing teacher wants us to draw a damn seed to scale. You're like damn fuckin' seed, can't see it, son of a bitch. And you're like [laughs] you're just like; it's like [laughs heartily]. I'm sitting in the corner. Talk about

interpersonal relationships. You start resenting the living crap out of people.

Denial and the Curriculum

Borderland blind children who receive their education in a main-stream setting and who are not deemed to benefit from a blindness resource room or itinerant teacher are assumed to be capable of performing at the same level as sighted classmates in all subject areas. There appears to be a denial of the reality of the experiences of borderland blind students. Making blind students perform along-side sighted classmates and then grading them on this unequal play-ing field reinforces the societal assumption that blindness causes incompetence, and may cause students to experience internalized oppression. Borderland blind students learn how to fake perfor-mance, to pass as sighted, to accept being chosen last on teams, to learn that they are not capable of high achievement compared to their sighted peers, and to suffer in silence—suffer not from their blindness but from the situation in which they are thrust. Border-land blind students may become riddled with self-consciousness because they stand out as different. For example, when I was in high school,

> one year during English class we were learning speed reading, which of course I couldn't do. After taking attendance, the teacher would dismiss me from class and I would be so embarrassed to walk out of that room with everyone looking at me. I was sent to the library to sit with kids who had been sent there for detention. I think this made me feel like going blind was a bad behavior—a disgrace. . . . I was ashamed of myself. At school, I sometimes sat at my desk in the classroom and dug at the top of my scalp until it bled, and then when it scabbed over, I'd pick it all open again. In P.E. [physical education] class I dreaded doing a headstand because the top of my head was so sore. I was scared and bewil-dered and I felt isolated and different from anyone else I knew. I had no one to talk to about it, no one who was going through the same thing.

Physical education is perhaps the most difficult situation that blind children grapple with as they are forced into competition with sighted students or expected to perform impossible physical feats for grades that cannot be earned on merit. One year I was assigned to a mandatory archery course:

> That was laughable, really. I hoisted my quiver full of arrows onto my shoulder and stepped up to the line. I shot all six arrows toward the target, although I couldn't see it, and then spent the rest of the hour hunting my arrows down, hoping I . . . I wouldn't get shot out there. I don't know what I was supposed to learn from all that [laughs].

Conclusion

This chapter traced the history of blindness education in Europe and the United States. I highlighted some problems encountered by borderland blind people as they made their way through an ocular-centric education system. Both Catherine's and my stories corroborate existing literature on many points. As Titchkosky (2003) reports, either (or both) institutional lack of knowledge about or denial of her impairment caused her early school years to take a personal toll on her. She did not receive much-needed accommodations; thus, she tried to pass as a "normal" learner. These efforts caused her anxiety, and the school system's judgments about her learning style were an assault on her own sense of self.

The stories in this study revealed that the education system in partnership with medicine and rehabilitation defined these blind students' identities and then acted according to these definitions. Education failed to listen to the student's voice even when the student spoke up—as much as a child could—to adults in positions of power and authority. All these stories are consistent with Titchkosky's (2003) assertion that "situations have in common the fact that such phenomena appear through narration by both self and by others" (p. 35). Both Catherine and I paid dearly for medical model–based institutional decisions to essentially declare us sighted, to educate us as if we were fully sighted, and to judge our performance using the same criteria as what was used for our sighted peers, despite obvious impairment-related limitations. Moreover, all these decisions flew in the face of the fact that medicine had already acted upon us by declaring us legally blind. Education was conflicted about the student's status: it embraced the medical diagnosis, and then treated us as sighted anyway. Education apparently denied the impact of visual impairment on us and chose instead to place us in standard curricula designed solely for the sighted. Ironically, education's choice to place Catherine and me into mainstream education for the purpose of integrating us into the mainstream actually caused us to feel even more on the fringes of the borderland between sightedness and blindness because we were subjected to the othering that the "squint-eyed" (Anzaldúa 1987) experience whenever we attempted to traverse the border into the mainland.

Education is usually considered the most fruitful path to meaningful and gainful employment, but blind people are often denied equal access to educational opportunities. Borderland blind people may experience even less access than totally blind students because of an education system that does not understand the borderland, does not tolerate difference, or is too unwieldy to accommodate specific access requirements.

6

The Perils of Rehabilitation

Historically and ideologically, rehabilitation is inseparably fettered to medical model theory and practice. Michalko (1999) observes that rehabilitation and the medical model assume that a "seeing life" is the "only good life" (p. 67). Michalko deconstructs medical, psychological, and societal ideas and practices around blindness. He notes that once ophthalmologists have diagnosed patients as destined for permanent blindness, they refer the patients out for rehabilitation. Michalko writes:

> Ophthalmology is recommending *agency* as an *actor* presented as qualified to speak about, and act upon, permanent blindness. This suggests that blindness requires agency and needs to be acted upon in order for it to be lived with. . . . Rehabilitation, too, conceives of the seeing life as the only good life. (pp. 66–67)

People who are unable to be "successfully rehabilitated" to "normal" or expected functioning may feel like failures.

Within an ocularcentric paradigm, blindness and sightedness are represented as a binary, and blindness is perceived to be a diagnosable aberration of nature. According to Michalko (1998):

> Diagnosis relies upon common sense in that it assumes what normal seeing life "looks like." "Normal seeing" provides the background against which an instance of blindness can be discovered. . . . Diagnosis enters the story of blindness at this point. It explains

the discovery of blindness by attributing a medical cause to it as well as giving it a prognosis. Diagnosis is the final arbiter: if the prognosis is positive, blindness is prevented; if negative, another blind person enters the world. (p. 5)

Because it is necessarily so that sighted people are the diagnosticians, it is sighted people who decide how blindness should be handled: "Sight is status and is a status former to blindness. Sight is not a mere shadow of its former self since it has no former self. Thus sight is not regarded as needful of restoration" (Michalko 1998, p. 68). But blindness is. Doctors, legislators, and policymakers work together to create categories of blindness; they determine who fits into those categories and then either grant or deny access to economic, educational, and/or social supports. When a patient's prognosis is permanent blindness with no chance for a "cure" anticipated in the near future, ophthalmologists exert their authority to either declare patients "partially sighted," "legally blind," or "totally blind." The importance of such a declaration is that patients may become eligible to apply for economic, educational, and/or social supports. Some doctors tell their patients that the medical documentation letter will open the door to a permanent Social Security disability pension. The message here is that patients are no longer able to support themselves financially; their blindness has rendered them unemployable.

Many ophthalmologists either do not know about or just do not concern themselves with "low vision" or "rehabilitation" options. They send patients away without hope for alternate ways of living effectively as blind people. Of the countless ophthalmologists I have gone to over many years, not one has referred me to either social or low vision services. I have had to ask for referrals or sought them out on my own. When ophthalmologists bother to refer their patients to low vision or rehabilitation services, they are done with them. It is "the ophthalmologist's method for bowing out as storyteller in the story of blindness and is its way to introduce the next speaker," which is either rehabilitation or special education (Michalko 1998, p. 67). Blind persons are then moved out of their role of "patient" in the world of ophthalmology into the "client" (or, more recently labeled "consumer") role of rehabilitation services.

Rehabilitation in Theory

It is no surprise that programs designed to "rehabilitate" blind people are created on an ocularcentric premise that blindness is a deficit; thus, service provision fosters negative attitudes toward blindness and blind people. Michalko (1998) asserts that the goal of rehabilitation programs is to make blind persons as ordinary as possible. Rehabilitation programs are predicated on the assumption that blind persons are just like everyone else and, as Michalko (1998) notes, "with the right techniques, they can do the things that everyone else does. Rehabilitation wants this for blind persons in that it wants blind persons to do the ordinary things that ordinary people do" (p. 65).

Rehabilitation assumes that sight is the superior sense since the other senses will be used to "see." Michalko (1998, p. 65) writes, "Restoring blindness to its former status is restoring it to what it originally was, namely, sight." This restorative theory of rehabilitation is especially ludicrous when applied to people who were born blind, since blindness is their "normal" lived experience.

An ironic feature of blindness rehabilitation—proof of its attempts to "normalize" blind people—is its emphasis on visual aspects. Kleege (1999) explains:

> [An] astonishing amount of "training" and "rehabilitation" of the blind deals with . . . the visible manifestations of blindness. Eliminate "blindness," the experts say, the physical traits to which the blind are allegedly prone—the wobbly neck, uneven posture, shuffling gait, unblinking gaze. Discoloured or bulging eyes should be covered with patches or dark glasses, empty sockets filled with prosthetics. (p. 19)

Rehabilitation books and pamphlets go even further, urging that the blind be extra attentive to personal grooming and that they choose clothes that are stylish and color-coordinated. Kleege (1999) notes that while rehabilitation workers' advice about keeping clothes in order and so forth may, indeed, be helpful in practicality, it instructs us that "blindness is unsightly, a real eyesore. No one wants to look at that" (Kleege 1999, p. 19).

Blindness rehabilitation is most often committed to helping teach blind people vocational, home living, and social skills so as to live as "normal" a life as possible. Rehabilitation maintains the medical model of disability, which presumes that sight is normal while blindness is deficit. Hence, blind people learn from their ophthalmologists and from the rehabilitation system that they are "less than." Michalko (1998, p. 67) asserts that the "commitment to restoring something to its former status suggests that the thing to be restored is itself of no value in its current status."

A primary goal of rehabilitation is "independent living," which sets blind people up for failure. Sighted people are not pressured to be "independent" in the same ways that blind (and other disabled) people are mandated. Sighted people do not have to think about whether they are performing independent of other people. Even though societies are inherently interdependent, self-reliance is demanded of blind people. The notion of "independence" implies that if blind people ask for assistance, they are dependent. "Dependence" is presupposed to be a one-way relationship in which helping someone has no reciprocity, as if blind people passively receive but do not give. In order to be considered rehabilitated, blind people must, at all costs, make their own way in the world. This is the foremost determinate of restoration of status. If a blind person gets lost and must ask for help in order to get oriented, this is failure to act rehabilitated. If a blind person does not find employment, this, again, is failure. The onus is misplaced on the blind person rather than on an inaccessible environment and lack of opportunity, or, worse, discrimination in the workplace. Barnes (1996) argues that professionals working within a medical model perspective "invariably pathologise the experience of impairment and in so doing compound the problems faced by disabled people; directing us into segregated schools and sheltered workshops as two good examples" (p. 43).

Rehabilitation rests on the assumption that it knows what is best for its particular population. However, the majority of rehabilitation workers are nondisabled, which makes it impossible for them to genuinely understand the lived experience of disablement. Rehabilitation creates its own set of values by which disabled people are expected to abide. And, many times these values are contradictory, leaving clients in a lose-lose situation. Knipfel (1999) reports his home skills instructor told him to rely on his fingers more than anything, but his orientation and mobility instructor told him *not* to rely on his fingers.

Rehabilitation implies that it alone can rescue disabled people from the tragic clutch of impairment. By addressing needs that arise out of impairment while ignoring social processes of disablement, rehabilitation seeks to fix the problem by fixing its client. According to the landmark study by Scott (1969), rehabilitation attempts to

> clarify for them [blind men] what they have lost because they are blind, how they must change through the course of rehabilitation, and what their lives will be like when rehabilitation has been completed. These ideas are given added weight by the fact that they are shared by all staff members who deal directly with the client and, in some agencies at least, by other nonservice personnel who have occasional contacts with clients. (p. 83)

Without actual supporting data, rehabilitation assumes blind clients experience tremendous feelings of loss, low self-esteem, and poor self-image, which can be remediated *only* through a series of training processes offered *only* by rehabilitation (Scott 1969; Michalko 1999; Gordon 1994). Rehabilitation workers are educated to believe they hold the proper and correct keys to blind persons' futures. They believe that by applying standardized adaptation techniques, blind people can be restored to their former (privileged) status—that of being sighted.

Michalko (1998) writes:

> Rehabilitation is fundamentally interested in the restoration of a condition or status in which, before restoration, a person lives in degradation with an attainment or, as Goffman (1986) might say, a "stigma." It is interested in restoring privilege, rank, possessions, character, and reputation. Living a life in the way it should be lived is rehabilitation's fundamental interest. (p. 69)

The problem with these goals is rehabilitation's assumption of knowing best how blind people should live. Hence, rehabilitation workers are placed in positions of expert authority on clients. If clients resist this authority, they are often perceived as either in denial, not adjusted, or angry at their blindness rather than angry about not having their uniquely individual needs met or having meaningful input into their rehabilitation plan.

In the main, rehabilitation services have been devised for totally blind people—despite the fact that most of their clients have residual vision. Therefore, when legally blind people enter rehabilitation, they enter a world in which the lines between legal blindness and total blindness have been erased. Such transformative labeling finds its equivalent in the American "one-drop rule" applied to black people, meaning that "a single drop of 'black blood' makes a person a black" (Davis 1991, cited in Rosenblum and Travis 2003, p. 40).

Rehabilitation in Practice

In her efforts to convince a client to enter rehabilitation, a social worker with the Texas Commission for the Blind challenged a newly blind person to "make a decision" to enter formal rehabilitation. "Do you want to be a blind person in a blind world or a blind person in the sighted world?" (Fittipaldi 2004, p. 33). Note the social worker's ocularcentric use of the articles *a* and *the*. This suggests it is merely "*a*" blind world, as if it is a murky place not worthy of specificity or identity, while "the" sighted world retains its dominant privilege as being "the" world. Additionally, the social worker's statement reestablishes a fallacious blindness/sightedness binary that berates the blindness experience as second-best and, moreover, assaults the blind person's essential personhood. When stated in such a way, the blind person is made to believe she has little choice but to enter rehabilitation or risk suffering an inferior life, perhaps, one not even worth living.

Fittipaldi's social worker reaffirms rehabilitation's belief that while it cannot "cure" blindness, it can instruct the individual about how to be as "sighted" as possible. The social worker places all responsibility on the blind person to "adapt" to a sighted society. The social worker attempts to have Fittipaldi recruited into the blindness system. Scott (1969) explains such pressure can be exerted on the blind person from many sides:

> Not all people who have been labelled "blind" can follow a course entirely of their own choosing. Strong pressures are often exerted upon them to begin to think of themselves as blind. These pres-

sures sometimes take the form of admonitions from others to "face the facts." More often, however, they are insidious, resulting subtly from the reactions of medical and welfare specialists, friends, family members, and even the impaired person himself to the new label that has been applied to him. (p. 73)

The first hurdle blind people face in the rehabilitation system is the qualification process. After filling out forms and providing appropriate medical documentation, clients meet face-to-face with a counselor. Here, they also meet a built-in catch-22 that is especially difficult for legally blind people. Legally blind applicants must demonstrate that they are blind enough to need rehabilitation, and then they must prove that they are capable of being successfully rehabilitated. In practice, this means legally blind people must be simultaneously disabled and nondisabled. At times, it may be necessary to fake being blinder than one actually is in order to pass initial requirements, and then fake being more sighted than actual to prove potential for success. Unlike totally blind people whose impairment is more easily understood, legally blind people must muddle around in the borderland—challenged to prove they are fit for the blindness world and for the sighted world, yet not belonging in either one.

However, being deemed eligible for services does not guarantee acceptance into rehabilitation programs. Like other blind people trying to enter the rehabilitation system have reported, Knipfel (1999) relates how he got caught in the politics and infighting of various blindness service agencies in New York City and was ping-ponged back and forth between them with no one providing what he needed. He writes:

My experiences with the Cane Lady [orientation and mobility training] and the Commission suggested that the various Blind Man organizations in the city hated one another with a passion and tried to undercut one another whenever they could, regardless of how that might affect the people they were supposed to be helping. (p. 215)

And, he writes: "No wonder the Commission was at war with the Lighthouse, which was at war with the American Foundation for the Blind, which was at war with the Associated Blind, which was at war with the Commission" (p. 216).

Rehabilitation clients may also encounter a federally approved process called Order of Selection. A brochure from the Oregon Commission for the Blind explains:

> The Order of Selection is a prioritization system required by Federal Regulations under which the agency serves clients with the most significant vocational rehabilitation needs first. Depending on the program's resources at the time they apply for services, clients may experience a wait time before receiving assistance from the agency.

This terminology is both upsetting and threatening; it is reminiscent of Nazi selection for extermination of blind people. The language is borrowed from social Darwinism, and could be argued to be a form of institutional vocational eugenics.

A disturbing disparity apparently exists between stated goals of rehabilitation services and what clients report about their actual experience with blindness agencies. Numerous writings describe being ignored, disrespected, dismissed, abused, lied to, or mistreated (Knipfel 1999; Gordon 1994; Scott 1969). Because of the failure of blindness rehabilitation to fulfill its stated goals of serving clients in the acquisition of education, training, and assistance in finding meaningful gainful employment, the system has helped to keep blind people in low income circumstances. Knipfel (1999) was told by the Lighthouse for the Blind he needed to take extended time off from his job in order to devote himself to being rehabilitated, but for obvious reasons, he was reluctant to do so. On top of that, he made too much money to qualify for any rehabilitation service to purchase low vision aids (such as a closed-circuit television to magnify print materials); yet, he did not make enough money to buy them himself. Eventually, he was able to purchase access technology. Incredibly, his rehabilitation case worker called him one day, asked him a few questions, and then told Knipfel she was closing his case, considering him successfully rehabilitated even though the agency had given him no help at all. This practice by the rehabilitation industry boosts statistics without having to invest in clients.

Rehabilitation's gatekeeping practices often dishearten people as they try to break down structural barriers and sometimes discourage them from pursuing services altogether. Hence, many blind people in the United States continue to subsist on Social Security Disability Insurance (SSDI).

The next part of this chapter examines the experiences of all four participants with the rehabilitation industry, especially regarding its ability or willingness to prepare borderland blind people for living and working as a blind person in a sighted world.

The blindness rehabilitation industry relies on fundamentally ocularcentric assumptions about blindness as "lack" (Michalko 1998), which necessarily assumes from the outset that blind people have "functional limitations," hence, limited potential. Thus, services are often difficult to obtain, inadequate in practice, and out of touch with clients' needs, personal potential, and career desires and goals. This attitude is not limited to rehabilitation, which is merely a reflection of the larger society. Even friends and family who mostly understand their blind loved one's abilities may question how far borderland blind people can go—how much they can succeed. Catherine said:

> Well, most of the people that I've been around like for forever, and they know pretty much how to do it. Sometimes they have the wrong expectations. Like I find people that actually know how to treat me have wrong expectations of where I should be going with my ambitions and my goals.

Catherine's observation strikes a familiar chord. I believe that my parents pushed me into getting married young because they were afraid I would not be able to take care of myself, pursue a career, or live independently. They believed what the doctors told them about what it means to be blind. The lack of faith in blind people's capacity for success begins with medicine's prognosis.

Larry's ophthalmologist commenced his role as medical gatekeeper when he first conferred the diagnosis of legal blindness on Larry. He told Larry, "Ah, you're legally blind, and I'll sign any paper you want." Larry's doctor exercised the traditional model Michalko (1999) describes:

> When ophthalmology does not have a "cure" the patient becomes
> a symbol of that failure; hence, ophthalmology remains silent and
> contributes nothing more to the story of blindness. (p. 45)

The doctor failed to tell Larry what the signed paper might do for
him. He neither told him about nor referred him to a low vision
specialist or rehabilitation agency. His doctor told him only that he
could receive Social Security disability benefits, which communi-
cated the underlying message that Larry was now unemployable
despite the fact that he was already engaged in a lengthy, successful
career as a public schoolteacher.

J. R.'s doctor also gave him a letter verifying his legal blindness
but did not tell him about blindness services in the community. J. R.
recalls that his sister, a schoolteacher, suggested he contact various
disability services in the area. J. R. proceeded to call three different
agencies and set up service provision himself.

Like J. R., Larry found his way on his own to blindness rehabilitation, where he requested orientation and mobility training but
was initially turned down for services. Larry said:

> You know there could be this great organization for blind people
> and it's run by sighted people. And then sometimes sighted peo-
> ple say, "well this is what, . . . this is what those four blind people
> in that room need." Do they ask for needs assessments for them?
> I have yet to be asked for a needs assessment in anything. And it's
> almost as if . . . if we could keep them frustrated long enough
> they'll leave us alone.

After J. R. received some services from the local blindness agency
but still needed more, his legally blind counselor took it upon himself to close the case because J. R. was employed full time. J. R. felt
that he did receive some needed services, but not everything that
would help him learn "how to deal with what I had to deal with."

Inconsistency and Quality in Service Provision

Because the role of client inherently places people in a vulnerable
position, it is especially important for those receiving services to

have consistency and familiarity with their counselors. Participants reported a range of experiences of inconsistent service provision.

In general, J. R.'s attitude toward blindness service provision was more positive than the three other participants. He described his experience with the state agency as "pleasant," although he felt they provided little more help than just buying him one piece of access software and so were mainly absent from the picture. Nonetheless, he was disgruntled about changes in personnel because just when he was getting to know one, he or she would leave. I experienced similar situations in Virginia, where I had four different counselors over six years, and the level and quality of service provision varied with each counselor:

> I was frustrated with each new personnel change because I had to start all over again letting the counselor get to know me and convince each one that I was both blind enough to warrant their services and capable enough to pursue a higher education. As each counselor left, I became more and more reticent to make an effort to establish any sort of meaningful relationship with the next one.

J. R.' s first counselor left after only two months:

> Just as I was starting to get to know him I lost him, and he left and I got reassigned to a new counselor, who had a very standoffish personality.

Of the six counselors I have been assigned to over the years, only two of them were supportive and genuinely seemed to care about my efforts to better my circumstances. Others were adversarial at times, clearly operating within the agency's medical model perspective that blind people cannot do much with their lives; they doled out services as if they were a gift from their own pockets, and they seemed to have no understanding that without us there would be no jobs for them.

> I even experienced abuse from one counselor in Virginia when I worked at the pie shop. She ordered a Thanksgiving sweet potato

pie, but when she came to pick it up, she demanded I give it to her at no charge. I explained that I had no authority to do that, so she begrudgingly paid for the pie, and then as she was leaving she said, "Oh, by the way. You won't be able to get the talking cash register you requested."

To the agency's credit, this counselor was terminated in response to numerous client reports of abuses perpetrated against them.

J. R. describes his experience with a legally blind counselor for whom he lacked respect because the counselor did not model a positive blindness identity:

> He had a credibility problem. I found out later he is, in fact, legally blind, but he wouldn't use a white cane. He didn't want anybody to know he was legally blind. . . . He didn't want people to know he was blind because of the subtle discrimination you get when you use a white cane.

J. R. told the counselor that clients would not believe him when he said, "I know exactly how you feel." J. R. said clients would say, "Like hell you do." This anecdote speaks to the idea that one self-defeating cost of "passing" is that the person is not being true to their needs (Omansky Gordon 2003), because the counselor lacked the credibility required for successful counselor-client relationships.

J. R. described another service provider from a different agency as "more agreeable" and, as a result, he enjoyed the experience of learning cane travel. But, the philosophy of service provision was inconsistent from agency to agency. At one local disability agency, when personnel changed, so did the philosophy of service provision. J. R. described one sighted orientation and mobility instructor as reluctant to "be that social" with those he was training, and so he did not endeavor to learn where his clients needed to go in the city. Therefore, the instructor's need for professional distance preempted the training needs of the people he was supposed to serve. The sighted trainer disbanded an established group of disabled volunteers who had been helping blind people learn to go where they wanted in the city. He chose to take on all the orientation training by himself, which is rather puzzling since most service agencies are terribly in need of additional personnel.

Fortunately, the rehabilitation counselor to whom I was assigned during my doctoral work had a PhD and very much appreciated the value of postgraduate education, believed blind people are capable of achieving their full human potential, and enthusiastically encouraged me as he provided services to support my education and training. He even went beyond the written rehabilitation plan by voluntarily suggesting services and strategies I had not thought of myself. He followed through on his word and rendered services in a timely, respectful, and helpful manner. I felt like we collaborated in the rehabilitation process, just as is legally mandated for rehabilitation agencies in the United States.

Who Chooses What? Power Struggles in Rehabilitation Service Provision

Larry's goal was to get a guide dog, but the guide dog school required him to first learn cane travel. Only through personal contacts and persistent networking was Larry finally approved to receive orientation and mobility training. Larry stated that he wanted to succeed with his orientation and mobility lessons not only for himself but for the people who "put an awful lot of energy" into making it possible. Apparently, he perceived these lessons more as a gift than a right; perhaps such a belief is a result of the charity model of disability.

Larry experienced problems with the blindness industry similar to what Knipfel (1999) observed as he was bounced from one agency to the other, a victim of competing agency interests and philosophies about best blindness skills. Larry learned during his initial interview with the guide dog school that there was a philosophical conflict and lack of coordination between the guide dog school and the cane travel training organization. The school representative subjected Larry to a type of test found only in the borderland of legal blindness, where sighted people hold the power to decide if someone is "blind enough" to warrant services. Larry describes his initial interview with a school representative:

> I hit what I call on the east coast a catch-22. And it's like this political ping-pong game going on. And the way I read it was [pause]

I read a couple of different scenarios here. Alright, so you're legally blind. It's been proven medically. Yeah you prove to me that you're legally blind. It's dangerous for you crossing the street. Um, and you don't trip too much over curbs and upraised sidewalks. But I can see that you're blind.

Okay? And then I find out, and I; she actually didn't; I didn't find out from her. She restated or reaffirmed the fact that you can't get a dog unless you have cane orientation. So I said bring it on, you know. So, all right. So the interview proved that I do have legal blindness, and that I have difficulty crossing the street. Okay, but this is part of the dance. That you know, and you just have to just accept it.

One catch-22 led into another during this conflict about how to train Larry; not incidentally, those involved in these decisions were sighted. The guide dog school wanted Larry to learn cane travel without using a blindfold, yet the organization that agreed to train him required him to use a blindfold. This is reminiscent of Knipfel's (1999) experience with one blindness professional telling him to rely on his fingers and another blindness instructor telling him not to rely on his fingers. Larry said:

Oh, then what happened with this political basketball that kept going back and forth was, well it's kind of silly to have to be blindfolded and the other, well it's not silly to be blindfolded. And I'm saying I really don't give a rat's patoot. Just get me my training. And ah, then the next catch-22 was, well you know like if you become proficient with the cane there really isn't any need for a dog. A representative of the guide dog school asked, "And why would you want a dog if you can use a cane?" And I said, "Well what about my comfort zone? What about having somebody to be with when I'm out at night?" [The representative] said, "Well the dog can't tell if the light is red or green." Well neither can my cane. You know?

The representative's line of thinking regarding cane proficiency as a reason to deny use of a dog illustrates how the rights of disabled people to rehabilitation services can be subverted—a practice that has been employed in the courts to significantly weaken the Americans with Disabilities Act. (See Supreme Court rulings in 1999 on

Sutton v. United Air Lines, Inc. [97-1943] 130 F.3d 893; *Murphy v. United Parcel Service, Inc.* [97-1992] 141 F.3d 1185; *Albertsons, Inc. v. Kirkingburg* [98-591] 143 F.3d 1228.)

Nearly all state and local jurisdictions and agencies use a fundamentally medical model testing tool called a "functional assessment" to determine eligibility for services and benefits. These tests are set up in ways that fail to accurately reflect the variety of environments borderland blind people encounter in everyday life. Paradoxically, it is impossible to know going into each different evaluation whether one is more likely to qualify for services by being less blind or more blind. This problem is of particular import to borderland blind people because their vision is variable depending upon lighting, season, time of day, amount of rest the night before, physical condition, nature of the eye disease, and so on. One day a person's vision could be 20/200 and another day 20/400. Someone might be able to see streetlights when the sun is at his or her back yet miss the entire intersection completely when facing the sun.

This is illustrated in my own experiences. For example as part of the application for paratransit in Tucson, I was required to demonstrate my mobility skills under the scrutiny of an occupational therapist who would recommend whether or not I could have accessible transportation.

> She took me to an intersection that had traffic signals and sidewalks on both streets. She walked with me around the four corners of the intersection and that was the whole assessment. The thing is . . . most of the streets in Tucson have either gravel, dirt, or no room at all for sidewalks. I was not tested in my own neighborhood, which was full of obstacles like cactus growing out from people's yards, telephone and utility poles in the middle of the walkway alongside the streets, and very few traffic lights. I can't see anything when I'm facing the sun, which happens a lot in that city where the sun shines 350 days a year. And, I wasn't assessed to learn how well I could find bus stops—which I can't do because I can't see bus stop or street signs. This alone would qualify me for paratransit. Anyway, when I left that interview, I had no idea whether I was "not blind enough" to qualify or whether my cane skills were too good, which would be a mark against me.

A good deal of pressure is exerted on applicants to fit specific criteria, which they may not be informed about in advance of the evaluation. Consequently, it is difficult for applicants to be genuine or candid with evaluators.

I asked Larry what he would do if the guide dog school requested a cane travel assessment knowing that if he did well he might hurt his chances for a dog. Larry said that first he would call someone he knows who works at a guide dog school in another state to find out what to do, and concluded, "I would do all that would be necessary to do in order to guarantee myself a pooch."

Blind People Are Not Cookies

The stories told by the participants in this book demonstrate that blind people experience hegemonic medical practices, including being subjected to functional assessment testing that may or may not be particularly germane to everyday life. The assessments concentrate solely on the person's limitations without taking social or other variable factors into account—as if blind people stand alone, unaffected by the world around them.

Rather than impose a battery of functional assessments on blind people as is done by professionals bound by the medical model, a social model practitioner would most likely ask disabled people what institutions, social services, and environmental barriers are disabling them and would ask what they needed rather than "determine" what they should have.

Blindness agencies regularly prescribe prepackaged employment programs with little regard for clients' talents, strengths, or interests. The agencies practice cookie-cutter vocational rehabilitation counseling by trying to fit clients to jobs rather than calling upon clients' personal desires and career goals. For example, when I was accepted for blindness rehabilitation in Virginia, the counselor decided I should enter the Randolph-Sheppard vending stand program, despite the fact that I had never expressed any desire to be self-employed in a capital-producing venture.

> I am not an entrepreneur, obviously since I'm not a capitalist. The counselor took me around to the biggest, most successful vending facility in the area to try to persuade me to do this. I think this

would have been the easiest solution for her because the program was in place and she wouldn't have to help me find a job, contact employers, or anything like that. It may have been easy for her, but it would have been hell for me.

As part of a summer work program through her state blindness rehabilitation agency, Catherine was placed in a job as a patient transport worker at a local hospital, but her experience was unsatisfying at best and degrading at worst. She reports, "They didn't trust me with patients because [of] my vision disability." (Note that Catherine resisted the messages of worthlessness of visually impaired employees covertly conveyed by her employers.) Catherine said:

> It makes no sense. It's like, haven't you seen how good I am? Have you not seen how compassionate I am? I just need to learn how to adapt. I need to do it differently than they do it. But they wouldn't give me the chance. It's like they had three weeks where they could've taught me to do it by myself—taught *me* to be self-sufficient, and do the job and do the job well. I mean being such a compassionate person I could've given so much to that hospital, and they don't want to do it. And it's not the hospital's fault; it's a couple of people that screwed it all up for me.
> And it's like they're giving me sub par which means that I don't get [pause]. The work program means it failed. The work program failed. The Commission failed. They did not teach me to work. And they also did not teach [the hospital] to hire workers that were visually impaired. And then they had a blind kid that all he did was shred paper all day. That's all he did. We were both on the same work program.

Catherine's anecdotal evidence was echoed in J. R.'s contention that the rehabilitation industry does not do enough to educate employers about blindness and blind people's abilities.

Conclusion

Due to its failure to respond appropriately to the needs of its clients; institutional stagnation; and a general lack of imagination, creativity, or desire to repair existing entropic service provision, the rehabilitation industry does little to help blind people achieve truly meaningful, gainful employment. Because the rehabilitation industry is captured in an impotent medical model, it fosters a cycle of exclusion from social and economic equality. When people cannot earn a living, they cannot participate in a consumer economy, which can lead to social isolation, poor health care, inferior housing conditions, and so on. Even though theories of rehabilitation support education and training of disabled people, its actual practice is often self-defeating in that it misuses or outright corrupts its programs and miserably falls short of its promise to contribute to the betterment of disabled people's lives. The participants' reports of their experiences with rehabilitation brought to life Michalko's (1998) thoughtful, incisive critique of both education and the rehabilitation industry. He asserts that these societal institutions

> evoke various techniques for solving the problem of blindness understood as the problem of knowledge. Their essential aim is to provide blind persons with skills which will allow them to adapt to a sighted world. Thus, "fitting in" society is what these programs have in mind for blind persons. They want blind persons to be like everyone else—just persons. Person is first, blindness is second. Persons who *happen* to be blind are what these programs hope to release into the world. (p. 6)

While all four participants reported some benefits from school and rehabilitation, not one of them expressed that they felt more "normal," nor did they at any time express the idea that they perceived themselves as "persons who [just] happened to be blind." Blindness took center stage in every area of their lives, and if they attempted to minimize the fact they were blind, society was right there to remind them. Even when the participants attempted to fit themselves into a sighted world, an ocularcentric society told them through attitude and action that they (blind people) were different, and so could not be equal partners in the broader community.

This is also expressed in the practice whereby the rehabilitation industry places clients in minimum wage (or below) jobs, presented as "training programs," where they are paid much less than their sighted coworkers. Catherine experienced this at her hospital placement:

> I was paid by [the hospital] but I was paid six, you know six what-ever, ninety-five or seventy-five; what it is, you know, minimum wage. Whereas a patient transport [person] makes like eleven, ten dollars an hour or something like that.

I had a similar experience working as a baker in a mom-and-pop pie shop. The discrimination experienced in rehabilitation programs continued through to the transition to work.

7

Work

According to the US Bureau of the Census (1996), although the average employment rate for people between 21 and 64 years old is 76.2 percent, among the 4,200,000 Americans with visual impairments, only 43.7 percent (1,751,000) are employed, and among the 568,000 Americans who are blind, only 30.8 percent (175,000) are employed. It therefore seems that despite passage of the Americans with Disabilities Act of 1990 (ADA), exclusion from the labor force is the rule rather than the exception. Approximately one-third of blind men ages 18–64 and blind women and men ages 65 and older live in poverty, but almost half (48 percent) of blind women ages 18–64 live in poverty. Only 19 percent of the legally blind NHIS respondents were currently employed (Zuckerman 2004). While these findings are different from the US Census reports, it is evident that blind adults in the United States are not adequately employed.

Public policy matters such as those laid out by the Social Security Administration are fixed firmly within the medical model of disability, which often perceives blindness to be the most tragic of all physical, sensory, or cognitive impairments. Paradoxically, the Social Security Administration engages in reverse discrimination with regard to blind people. In the next section, I examine how ocularcentrism manifests itself in economic policies, education, and employment through segregation of blind people. For instance, the US Social Security Administration separates blindness from all other forms of impairment and administers higher monetary compensation to blind people than to sighted people who are otherwise impaired. In 2010, blind recipients of US Social Security Disability Insurance are permitted to earn $1,640 per month before their employment is considered "substantial" (personal communication with Social Security personnel, September 7, 2010). Once they earn even one dollar more than $1,640, they lose all their SSDI benefits (which often include Medicare insurance). However, SSDI recipients with impairments other than blindness are allowed to earn only $1,000 per month before their benefits are withdrawn. US Internal Revenue Service tax laws reflect a similar bias: every year, blind people are allowed a deduction equal to "dependent" deductions, while people with other impairments have no such allowance. Although these rules are inequitable, they are realistic in light of statistics that indicate abysmal rates of unemployment and under-employment of blind people.

Rehabilitation agencies routinely close cases they consider successfully rehabilitated, when, in actuality, clients are left in poverty-level, dead-end jobs. The rehabilitation system is big business, employing thousands upon thousands of sighted and, much less frequently, blind workers. The rehabilitation industry is designed to discourage or altogether prevent blind people from pursuing a higher education because it does not want to pay for it. Traditional blindness rehabilitation practices rob blind people of the possibility of pursuing their goals—of living up to their potential.

As explained in the previous chapter, the advent of blindness rehabilitation sprang out of residential institutions for the blind, especially from the Saxon model of workshops as education. In the United States, the idea was to set up workshops not affiliated with schools so that blind people could live in the community and go to work each day. The first such workshop, the Pennsylvania Working Home for the Blind, opened in 1874 and was the precursor of modern-day sheltered workshops.

The Government as Employer and Customer: Vending Stands and Sheltered Workshops

In the 1930s, two federal laws, the Randolph-Sheppard Act (US Federal Government 1936) and the Wagner-O'Day Act (US Federal Government 1938) established employment programs specifically for blind people. These programs are still active. While they do provide employment for blind people, they also render them dependent on government funding. Because of these two laws, some blindness vocational rehabilitation services are preprogrammed, which makes for a limited choice of career goals. Budget restraints direct rehabilitation services be rendered as cheaply, swiftly, and effortlessly as possible; consequently, blind clients are urged to accept jobs in these preexisting programs.

The Randolph-Sheppard Act of 1936 established a program specifically for blind persons to operate vending stands in federal buildings (US Federal Government 1936). Since its inception, the program has expanded to include state buildings as well. The Randolph-Sheppard program is part of the rehabilitation industry and is most often administered by state rehabilitation agencies. For example, in Oregon, the Business Enterprise Program (BEP), administered by the Oregon Commission for the Blind, has six "dry stands," seven "snack bars," four "cafeterias," and seven "vending routes." In fiscal year 2002–2003, the "dry stands" net sales ranged from $4,161.51 to $27,086.42 per annum, with four of the six facilities earning less than $8,000. Snack bars fared better, with highest net sales of $44,639.58 to a low of $812.55. One cafeteria earned net sales of $25,238.65, while the other three each earned less than $16,000. Two of the vending routes earned more than $35,000, while three earned less than $20,000 (lowest net sales were $13,236.23). Among all the BEP stands, only two vendors had net sales over $40,000 while six earned less than $10,000 (unpublished report from Oregon Commission for the Blind Business Enterprise Program, October 1, 2002, through September 30, 2003).

According to the US Bureau of the Census (2004), the poverty threshold for one person under age 65 years old (working age) was $9,573. This means one-quarter (six of twenty-four) of the BEP venues in Oregon earned net sales beneath the US poverty threshold for one person; moreover, it is not known if households of two or more depend upon the income generated from BEP business, which would place them into higher poverty threshold levels incrementally.

At a national level, Randolph-Sheppard vendors organized their own advocacy organization, the Randolph-Sheppard Vendors Association, which is under the umbrella of the American Council of the

Blind. This association promotes "their independent and effective participation in the systems which serve them, as well as in all material aspects of their work" (American Council of the Blind 2004). (Note the primary emphasis on the value of "independence.")

Under the Wagner-O'Day Act of 1938 (later amended to be the Javitz-Wagner-O'Day Act), the National Industries for the Blind (NIB) was established to employ blind people as factory workers producing products for government agencies (US Federal Government 1938, 2005). Currently, NIB claims it is the largest employer of the American blind. NIB and its business partners employ blind and other "severely disabled" workers in 100 locations across forty-four states (www.nib.org). National Industries for the Blind is big business, making money from purchasing and supply, clerking, and secretarial services, but mostly manufacturing. Blind workers make more than 3,000 products such as pens, cleaning products, and military uniforms. NIB and its associates sell to federal agencies—the military, government offices, and correctional institutions. As a private not-for-profit organization, NIB profits from its partnerships with state rehabilitation agencies, which has the American military-industrial complex as one of its best customers. NIB declares it is "helping the war effort" (www.nib.org, December 19, 2004). Their 2003 annual report boasts about their blind workers making jackets like the one former US president George W. Bush wore to Iraq. The war in Iraq resulted in increased demand for manufacturing by blind people, which was very good for NIB and its associate agencies, such as the Columbia Lighthouse for the Blind and Travis Association for the Blind. They reported total sales of $407 million in 2003. NIB manufactures T-shirts, military uniforms, and equipment belts for all branches of the military. Perhaps blinded veterans returning from Iraq and Afghanistan will find employment at NIB cutting and sewing uniforms for their former comrades-in-arms.

NIB's annual report freely shares information about gross sales, organization growth and expansion figures, affiliated agency sales, and so on. Nonetheless, facts or figures about workers' wages are nowhere to be found. Although efforts were made to get this information from the National Industries for the Blind headquarters, I was told that these figures are not disclosed, and that if I wanted the information, I would have to seek it through the US Freedom of Information Act process.

When I contacted the Oregon Blind Enterprises (OBE), an associate agency of NIB, to learn about their operation, my inquiry was met with caution. After asking several questions about the number of employees and what they do, I then asked about workers' wages. The OBE employee's tone of voice changed, and then she asked who I was and why I wanted to know. After I told her I was doing research that involved, in part, learning about job opportunities for blind people, the woman was more forthcoming. She reported that OBE employs seven workers who make name and service tags for the US Marine Corps. The agency's gross earnings in 2003 were $300,000. Wages range from $7 to $12 per hour, with the average being $8 per hour. This means that if one person makes $12 per hour and another person makes $9 per hour, five people make $7 per hour. The majority of employees have worked there at least ten years (telephone communication with OBE, December 15, 2004).

Another example of manufacturing and distribution endeavors in the United States can be found at the Virginia Industries for the Blind (VIB), which has two main plants and fourteen federal supply store centers around the Commonwealth of Virginia. In VIB's sheltered workshops, blind people package spices, and manufacture mattresses, mop heads and handles, gloves, pillows for prisons, as well as 144 different writing instruments (www.vdbvi.org/vib, November 2005). These circumstances suggest that little has changed since the early nineteenth-century blindness institution in Edinburgh, Scotland, where blind residents learned how to make mattresses.

Blind people learn the same stereotypes about blindness as do sighted people; therefore, they may hold beliefs that their employment potential is limited. As a newly blind person, Rod Michalko (1999) believed

> society did not present "positive" conceptions or collective representations of blindness. The opposite was the case. Since I did not possess any extraordinary musical ability, something which is often assumed blind persons do possess, I thought my future career would consist, and I mean this quite literally, of selling pencils on a street corner or working in a broom factory. (p. 132)

Modern innovations in blindness vocational rehabilitation created preprogrammed opportunities in customer service clerk training at chain retail stores. Retailers benefit from participating in these training programs in three ways: first, blind persons are paid less than minimum wage during a nine-month-long training period; second, the retailers gain special tax benefits for hiring disabled people; and, finally, they gain social capital through making it known that they "hire the handicapped."

Blindness rehabilitation also engages in technology training. Advances in access technology for disabled computer users have been impressive over the past decade. However, this is very expensive and few blind people can afford to purchase computers and access software out of their own pockets. Again, budget restraints limit the ability of state rehabilitation agencies to provide equipment to clients. Moreover, when agencies agree to purchase computers, they often either influence or outright determine which equipment and brand the user should have, whether it is best for the client's particular tasks or not. This is because agencies often have contracts with certain vendors at reduced rates for multiple purchases, so a client who requests something out of the agency's norm may be turned down.

Under the Americans with Disabilities Act (US Federal Government 1990), employers are required to provide access technology for qualified disabled employees. Now we encounter another catch-22. In order for blind people to compete on a level playing field with sighted job applicants, they are required to demonstrate equal competence on the computer, but, without advance training and practice, this is a fairly impossible endeavor. Technology is frequently promoted as the great equalizer for disabled people. But, because of the high price of computers equipped with access technology, the increase in graphics-oriented websites that are out of compliance with disability access-related federal laws and regulations, and an 81 percent unemployment rate for blind people, it is impossible for technology to accomplish this feat. Only when the workplace ceases to shut blind people out of the workforce can technology possibly begin to act as a great equalizer.

None of the participants in this study is currently employed in substantial gainful employment. This is not surprising considering the approximately 19 percent employment rate among blind people.

Taking Advantage

When I applied for a job as a baker in a little pie shop, my rehabilitation counselor advised me not to disclose my blindness until after
the owner made a job offer. With disability antidiscrimination law
to guide and back me, I did not disclose my blindness until after he
offered the job. I felt confident that I'd do fine at this job because I
am a very good cook and a loyal, reliable worker with creative ideas.

> Once my future boss made the offer, I told him about my eye
> impairment and requested two reasonable accommodations; first,
> that they enlarge the print of the recipes, and secondly, that they
> allow my rehabilitation counselor to place raised marks on the
> measuring cups and steam kettle knobs so I could measure accu-
> rately and adjust temperatures. He agreed to do this, but then he
> reduced his initial wage offer by 50 cents an hour. I knew this was
> discriminatory, but I really needed and wanted that job, so I
> agreed to it. In the year and one half that I worked there, I never
> did get caught up to parity with my sighted coworkers.

Larry Lets His Career Go

As soon as Larry was diagnosed as legally blind he decided to tell his
boss. He felt it was something he could not hide.

> I didn't tell too many people. I told my boss because she had to
> know. [I told her] almost immediately. We had that relationship. I
> figured, "Oh, this is like trying to hide a murder and not washing
> the blood off your hands." You know, it doesn't quite work.
>   I just went to work and I sat down with my boss . . . I told her,
> I said, " . . . my eyes are all fucked up. And, I really can't see any-
> more. And, uh, you know, I'm going to do the best I can, and then
> when I think I can't do it anymore, I'll let you be the first to know.
> And then I'm just going to pack it in."

Larry continued to teach but became increasingly uncomfortable about his ability to do a good job "not because I didn't have
anything to say" but because he was concerned about the students'
safety in his classroom. He thinks this goes back to the disdain for

bullies he has felt since childhood. Larry said, "I didn't know if Johnnie was in the back of the room goofing around or being cruel to somebody." Larry was not offered any reasonable accommodations such as a student intern or assistant to monitor the back of the classroom. He was not informed about access technology or referred to blindness rehabilitation where he could have explored options that would have made it possible for him to continue working. Apparently, the administration did not know what to do with Larry's blindness and so they did nothing. He took an early retirement, which has directly affected his economic status.

J. R. Experiences Insidious Employment Discrimination

J. R. demonstrated superior competence throughout his life. For example, after completing a master's degree program, he went on to graduate fourth in a military transportation officer's course. J. R. had a successful career for thirty years, working as a traffic engineer for the state in which he lives. Even though he had vision difficulties, he drove to and from work each day and also drove from site to site to examine construction design needs. Then when he could no longer drive, his first wife took him to and from work. He worked diligently, putting in ten-hour days and was "the first one at work and I was the last one to leave, and I had a key to the office, to the building." But, later on:

> my boss kinda had reassigned me—you know stupid little boss—
> to a traffic investigator, which is a subengineering . . . you know
> someone you don't get a professional engineer for.

When J. R. told me the boss "had no idea what I was capable of doing," I asked if this demotion was a result of his vision loss. He answered, "It's regardless . . . I think he was too stupid to remember I had vision impairment." Be that as it may, as our interview session proceeded, J. R. began to recall experiences of disablement in the workplace; he related experiences from when he worked at a state agency wherein he found himself with no opportunities for advancement. One time he went in to have brain surgery. The doctors prognosticated he had six months to live, so while he was still in the hospital, the agency replaced him. He had been heading up a $50 million federally funded program, and they gave his job to someone who was not even an engineer. They had reassigned him. J. R. explained: "I had a job, I didn't have the same job. I had a position but no job." Thus began J. R.'s downward spiral into a series of menial tasks that were fairly impossible for a man with a vision impairment and partial paralysis of one hand to do. He recalls:

> One day they came in with a whole boxful of pamphlets that they'd had printed at State Printers and another box full of changes that needed to go in the middle of these. They wanted me to take the staples out of 'em, insert these other pages . . . and restaple 'em . . . with one hand.

This story is reminiscent of Catherine's experience working in the hospital and being assigned the task of collating papers, as well as the blind boy she saw sitting in a room shredding paper all day. It also speaks to my experience in high school where I was required to participate in archery in the physical education class. These stories uncover a subtheme about how sighted people in positions of power and authority set blind (and other disabled) people up for failure, which serves as a self-fulfilling prophecy on the part of authority figures. J. R. explains his observation of the situation:

> Yeah. And because I had trouble doing it just shows of course that you're; you have a mental deficiency. We don't want you around here. . . . Well finally, the boss went.

When J. R. was ten years into his career at the transportation agency, his boss began a systematic campaign to fire him. As soon as J. R. realized this, he kept a daily journal, which he titled, "Chickenshititis," documenting everything his boss was doing. He took the journal down to one of the internal offices to have it bound into a professional-looking volume. J. R. maintained inner resistance and his sense of humor during these ongoing attacks by keeping the journal on top of his desk in plain view of anyone who came by; he took satisfaction that "they never caught on." Finally, he built up a case. He ran it through and he "got somebody to sign it to say I was fired. That's it." J. R. then filed an appeal and his case went to a one-year-long binding arbitration process during which he remained unemployed. J. R. recalls:

> The arbitration went on until I filed a discrimination complaint with the, with the federal government on discrimination against my handicap. Filed one with the state and one with the feds. They weren't too worried about the one with the state, but as soon as they got the one; heard about the one with the feds, their attorney was on the phone to my attorney and wanted to settle out of court.

The settlement money made up for the salary J. R. lost during the previous year of unemployment, and then they transferred him to another city within the same agency.

After he returned to work, J. R. continued to encounter roadblocks. For instance, his computer was hooked up to a local area network, which the information services employees insisted be left on at night so they could check everyone's computers to make sure no unauthorized software had been loaded onto any computer terminal. Several times, J. R. came to work only to find that the information services technicians had removed his screen magnification and speech software. He used to take the software diskette to work-related computer classes and load it onto any computer so that he could access the class. Apparently, his bosses had some strong feelings toward this software as evidenced by J. R.'s report: "In fact when I left they told me to take it with me. They said, 'get it out of here. We don't want it anymore.'"

The job J. R.'s boss had assigned him was blatantly inappropriate for a person with vision impairment. He recalls:

> [laughs] So I, all I have to do; all I had to do was take that to my doctor and said, "Okay now is there any way that I would be unable to do this job description?" [Changes vocal tone to be in character] He said, "You can't do this job description."

As a direct result, J. R. took an early retirement at age fifty-one because he was "tired of that kind of hassle." Unlike the other participants in this study, J. R. benefited financially by being out of work because a combination of his retirement income and Social

Security disability benefits brought in more money than his salary alone.

J. R. believed that during his career he was denied jobs due to being visually impaired because he "didn't make good eye contact" with job interviewers, despite the fact that he had his white cane with him. Eye contact is an ocularcentric value that is fairly meaningless to people who cannot look into another's eyes. The committee's expectation and demand that J. R. participate with eye contact was no more realistic or fair than expecting him to become a woman or African American during the interview.

J. R. recounted another incident: when he wore an eye patch over one eye during a four-member interview committee—three across from him and one out of his field of vision. At the end of the interview, J. R. shook hands with the three across from him but not the woman out of his field of vision. Later, he was told he did not get the job because he failed to shake hands with the fourth interviewer. I reflected, "Why didn't she identify herself to you?" and J. R. responded, "Why didn't she say anything? Why didn't she say something, yeah?"

My Career Decline: From Politics to Poverty

I had no job when my husband and I started the divorce process. This was two decades before the implementation of the ADA—before disabled people won their civil rights. Within the first two years of our separation, I was fired from three jobs because of my eyesight, despite the fact I told employers in advance of being hired exactly what I could and could not see. I could not support my children and had to resort to feeding them nutrition-deficient welfare food. Things went downhill from there.

Finally, I got back on my feet and got jobs in politics and community relations. I was able to support myself, but then made a similar decision as Larry did, for similar reasons as his. Here is what happened:

> Increasingly, I was finding it difficult to "work the room" at political functions because I couldn't spot people more than, say, ten feet away. I knew I was losing ground. I couldn't drive at night so

I had to depend on other people to take me to evening functions and there's an awful lot of those in politics. Then, one day, Jim, my boss and comrade, took me into one of the offices at the "Fed" [which is the County Federation of Labor, AFL-CIO], and pointed to a computer screen. "Can you see this?" he asked. I looked at the small lines of print on that DOS screen and answered, "No." I got a sinking feeling—dread. The labor movement was keeping up with the times by computerizing all its member lists, precinct information and all. While they accommodated me as well as any of us knew how at the time, I ended up leaving that job. I never told them or anyone else the real reason—that I felt totally inadequate and unable to pull my weight or keep up. Somehow I had gotten the idea that I could never use my vision loss as a reason because I believed a reason was an excuse. I went on Social Security disability and stayed unemployed for nine years.

Conclusion

With regard to employment, three of the participants have postgraduate education and the other is a college graduate. The data are in agreement with fundamental social model concerns about disabled people being systematically excluded from the workplace for a variety of reasons other than individual functional limitation. Oliver (2004) explains that the social model

> refuses to see specific problems in isolation from the totality of disabling environments: hence, the problem of unemployment does not entail intervention in the social organization of work and the operation of the labour market but also in areas such as transport, education and culture. (p. 20)

Additionally, all the participants' personal experiences support recent statistical data in the United States (Zuckerman 2004) that reports unemployment rates of blind people around 81 percent. Finally, the stories in this chapter reinforce Oliver's succinct contention that education, rehabilitation, and the workplace all have fundamental problems in common: "Government policies are, by and large, targeted at equipping impaired individuals for the unchanging world of work rather than changing the way work is carried out in order that more people might access it" (p. 21).

J. R. believes the state blindness agency should do more to educate employers about blindness, which is in agreement with Oliver's (2004) view that the workplace wants disabled people to fit into the status quo rather than adjusting itself to become a more inclusive environment. J. R. states the case poignantly:

> Yeah, the employer is the weak link in this whole thing. He doesn't understand what he's dealing with in terms of someone who's blind. . . . You know I had a boss that believed I was incapable of doing anything. He had no understanding of what my educational background or experience was.

J. R. voiced similar comments as Catherine when each expressed that their employers had no idea what they were capable of doing. These statements express the subtheme found in all four participant stories—stories of oppression as a result of ocularcentric perceptions. No matter how educated, talented, dedicated, enthusiastic, intelligent, skilled, or otherwise accomplished the participants are, our dominant sighted society remains either reluctant or incapable of inviting them in from the borderland. And, like countries that erect fences to keep unwanted "aliens" out, nondisabled people erected and maintained barriers that made the participants' chances to participate in the labor market remain thoroughly uncertain. Meanwhile, economic and social supports maintain blind people at poverty-level status. The 2010 US Census survey short form, which went out to every household, contained no questions about disability, which does not bode well for future funding of rehabilitation and employment programs. Only the American Community Survey, which is offered to a limited number of people, contains disability- or impaired-related questions. A population that goes uncounted is a population that goes unfunded.

PART 3

Social Life Outside, Inside, and Across Borders

8

Constructing Blindness

Sighted people's reactions to blindness create social distance and marginalization of blind people. The public regularly misunderstands legally blind people, especially because they do not fit the stereotypical image of blindness. In fact, sighted people are frequently surprised when a person with whom they are casually acquainted reveals he or she is legally blind. When sighted people respond with something like, "But you don't *look* blind," they are expressing the same stereotypical thinking that prompts someone to say, "But, you don't look Jewish," or "I never would have guessed you are gay."

Even when people are aware of legal blindness, they may harbor misconceptions about how going blind affects social life and daily living skills. For instance, a woman who serves on a disability advisory council for her local government jurisdiction stated, when people become blind, they become "de-socialized" and "illiterate." Such misperceptions are especially disabling when they are carried by people who are actively working on behalf of people with impairments.

Misapprehensions About Sightedness and Blindness: The Medical Model Approach

Despite assertions of objectivity, of unbiased methodologies, science does not stand alone; it lives within society and is shaped by culture.

Scientific descriptions of vision and sight are located within physiology, but science's explanations fail to acknowledge how vision and sight are expressions of socially constructed, emotionally linked experiences.

Society misunderstands working elements of sight and blindness because it constructs ocularcentric notions that fail to notice that what we choose to see and how we see depends upon what we fear, what we avoid, what we desire; these emotional reactions are also socially and culturally constructed. For example, one culture might teach its inhabitants to look at women's naked breasts in an unconcerned way, while other cultures instruct people to avoid looking at women's "private parts" at all. Some cultures create fashion that exposes human bodies, while others, such as Muslim and Orthodox Judaism, use covering of women's bodies and hair ostensibly to help men avoid inappropriate lust. Sight becomes a point of entry for sin.

Even though French philosopher Denis Diderot seems to understand this point, he uses it to pose questions about blind (and deaf) people's capacity for morality. In 1749, Diderot wrote, "Letter on the Blind for the Use of Those Who See," in which he asked:

> How different is the morality of the blind from ours! And how different again would a deaf man's be from a blind man's; and how imperfect—to put the matter kindly—would our own system of morality appear to a being who had one more sense than we ourselves! (Diderot 1966a, p. 62)

Science erroneously assumes sight is opposite to blindness; yet, as Elkins (1996) points out, sight actually has blindness as an essential coexisting functional component. He asserts there are things we miss even when we are looking directly at them, while "other things we stare at obsessively, so that we are blind to everything else" (p. 12).

Elkins's belief that blindness is a constant companion to sight situates sightedness and blindness as collaborators. Furthermore, Elkins examines sight as socially and psychologically constructed at an unconscious level, claiming that people are blind to their blindness. "We need to be continuously partially blind in order to see. In the end, blindnesses are the constant companions of seeing and even the very condition of seeing itself" (Elkins 1996, p. 13).

However, when blindness is conceived of as a deficit, a lack of sight, blindness becomes abnormal, as something to be fixed in order to have the afflicted person made normal. Michalko (1998) asserts traditional medicine constructs blindness in comparison with sight; consequently, blindness becomes a thing to be cured (Michalko 1999). But, as Barasch (2001) points out, blindness is as natural a phenomenon as is sight. He contends that medical treatment is not intrinsically part of blindness. Furthermore, Barasch argues that cultural meanings of blindness change, but blindness itself does not. For example, attitudes toward blind people were chronicled in the 1870s edition of the authoritative and highly respected *Encyclopaedia Britannica*:

> The sedentary life, to which they are doomed, relaxes the frame, and subjects to all the disagreeable sensations which arise from dejection of spirit; hence the most feeble exertions create lassitude and uneasiness, and the natural tone of the nervous system, destroyed by inactivity, exasperates and embitters every disagreeable impression. (Quoted in Artman and Hall 1872)

Contemporary disability studies sometimes assumes that resistance to oppressive constructions of impairment and disability are something recent; this is not the case, however, as evidenced by several antiquarian books about blindness, usually written by blind people. For example, more than 100 years ago, William Artman and Lansing Hall wrote:

> Diminished expectations of blind people can be devastating: . . . the prejudice his condition creates, opposes him on every side. Without hesitation we say, that all the most painful disadvantages with which we have been obliged to contend under the absence of sight, have arisen entirely from ignorance, on the part of community, of our capabilities and resources. (Artman and Hall 1872, p. 10)

James Holman, for example, was a famous British traveler and writer at the turn of the nineteenth century. Accused of being a spy in Russia, Holman was asked to leave the country. Holman challenged ocularcentric attitudes that attempted to negate the value of travel by blind people. Sadly, two centuries later, I have been asked the same question posed to Holman: "What is the use of traveling to one who cannot see?" Holman responded by describing his phenomenological experience as a blind traveler and by presenting the possibility of blindness having distinct advantages over sightedness; for example, the blind traveler might examine the surroundings more closely and be less likely to be "deceived by appearances" (quoted in Artman and Hall 1872, pp. 102–103).

During the last half of the twentieth century, new models of "diversity" and "multiculturalism" were developed that a few people applied to impairment. In 1956, Marguerite Vance wrote a children's book, *Windows for Rosemary*, reframing blindness as merely "difference," as opposed to pathology. The book is clearly meant to resist and challenge societal stereotypes about blindness and educate the next generation about honoring difference. Vance (1956, p. 13) uses first-person narrative from the point of view of a little girl to describe the phenomenological experience of blindness thus:

> Most people see with their eyes, but I do it differently. I see with my ears and nose and lips and tongue and fingers and at the seashore with my toes. That is my way of being different, and people have a word for seeing that way: they call it being blind.

To discuss blindness as "difference" rather than pathology is not merely a matter of semantics. In the next section, I will explore how language works multidirectionally to transmit societal attitudes through the use of representational metaphor, and how such language perpetuates negative stereotypes and oppressive cognitive schemas.

Hazards of Blindness Metaphor

Blindness bears countless negative metaphorical connotations. Watch television or listen to casual conversation and it is common to hear that someone was "blinded by love" (unable to think clearly) or "blindly following" (unable to think independently). "The blind leading the blind" describes two or more people who are incapable of solving a problem. "Blind" is sometimes used as an adjective to emphasize negative emotions, for example, "blind rage" and "blind concentration" (obsession). People are "robbed blind" (victimized) and "blind to faults" (unprepared and unwilling to understand). If a person makes a decision "blindly," the implication is that the decision was not founded in reason.

Roget's New Millennium Thesaurus (2006) cites numerous blindness metaphors to describe ignorance, denial, naïveté, confusion, unintelligence, crudeness, incompetence, mystery, defect, isolation, befuddlement, perplexity, disregard, or unawareness. "Blind" represents something tricky that is intended to conceal the true nature of a thing, as in "blind taste test" and "double blind" research study. In botany, a plant is "blind" when it fails to flower. Artists and writers used blindness as metaphor throughout written history; it plays well to people's fear of becoming blind themselves.

Some blind people are fully aware of the stigma attached to blindness and often resist using "blind" to describe their condition. They might expend much effort either trying to conceal their blindness or using various terms that describe blindness without uttering the word in order to make themselves and others more comfortable. Kleege (1999, p. 19) reports that people with all levels of visual impairment are encouraged by social workers or family members to "sham sight," because blindness connotes darkness and despair. "Shamming sight" or "passing" has personal costs—exhaustion, hypervigilance, being found out, physical injury, limiting freedom of choice, and not getting personal needs met (Omansky Gordon 2003). We are taught to distrust people who "don't look you in the eye" and that "the eyes are windows to the soul." The underlying message is that blind people cannot be trusted and are empty of spirit.

The nondisabled majority population has, until very recently, been the creator and definer of language; it retained access to and control over the dissemination of information. Nondisabled people's words have governed language that shapes cultural values. How people say things reflects how they feel about those things: words reflect people's worldviews. As is the case with other stigmatized minority groups, the majority views blind people as deficient in comparison to sighted people.

Barasch (2001, p. 61) writes, "In being an embodiment of nothingness it is also a negation of one's self." Like water trickling over rocks, blindness metaphors, almost imperceptibly but steadily, wear away at society's confidence in blind people's abilities. The end products of negative values about blindness are attitudes of prejudice and acts of discrimination.

Even though much of polite society in the West has learned to refrain from using metaphors that have racist or sexist undertones in public venues, disablist metaphors continue without a trace of notice. Language has partners in the advancement of negative portrayals of blindness. Damaging messages are easily found in all cultural representations of blindness.

Media Images of Blindness

Time and again, television and movies portray visually impaired people as objects of ridicule, buffoonery, and trickery, or show that it is funny to deceive blind people (Norden 1994). Film plots often employ a cure for blindness as the happy ending. Norden (1994) notes that along with the cure comes a new sexuality, thus the hero or heroine becomes relationship worthy. Harking back to ancient Greco-Roman influences, moviemakers sometimes portray blind people as asexual, although these characters are endowed with "insight" into the spiritual world as compensation (Norden 1994).

Because the appearance of blind eyes is distasteful to sighted decisionmakers, blind people are not hired—even to play blind characters. They are often objects of comedy in the media, for example, driving a car, walking into walls, being deceived, or masters of self-deprecating jokes or metaphor. Movies do not tell stories from the experiences of real blind persons.

According to Norden (1994), from the mid-1930s to the mid-1940s the "Saintly Sage" stereotype had its heyday. This character is a "pious older person with impairment (almost always blind) who serves as a voice of reason and conscience in a chaotic world" (p. 131).

Whenever media makers develop representations that either debase or exalt by portraying disabled people in the extreme, it discredits natural difference and dramatically makes apparent the stigma of disability. Goffman (1986) distinguishes between the discredited, whose stigma is immediately apparent to an observer (e.g., race, sex, some physical impairments), and the discreditable, whose stigma can be hidden (e.g., sexual orientation, social class). When someone is discredited, it means that one's stigma is immediately apparent to others. Hence, those who value sight as the only legitimate ontology impose these beliefs through cultural, economic, political, and social practices.

The Use of Blindness in Religious Contexts

In the main, disability studies prefers to distance itself from religion except to critique historical and current representations of disability as evil, tragic, pathetic, and so on. Some religious practices represent and exploit disabled people as "special" children of God (particularly applied to people with developmental disabilities) or as having supernatural connections to a Supreme Being and deserving of charity—a position vociferously contested by disability rights activists who advocate for opportunity, not charity. Disability activists advocate for equal access to churches, synagogues, and other facilities where religious communities meet. Rarely does disability studies examine the positive role religion and spirituality play for large numbers of people living with impairments.

I did not set out to learn about the participants' faith or religion. Rather, it emerged as a subtheme on its own. Through self-exploration of their faith and religions, three of the participants discovered meaning and reason for their lives as blind people, which is congruent with both old and new literature. Helen Keller wrote extensively about her spiritual beliefs, how they helped her to understand, accept, and find meaning in herself as a blind person and as a citizen of the world. Jim Knipfel (2004) asserts that elemental to "any question of the spirit, to my mind at least, is the body we're saddled with" (p. 1), and further opines that "true 'spirituality' is reflected in how you deal with things in the face of unexpected and uncomfortable circumstances, regardless of whatever rule system you might swing about" (p. 1).

This section traces the history of representations of blindness in religious writings as well as how blind people use (or do not use) faith to make sense of their blindness.

Constructions of Blindness in Religion

Ancient Greeks used the same word, *ate*, to describe both physical blindness and as metaphor to denote "a whole complex of conditions—psychological, social and religious" (Barasch 2001, p. 34). They also used blindness as a metaphor for death, because they believed light *is* life (Barasch 2001). Characters with multiple eyes signify eternal watchfulness (Monbeck 1973, p. 126). Both Greeks and Romans discussed sexual taboos in ocularcentric terms—as "offenses are committed by the eye; they are sins of vision" (Barasch 2001, p. 26). Postmodern suppositions about sight and vision reinforce the idea that sight and vision are inextricably linked to desire (for a thorough discussion, see Elkins 1996). Using sight to represent culturally positive things is, nonetheless, another expression of ocularcentrism. An ancient Chinese myth, for example, claims that the day begins when the creator opens an eye (Monbeck 1973). Even today, the concept of the "evil eye," whose roots are found in ancient symbolic mythology, is common in many cultures (Barasch 2001); it represents supernatural surveillance and power. Friedrich Nietzsche used "evil eye" to describe envy: "One must not look back toward oneself, or every glance becomes an evil eye" (in Levin 1993, p. 127). Again, sight is coupled with desire.

Ancient Judeo-Christian texts contain both narrative and proscriptive representations of blindness and other impairments. According to Barasch (2001), sixth-century Christian iconography used the restoration of sight to represent spiritual awakenings—the move from paganism to Christianity. Across the thirteenth and fifteenth centuries, society began to represent blind people less as objects of spirituality and more as recipients of charity. Either way, blind people were marginalized from mainstream society and were afforded little opportunity to earn their own keep.

Religion, especially fundamentalist sectarianism, has grown in popularity in the United States and elsewhere in recent years, bringing along with it increased exposure to religious literature such as the Hebrew Bible and commentaries, the Christian Bible, and the Quran. While religious texts serve to comfort and help make sense of strife and chaos through faith, readers of such texts may also be learning meanings of illness and impairment as transmitted through story, metaphor, and legal doctrine. Negative metaphorical and allegorical references to blindness date back to biblical times. Here, I trace the roots of modern-day beliefs about blindness and blind people through metaphor, representation, and proscriptive ritual and law.

Hull (2001a) advises blind readers to keep in mind that the Bible was written by sighted people for sighted people. He writes that the way blindness is portrayed in the Bible is "not a permanent or particularly significant aspect of the message of the Bible" (Hull 2001a, p. 67). He asserts that the authors of the Bible did not have meanness toward blind people in mind; rather, their representations of blindness were reflective of the worldview of the times in which they lived. Then Hull illustrates ways in which these biblical references had profound and devastating results for blind people over centuries. Given both historical and modern roles of Christian charity in "services" to the blind, the power of biblical language cannot be dismissed, especially in texts as ancient and enduring as the Bible. While writers of the Bible may have written about blindness in shaming and exclusionary ways at a "subconscious level," as Hull (2001a) contends, the power of biblical language remains firmly in place and potently influential. As a student and teacher of religion, Hull (1990) struggled with the metaphor of blindness and light represented in the story of John in the Christian Bible. He concluded that he had to reject the notion of goodness (God) as light in order to affirm his existence:

> "God is light, and in Him there is no darkness at all" (I John 1.5). This is of limited use to me. God may be in light but I am in darkness. This alternative archetype only oppresses me by the brightness of its contrast. By obliterating the darkness, it obliterates me. The archetype of light cancels the archetype of darkness but does not transcend it. It cannot transcend the darkness/light because it is one side of it. I need to find an alternative archetype of a higher order. (p. 65)

The metaphor of blindness as a cultural representation of darkness with another form of otherness (disability) is important because it links blindness to evil, tragedy, ignorance, or punishment for sin—themes that continue to resonate in literature, drama, art, and current everyday language. Blindness as personal tragedy has become a "grand narrative" (de Sena Martins, 2004). Language constructs realities, and metaphor distorts the edges of those realities. Metaphors help control both fears and the objects of those fears. Hidden within metaphors of blindness are messages of misunderstanding, fear, devaluation, and contempt.

Many religious denominations (especially fundamentalist sects) are biblical literalists and, as such, are more likely to accept notions of illness as punishment for sin and as tragic conditions requiring prayers for cure. Writers of ancient Jewish texts copiously employed metaphors of impairment and illness to dramatize moral, ethical, and religious lessons; thus, impairment and illness have become bound up in Judeo-Christian discourses of God-decreed punishment for sin, physical "imperfection," and ritual impurity as well as objects of sorrow and pity. Bryant (1993) reports "disabled" is mentioned only one time in the Hebrew Bible (in Leviticus 22:22); nevertheless, the language of illness, impairment, and physical imperfection is used repeatedly to define human beings in relationship with God and within Jewish society.

In his study of the representation of blindness in art over many centuries, Barasch (2001) writes:

> The intervention of gods or demons in blinding is usually understood as a punishment for the transgression of a basic natural, moral, or religious law. In some way, then, the blind one is delinquent and his blindness always reminds us of his grave guilt. (p. 9)

Consequently, blind people became objectified as representative of sinfulness because there was a "blurring of the division between physical and metaphorical blindness" (Barasch 2001, p. 9). During the twelfth century, Moses Maimonides, a brilliant and influential Jewish philosopher, postulated that the Bible intended to enlighten through metaphoric language. Believing that metaphor was an effective tool to bridge a gap for people who believed in science, yet wanted to have faith, Maimonides, who was a physician and jurist, ascribed to a positivistic-type notion that truth is found through science. He asserted that the Bible was written within the confines of human language and to read it literally was to miss the "truth" (Goodman 1976). Conversely, Professor Emeritus of Communication Anita Taylor at George Mason University asserts, "Metaphors are driven by unstated assumptions and are windows into our thought processes. They render invisible any other way of constructing a subject" (personal communication, 1999).

While the writers of biblical texts used earthly language to describe and explain the inexplicable (God), one need only scratch the surface of metaphors of impairment to unearth negative attitudes, societal stereotypes, and damaging consequences. "You shall not curse the deaf or put a stumbling block before the blind" (Leviticus 19:14) presents deaf or blind people as "other"—separate from the general population—and, as such, they are represented as needing "special" treatment. Additionally, this metaphor implicitly fosters the stereotype that people with sensory impairments are easily taken advantage of. In *Judaism and Disability* (1998), Judith Z. Abrams offers a comprehensive examination of how disability is portrayed in ancient Jewish texts. She illustrates that several different metaphorical meanings were found in the metaphor of the stumbling block and the blind: The Bavli (Babylonian Talmud) used it in cases of serving wine to those who ascribe to prohibitions against drinking wine (Avodah Zarah 6a–6b); lending money without witnesses (B. Baba Metsia 75b); or deliberately irking someone to test their temper (B. Kiddushim 32a). In these examples, blindness is used to illustrate enticement and temptation, inability to control one's desires or deliberately acting wrongly toward another human being. All the examples equate blindness with helplessness.

Blinding someone seems to be the weapon of choice in the following examples: In Genesis 19:11, young and old alike were struck with blindness so they would wear themselves out groping for the exit; Samson was blinded by the Philistines (Judges 21). The stigma ascribed to visual impairment is found, for example, in the story of Leah, who was devalued as a potential wife because she had "weak eyes" (Genesis 29:17). Under the cover of darkness, Leben, Leah's father, deceived Jacob into marrying Leah (Genesis 29:16–25). The inference is that darkness allows for trickery, which is consistent with the misperception that blind people are easily fooled, and despite knowledge demonstrating that touch is the most reliable of the five corporeal senses, vision is valued above the rest. Exodus 23:8 warns, "and you shall take no bribe for a bribe blinds the officials, and subverts the cause of those who are in the right." Again, blindness represents corruption and deceit. Blindness is also characterized as punishment for failure to obey God's commandments: "The Lord will strike you with madness, blindness and dismay. You shall grope at noon as a blind man gropes in the dark" (Genesis 28:28–29).

Even though other impairments and diseases are far from exempt as means of punishment in the Bible, by sheer number of mentions, blindness appears to be the favorite impairment or disease. In common with ancient Greek literature, the Book of Lamentations goes so far as to compare the blind to the dead: "He hath set me in dark places, as that they be dead." In his commentary, eleventh-century Hebrew scholar R. Samuel interpreted this as referring to the blind (Freedman and Simon 1961).

As value-laden as metaphor is, ancient legal doctrine is equally so. The Hebrew Scriptures and subsequent commentaries devote lengthy passages detailing the inferiority of "physical imperfection" and lay down extraordinarily detailed laws governing people with these "imperfections."

According to Abrams (1998), a later commentary by Torah scholar Rabbi Yehudah places restrictions on blind men, who are prohibited from reciting the holiest prayer in Judaism: "Anyone who has never in his lifetime seen light may not spread [a cloak] over his head and recite the prayers preceding and following the Shema [the watchword of the Jewish faith]" (M. Megillah 4:6). The rabbi reasoned that a person totally blind from birth has never seen light and is not equipped to thank God for light (Abrams 1998).

The human desire to rid the world of illness and impairment is a "natural" consequence of negative attitudes toward physical, sensory, or cognitive difference. For example, the Western practice of faith healing with its roots in Holy Scripture personifies society's commitment to and production of a "naturally ordered body." Hence, it is significant to examine faith healing more as an artifact of social beliefs about an "ideal" embodiment rather than merely as a creation of religion. The ultimate manifestation of this desire to ensure "normal embodiment" can be found in a biblical description of what will occur when God returns to this world:

> Strengthen ye the weak hands, And make firm the tottering knees. Say to them that are of fearful heart: "Be strong, fear not"; Behold, your God will come with vengeance, With the recompense of God He will come and save you. Then the eyes shall be opened, And the ears of the deaf shall be unstopped. Then shall

the lame man leap as a hart, And the tongue of the dumb shall sing. (Isaiah 35:3–6)

In the Christian Bible, blindness is used as metaphor for spiritual revelation, such as Paul's temporary blindness as a precursor to his conversion. Koosed and Schumm (2005) examine the use of metaphors of light and darkness in the Gospel of John (John 9) to illustrate the "foreshadowing of resurrection." The authors report that one of the seven signs cited by John is restoration of sight to a blind man. Hull (2001b) also provides analysis of blindness in the Christian Bible in which he compares and contrasts his own experiences as a blind man with stories in the Christian Bible and imagines how events actually occurred at the time.

Metaphor used as a literary device is often poetic and beautiful. However, it is important to be thoughtful about underlying meanings and messages. Metaphors of illness, impairment, and disability have, in fact, been interpreted literally and used to stigmatize and disable people with illness or impairments. Many disabled people have stories to tell about well-meaning, faith-filled folks who perceive them as pitiful people, who believe that, if only they would seek answers to their ills in the Bible and believe in God's word with all their being, they may find that God will save them and heal their "tragic" bodies and minds.

Hull (2001b, pp. 37–38) relates a story about going to a faith healing service with his mother. When Hull went up on stage, the evangelist prayed over him, laid his hands upon him, and then exclaimed, "He can see!"; two of the evangelist's men grabbed Hull by each arm and escorted him off stage before he had a chance to protest. When he returned to his seat, his mother was crying. He told her that nothing had changed and they went home. Hull lays out biblical evidence demonstrating that modern-day faith healers do not act in the same way Jesus did.

Finding a Higher Purpose

John Hull's writings link phenomenological descriptions of blindness to his strong religious beliefs, including his journeys back and forth between doubt and faith. *In the Beginning There Was Darkness: A Blind Person's Conversations with the Bible* examines interpretations of the Bible (both Hebrew and Christian) from both sides of the border between blindness and sight (Hull 2001b). Hull explains that he wrote the book for sighted people to learn that the Bible was written by sighted people—from an ocularcentric point of reference. He explains how he felt alienated from the Bible when he first became blind, and then found meaning for his own blindness by coming to a new understanding of the equal importance of darkness and light in the Scriptures (Hull 2001a, 2001b).

Michalko (1998, pp. 133–134) does not address religion specifically; however, he discusses humanism's perspective on the "human spirit's capacity to cope with adversity, and that blindness is often perceived as another 'teacher' in this regard" (p. 133–134). Larry found his way to religious faith near the time of the onset of his blindness and used this faith to bring meaning to the experience, saying, "I honestly do believe that it's God's will." He stated that faith in God "turned around my attitude" toward going blind, and that he is "sure that whatever that [God's] design is that we have the tools to be successful in it." J. R. attends church regularly. When I asked him if he found a correlation between his religion and his blindness, he said, "No." He thinks that he is probably the only legally blind person ever elected "junior warden" at the church, which put him in charge of the physical plant. He feels he was well equipped to take on this responsibility because he has known "every nook and cranny" since childhood. Like Larry, I found particular meaning to my blindness through my faith:

> I was diagnosed with my eye disease during my fourth year of preparation for my Bat Mitzvah, so religion was already in the forefront of my daily life. I never prayed to be cured; I never bargained with God. But, I found strength in my religious faith. I also found Helen Keller's small volume of spiritual thoughts, *The Open Door*, and kept it on my nightstand. When I graduated from high school, I gave it to my high school counselor, a woman who encouraged me to write and who helped me through some rough patches with my family situation. I gave the book to her because I wanted to give her the possession I valued most.

Catherine recently "converted from nothing" to Christianity and regularly attends a Catholic church in her community. She seeks peace through meditation and prayer. None of the participants expressed cognitive dissonance between negative attitudes of organized religion toward blindness and their own spiritual beliefs or affiliations with their chosen places of worship. However, perhaps because of my interest and research into metaphors of blindness, I find myself annoyed when rabbis invoke such language, and most recently, I challenged a visiting rabbi to rethink her invocation of ancient references that perpetuate negative stereotypes.

The next section demonstrates some ways ancient stereotypes and representations of disability and blindness are alive and acted upon in this day and age, not merely benign sets of words and pictures from the past.

Social Barriers

Blind people encounter barriers to social life in both obvious and subtle ways. Hull (1990, p. 92) writes that the "social demands of public life and the personal demands of family life seem to create so many situations in which I become not only aware but painfully aware of blindness." Sighted people may feel awkward around blind people, and they act out their awkwardness, oftentimes incorrectly believing the blind person cannot see or observe them.

Sometimes the physical environment creates social hardship on blind people because they cannot access the everyday world with the same ease as do sighted people. Blind people take longer to do things, and they must do much advance planning. Sighted people more likely than not fail to take heed of particular problems encountered by legally blind people as they attempt to participate in social relations, as French (1999, p. 27) explains: "We cannot always engage in the same activities as sighted people, we cannot do things as fast, we need more time to see, and we need opportunities to use our other senses to the full."

Like French, Hull (1990) and Kuusisto (1998) note that time makes blind people's lives unlike those of the sighted. For example, Hull (1990, p. 79) explains his practical philosophy toward time and blindness as merely that "inexorable context within which I do what must be done."

Because blind people do not drive cars, they cannot make spontaneous trips to a friend's home, for example. They must make out their grocery lists by how much their bags will weigh on the way home. They must rely on public transit schedules, or wait for taxicabs, or figure in walking time and weather conditions. Sometimes they can get rides from people who drive, although there are potential drawbacks to giving over one's independence to another. When J. R. gave up driving, his wife drove him back and forth to work. One time they had an argument on the way home. J.R. recalled:

> Instead of turning left to go into town she turned right. And the other way there's a subdivision over on that side. She pulled into that subdivision. She pulled up to a place to turn around. She parked. She said, "Get out!" Yeah. And so here I am getting out, and she drives off—just left me. You know how to get rid of your blind husband [laughs]. And so the ah [pauses] the blindness. . . . But the, ah. . . . Well, if blindness could be cured that easily just by kicking you out of the car. But, yeah. But I; yeah so I walk along the subdivision. . . . It was a nice warm day so there's somebody out in their yard there, and I just asked if they'd call 911, and they called 911. A police officer came and he gave me a ride home.

You Can't Get There From Here: Public Transit

Another barrier to full and equal participation in social life is inaccessible transportation. Bus stops are not placed uniformly in intersections; bus signs are placed up high and in small print; and bus drivers routinely ignore federal regulations requiring them to announce stops audibly.

Federal law allows local transit districts to decide who is eligible for transit services for disabled people; therefore, disabled people are at the mercy of local decisionmakers who are chiefly trained within the medical model of disability and are often motivated by availability of funds rather than by lawful eligibility. The majority of these gatekeepers are most likely sighted and probably drive, leaving them with a total lack of knowledge about what it is like not to possess driving privileges. All these factors profoundly influence blind people's opportunities to do such mundane things as visit a friend's home, go shopping, or attend religious services, for example. The issue of inaccessible transit becomes even more critical to blind people who need to get to and from work on time each day.

In our society, and especially in suburban sectors, driving is the norm. Cities and towns are built around roads and streets, while sidewalks are most often not considered a public policy priority. Despite government's urging of its citizens to help the United States reduce its dependence on Middle Eastern oil-producing nations, to get out of their cars and walk in order to help relieve traffic congestion, or to get proper exercise, the lack of sidewalks makes it painfully apparent that it is largely lip service. As Bob Dylan (1965) writes, "You don't need a weatherman to know which way the wind blows." Three of the four participants used to drive but had to give it up because of their blindness, and this loss complicated their lives and changed basic lifestyles, including where they chose to live, how they thought about themselves in relation to the built environment, and how they felt about their blindness.

J. R.'s situation was particularly ironic in that his entire career had been in traffic engineering. As we read earlier, his ex-wife used driving as a method of control over him. Power over the wheel was wielded against him in the same way other disabled people experience caregiver abuse. J. R. had been used to driving from site to site to survey traffic problem areas and assess possible solutions, so not driving severely limited his ability to perform his job. His employer did not offer a driver as a reasonable accommodation. For a while he relied on his (then) wife to drive him to his office and back, but as we learned, this arrangement proved less than satisfactory. J. R. then had to go to human resources to ask for someone with whom he could ride to and from work. J. R. also had to give up a home he had built—one he loved—in favor of one closer to work.

Social Engagement

Blind people who do not see faces do not have the same choices as sighted people about whom they decide to greet on the street. They regularly draw unwanted attention as objects of curiosity and find it difficult to achieve a balance between being ignored or becoming the center of attention (Hull 1990). Dimly lit nightclubs, bars, and restaurants make access to menus, food, and beverages difficult, and sometimes, blind people's "mistakes" in these settings are misinterpreted as clumsiness, lack of social graces, or even drunkenness. Because blind people rely on hearing rather than lip reading or facial cues as part of interpersonal exchange, noisy venues make conversation nearly impossible, leaving them left out—isolated. Hull (1990, pp. 173–174) explains:

> When somebody turns the juke-box on in a coffee bar, the sound literally obliterates the voices of my friends. It is as if I was alone. They disappear. . . . This must be why I find noisy parties, especially discos, so lonely. . . . It is like having headphones on and not being able to take them off.

Cocktail party settings are social death for blind people because they cannot scan a room to see people's faces and make convivial conversation, even though they may be feeling isolated and out of place. It is difficult for sighted people to know how to share the pleasure they are experiencing through their sight and vision, and it is just as difficult for legally blind people to stay interested in the visual experience being described to them (Hull 1990). Such situations push blind people to the margins of polite society.

Guide dog users endure harassment or are denied admittance to public places altogether despite specific Americans with Disabilities Act (1990) regulations that protect the rights of disabled people and their service animals from this type of discrimination. Such experiences leave guide dog users in a state of uncertainty about where and when they may be harassed again.

On top of attitudinal obstacles, physical barriers to social participation remain an everyday part of blind people's lives. Fast-food restaurant menus are located up high against walls behind counters. Buffets are inaccessible. Mirrors in public restrooms are situated behind sinks. In libraries and bookstores, large print books are stacked in floor-to-ceiling units instead of at eye level, rendering the books inaccessible to the very population they are designed to accommodate. All of these instances force blind people to ask for help from strangers, who sometimes ignore requests for assistance or respond as if the blind person is stupid, intrusive, or inept.

Even though closed captioning is a widely used access tool for deaf and hard-of-hearing people, audio description (sometimes called "descriptive video") for the blind and visually impaired is rarely available on television, in movies, or at live performances. Cable television providers often choose to use the second audio band (required for broadcast of audio description) to run Spanish-language translation instead. Theaters and concert halls have designated accessible seating for wheelchair users, event venues provide sign-language interpreters upon request, but blind people are left out of the accessibility equation. When legally blind people request accessible seating, they are most likely offered the "handicapped" seats for wheelchair users, which are at the ends of aisles and often far back from the stage—thoroughly inaccessible to blind performance-goers. I have experienced this many times. Here is one example:

> One summer I called the office of an outdoor amphitheater to request seating close to the stage. The head of security told me to sit in the wheelchair section, that it was the only place they could accommodate my request even though it was halfway up the hill away from the stage. During the concert some of the wheelchair users told me I didn't belong there and should move. Several volunteer security people came by and asked me to leave. I showed them my white cane but no one seemed to know what to do with me. Between the venue personnel and the wheelchair users complaining to me about sitting in their section, I felt harassed from all sides. I stayed but I could not see the stage because it was too far away and I was sitting on the ground behind wheelchairs. The second concert I attended was no different—hassled and pressed to move. The third concert I attended there was an uneventful, enjoyable evening.
>
> After each event, I called the safety office and they assured me I would be allowed in the wheelchair section. It was kind of weird advocating for a location that was still too far from the stage for me to see but that seemed to be my only choice.
>
> The fourth time I went, a security guard blocked my entrance to the wheelchair section. We ended up in an argument.
>
> I said, "I was told by your security department to sit here."
>
> "We had a meeting and you're not allowed."
>
> "When was that meeting? I just talked to the person two days ago."
>
> "Umm . . . about a month ago."
>
> He told me I should talk to the security person in charge that night, and that he would bring him to the wheelchair section entrance. When that person showed up a little bit later, he said I couldn't go into that section. I told him the other guard told me they had a meeting about it, and he said that wasn't true and they hadn't decided anything. I felt very much stuck in a runaround.
>
> I asked, "Well, if I can't sit here, will you take us to the front to see if there is room for us?" He begrudgingly agreed but when

we got to the front it was full. He said, "You can sit right there but your friends can't." "Sir, that's against ADA regulations. My friends are allowed to sit with me." He told me I better know what I'm talking about because he did.

I said, "This whole experience is humiliating."

"No, humiliating would be for me to have to ask someone to move to accommodate you."

I felt stung by such an abusive statement. He turned his back and walked away from me. I followed him.

"Don't walk away from me when I'm trying to talk with you."

"I don't want the public to hear this," he said.

I replied, "When you ask someone to leave the wheelchair section, you are not humiliated." He said, "You're asking me to kick someone out of the wheelchair section for you?" I replied, "That is not at all what I said. I'm saying you have no problem keeping people out of the wheelchair section, but you will not ask someone to move so I can be accommodated at the front. May I have your business card?"

"I'd give you one but I don't have any with me," he said, still walking away. He told me to look for him at the end of the concert and he would give me a card. I held up my white cane (which had been in my hand during the entire event), and said, "How do you think I can find you?" and he walked away, saying, "Just look for any of the blue shirts."

After all that, I still didn't get accessible seating. I was self-conscious and embarrassed for my two nondisabled companions. Ironically, we were all there to see Blind Boys of Alabama perform.

After that fourth concert, I wrote a letter to the venue director documenting my experiences; they changed their policies about how to treat disabled patrons. But I haven't gone there since then even though there have been performers I wanted to see.

When blind people request seating front and center, they are sometimes misunderstood or made to feel as if they are demanding "special" or privileged treatment. Many performance promoters hold these seats back from public sale; instead, reserving them for influential people or for season ticket holders. If blind people succeed in reserving front row seats, they must pay the highest ticket price for the privilege. Occasionally, a blindness agency arranges special audio-described live theater performances. Audio-described (Descriptive Video Service, or DVS) movies on DVD are increasingly available, although it is difficult to get current films that include this feature.

Legally blind people's access needs are beyond the margins occupied by other disabled people; hence, these needs are sometimes dismissed or totally ignored. Moreover, legally blind people are sometimes assumed to know braille; consequently, they may be handed information materials that are as inaccessible to them as 8-point type.

"Polite society" sometimes loses its manners in interactions with disabled people; disabled people are somehow perceived to be public property of the nondisabled in that they are, at any time or place, confronted to explain their impairments. Strangers unabashedly ask legally blind people invasive questions about their medical conditions, ask what they can or cannot see, wonder out loud why they are looking closely at objects, and then act huffy when blind people refuse to answer such rude inquiries. The borderland called legal blindness leaves its inhabitants susceptible to accusations of either "faking" sight or of "faking" blindness.

"Which Side Are You On?" (Florence Resse, ca. 1930s)

Sally French's (2003) personal account, "Can You See the Rainbow?" receives the most comments of her entire body of work (personal communication, September 2003). Evidently, her story of enforced denial resonates with many involved in disability issues. In this piece, French recounts how the adults in her life responded to her visual impairment:

> Having adults pretend that I could see more than I could, and having to acquiesce in the pretence, was a theme throughout my childhood. . . . Adults who were not emotionally involved with the issue of whether or not I could see also led me along the path of denial. This was achieved by their tendency to disbelieve me and interpret my behavior as "playing up" when I told them I could not see. Basically they were confused and unable to cope with the ambiguities of partial sight. (p. 209)

Two of Larry's anecdotes are consistent with French's reminiscences. Larry's (former) girlfriend urged him to call colors by the names most commonly used by sighted people despite the fact that he does not distinguish them the same way. For example, if he sees a building as brown even though he knows it's red, he calls it brown, but she thinks he should call it red because that's what it is to sighted people and also how he used to see it. She is more comfortable with him pretending to see as sighted people do, and as he used to, even though she did not know him before he went blind. Colors are important to Larry's profession as an artist and photographer; so now he encounters a conundrum common to legal blindness. Which is more valid, an accurate description of what the borderland blind person sees, or the sighted population's naming and interpretation of things? And if the latter is accepted as "truth," does this put border-land blind people in the position of having to lie about their own experience to satisfy sighted people's perception of "reality"—of truth? Michalko (1998, 1999, 2002) speaks to this as a core problem in the medically constructed sightedness/blindness binary.

I, too, have often experienced people placing me on the sighted ("normal") side of the border despite my own choice to stake my claim on the blindness side. On two separate occasions, sighted people grabbed my white cane away from me when my picture was about to be taken. As I posed in front of a statue of George Mason on the campus where we had just attended my master's degree grad-uation ceremony, one of my relatives walked up and took my cane from my hand. I understood and appreciated his good intentions, but I didn't like it. I didn't say anything because I didn't want to cause tension between us or hurt his feelings. Another time, I was getting my picture taken at the Molly Malone statue in Dublin, Ire-land. The man in charge of the statue looked through his camera to set the pose and then reached up in an attempt to remove my cane from my hand. I was not as surprised as I was at graduation, so this time I refused to hand it over and got my picture taken as I am. I guess they both thought the cane was unsightly.

Stephen Kuusisto's family left him with a mixed message that placed him on the fence of the border, ill-equipped to fit in on either side; first, he was taught that he was blind, and next, he "was taught to disavow it" (1998, p. 13). He explains the emotional consequences thus: "I grew bent over like the dry tinder grass. I couldn't stand up proudly, nor could I retreat" (Kuusisto 1998, p. 13).

Sighted people do not always attempt to place blind people on the sighted side: a critical factor is acceptance of their loved one's blindness. For example, Larry's daughter accepted his blindness from the outset, and she understands the limitations of an ocular-centric built environment. Every year, she sends him a new bright yellow parka because she wants him to be easily seen by motorists. Soon after Larry told his family that he had become blind, one of his sons offered to act as driver on a trip across the country—a role Larry traditionally assumed. His son told him that he would drive, and Larry still could take photographs of the Southwest desertscape, just as he had always done on previous trips.

Resistance and Challenge in Everyday Life

Larry, Catherine, J. R., and I have been subjected to social treatment based on common myths about blind people, and we each found various ways to challenge these stereotypes. We all used humor as a strategy to resist and challenge societal misperceptions about blindness. J. R. believes that those who use humor are the ones who "survive" blindness.

For instance, when Larry shook hands with someone to whom he was being introduced, he made a "lucky guess" that the person was a piano player. The person making the introduction cried out in amazement, "Oh, my God! How did you get that?" Larry then spun a yarn about how his blindness gave him special hypersensitivity to touch. Larry laughed as he told me, "So you know I am definitely just perpetrating a hoax."

One of J. R.'s anecdotes speaks directly to the stereotype that blindness means darkness (Monbeck 1973), and it also highlights what it is like to be both observer and observed. When J. R. goes to the optician's office, he is aware that people notice that he wears tinted (not dark) glasses, yet he carries a white cane. He jokes, "They think, 'Oh you have glasses, you're not blind.'" But then, there is the presence of the white cane. J. R. suspects the observers wonder about the optician's abilities, thinking, "This is the best they can do?" His anecdote illustrates the cognitive dissonance sighted people experience when they witness the alterity of legal blindness. But J. R.' s social commentary was not as funny to me once I connected the dots back to when I was fired from my much-needed receptionist job at an optician's office because "it looked bad" for the optical company.

J. R. told about when he was using his white cane during an outing, and a child asked her mother, "Why is that man using that white stick?" The mother explained that he used the cane because he is blind. As J. R. passed them, he said to the mother, "Don't tell her about the 25 bonus points," which refers to the old joke about drivers earning "bonus points" for running over a blind person. He made his point that he is well aware of blind jokes.

None of the participants reported engaging in self-demeaning humor; instead, they turned the joke onto society in the form of social observation, and they all used humor to resist internalized oppression—a strategy used by many of the authors cited earlier (e.g., Hull 1990; Knipfel 1999; Kuusisto 1998; Michalko 1998, 1999).

Blind People as Public Property

Frequently, acting blind (i.e., using low vision aids and other blindness skills) elicits invasive, infantilizing questions from strangers such as, "Oh my, what happened to you?" or "How do you cross the street by yourself?" or "Aren't you afraid?" Sometimes this line of questioning is followed with something along the lines of, "Oh, you're just so brave" or "You're such an inspiration." Strangers seem to have no compunction about prying into private medical and even financial matters, as if they have a right to know; and if the blind person refuses to answer, the strangers either redouble their efforts or turn away as if they were the ones insulted. Larry manages blindness questions in different ways depending upon whether they come from strangers, acquaintances, or family. He said:

> It's like they wonder what it is that you see . . . if it's like my niece . . . I'll take more care in analogies and stuff like that, whereas if it's my brother or my sister-in-law or one of the guys I'm with, um, I would just give them a couple of different things.

Larry reports, however, that as for the general public, he doesn't "give a shit what they think." Be that as it may, he remains aware of how people might perceive him.

Borderland blind people report that they make decisions about whether they should disclose their visual impairment from moment to moment and situation to situation. Act sighted or flaunt blindness? Or should they just do what they need to do to get around without feeling the need to explain themselves to anyone? Self-disclosure decisions are aroused by the needs of embodied consequences of blindness, by awareness of societal attitudes and predictable consequences of presenting oneself as blind, and by issues around identity. All these factors influence how blind (and other disabled) people negotiate a world "from the vantage point of the atypical" (Linton 1998, p. 6).

As illustration, fast-food restaurants always hang their menus high up on walls several feet behind the service counter. Blind people cannot read the sign for two reasons: first, their impairment limits their sensory ability to read print from a distance; and second, the location, position, and font size of the menu make it inaccessible because the restaurant designers falsely assumed their customers are all sighted. Faced with the barrier of an inaccessible menu, borderland blind customers must decide whether to "ask for help" (request access), knowing through past experience their request might evoke pity, disdain, or that they will be outright shunned. One alternative I adopted in the past is to memorize what I wish to order and just order the same thing every time I go to that restaurant. Blind people often choose this option to avoid making themselves vulnerable to stigmatization, rudeness, public embarrassment, or pity, but the downside is that they surrender gastronomic variety (Gordon 1996; Linton 1998).

Restaurants can be particularly troublesome for borderland blind people because the ocularcentric environment and the embodied experience bump up against the pressure of social graces. The fancier the restaurant, the dimmer the lighting most likely is. People sit across from each other, so the table width breaches any possibility of eye contact. Add flickering candles, an undercurrent of simultaneously humming conversations punctuated with loud laughter, and now the setting becomes a recipe for social faux pas and other mishaps. Catherine said:

> They just think you're absolutely stupid. And it's just like you can't get away from that. That's your embarrassment. . . . And then it's all over. It's all over. [Laughs] And then you go to the bathroom and cry. . . . breathe . . . panic attack. It's like, Christ! Why can't anything go right? Why couldn't the mashed potatoes be over here? Why couldn't the butter be . . . ?

Finding the bathroom in a dark restaurant is like running an obstacle course—wending one's way through tables, booths, wait staff carrying head-level trays, feet and handbags in aisles, coats on chair backs, swinging kitchen doors with wait staff moving quickly in all directions, and the dark hallway that inevitably houses the restrooms, which are more than likely not clearly marked because the signs are hung high above eye level, written in fancy script, or marked with artistically gender-specific designs with no print as clues:

> I cannot count on both hands how many times I've walked into the men's room in restaurants because no one was around to whom I could ask direction. When I see a urinal on the wall, I turn around and head off into the restroom next door, hoping no one saw me enter or leave.

Asking for Help

When borderland blind people ask for impairment-related assistance, they must identify themselves as blind. It is very difficult to pass as sighted and ask for help reading a street sign six feet above where you are standing. Identity is a two-way social process; people identify themselves and people are identified by others (Rosenblum and Travis 1996). Since borderland blind people may not use typical blindness artifacts, such as white canes or dark glasses, the sighted public may respond to requests for assistance in demeaning, curt, or other unhelpful ways. Sighted people might be more ready to offer help to someone who is obviously blind; yet, they may feel intruded upon by an unidentifiable borderland blind person. Catherine said:

> Yeah, you have to ask everyone, and it's like people, they can be really . . . brush you off mean. You have to be really cordial and demure as a blind person.

Larry's reluctance to ask for help is bound up in his desire for self-sufficiency. He said:

> To find out that, yeah, you know, damn it, I need help reading this label because I don't know if it's apple juice or apple vinegar. . . .

So um, there was a time when I wouldn't have bought it. That's, that's the thing that can eat at you. You know?

Conclusion

The borderland of legal blindness is a confusing place for both sighted and blind people. Social interactions in the borderland are complex and sometimes awkward for all concerned. The participants' stories are congruent with previous writings of borderland blind scholars (such as French 2001, 2006; Hull 1990, 2001a, 2001b; Kleege 1999; Kudlick 2005; Kuusisto 1998; Michalko 1998, 1999, 2002; Omansky Gordon 2003), who all report they spend a good deal of time and energy plotting strategies for presenting themselves to the sighted world. Some of the reports, such as ways to make eye contact, articulate that ocularcentric values run deep— even among those who adopt a social model of disability.

The participants' perceptions about living with blindness emphatically challenge traditional medical model beliefs that "blindness is a profound misfortune, a calamity, really, for ordinary life can't accommodate it" (Kuusisto 1998, pp. 20–21). None of the participants expressed any indication of feeling either like a tragic figure or as someone heroically overcoming blindness. On the contrary, they consider themselves merely doing what they need to do to accommodate their blindness in an ocularcentric society and consider their blindness to be but one portion of a whole life. How they feel about themselves and their blindness directly challenges traditional medical model and cultural stereotypes of blindness and blind people.

9

Being Blind:
From the Inside Out

This chapter turns its attention to a more inward aspect of legal blindness. Some phenomenological features of impairment are located expressly within the individual, such as what and how a person sees—how blindness becomes what Hull (1990, p. 217) calls a "whole-body" experience. Blindness cannot be adequately addressed solely within an orthodox, materialist social model of disability, as that would ignore fundamental elements of the everyday experience of being blind. While not at all rejecting the social model, I call upon the medical model to discuss particular individualized features of the blindness experience. This book, however, delves further than the medical model because it seeks to hear what blind people have to say rather than simply offer biological, measurable descriptions of sight, vision, and blindness from the viewpoint of ophthalmology. Such an approach fulfills the original aims of this study as argued from the outset, that in order to adequately examine the life stories of blind people, embodiment could not and should not be ignored (Morris 1992; de Sena Martins 2004). During the entire research process, and especially with regard to phenomenological description and analysis, I remained vigilant about the pitfalls of mimicking techniques or goals of "freak shows" that "delineate the distance between the writer and the reader and emphasize the alien nature of blind experience" (Kleege 1999, p. 3).

However, in no way do I mean to infer ignorance or endorsement of hegemonic practices associated with the medical model, nor do I cast aside or even downplay the importance of social facets.

Many features of legal blindness are interrelationally entangled with social aspects and identity issues as well. Phenomenological experiences of legal blindness are important to learn about because therein lie the details of a rich ontology and epistemology. Kuusisto (1998) describes his view from the inside out, "I see like a person who looks through a kaleidoscope; my impressions of the world are at once beautiful and largely useless" (p. 21). How blind people use residual vision, touch, emotion, hearing, and taste, as well as what meaning they make of their "whole-body" seeing (Hull 1990), tells us much about living in the borderland of legal blindness.

An Existential Phenomenological Approach

Existential phenomenology, a branch of modern and postmodern phenomenological inquiry, was developed by such philosophers as Edmund Husserl, Martin Buber, Viktor Frankl, and Simone de Beauvoir. This model is especially appropriate for a study of blindness because existential philosophy concerns itself with the meaning of one's own existence, with one's relationship to society and the built environment, interpersonal associations, and relationship with self. Blindness is an embodied ontology and epistemology, a permanent companion to every facet of the lived experience; consequently it affects how blind people confront the meaning of existence, matters of life and death, of questions of freedom and responsibility. As members of an oppressed minority group, blind (and other disabled) people are habitually excluded from mainstream society, which denies them basic freedoms and renders them unable to take responsibility for themselves, no matter how much they desire and attempt to do so.

Phenomenology seeks to discover the essence of the blindness experience by engaging in "re-presentation (e.g., expectation, imagination and memory)" (Husserl 1900–1901; Embree 1997 cited in CARP 2006). Expectation, imagination, and memory all play significant roles in the phenomenon of blindness. My experience has included many instances, for example,

> due to the degenerative nature of my eye disease, I found it increasingly difficult to read the printed word. I remember that

Top Ramen soup had just become popular, so I bought some; but, when I went to prepare it, I found that I couldn't read the cooking instructions. I had to wait until a neighbor came home so he could read to me. I relied a lot on my memory. Someone would read directions for this or that and I'd just memorize it so I wouldn't have to ask again.

In *The Object Stares Back*, Elkins (1996) challenges socially constructed ideas about how sight operates. He asserts the actual phenomenon of sight is neither simple, sensible, nor one-directional. Elkins (1996, p. 11) observes that sight is "irrational, inconsistent, and undependable"—attributes that do not warrant society's dependence on sight as the ultimate sense. Elkins further asserts that eyes are not as controllable as one would think, and that humans are subject to vision's vagaries since vision is at the mercy of emotional response. He writes that sight is "entangled in the passions—jealousy, violence, possessiveness; and it is soaked in affect—in pleasure and displeasure, and in pain. . . . Seeing is metamorphosis, not mechanism" (Elkins 1996, p. 11).

He argues that blindness resides alongside sight, and, thus, shapes our essential experiences. His observations demonstrate that sighted people also experience blindness. Elkins (1996, p. 205) asserts that there are

> things we [sighted people] do not see and things we cannot see and things we refuse to see, and there are also things we can't make out, puzzling things and sickening things that make us wince. There are things too boring to see, too normal or unremarkable to ever catch the eye. . . . There are things emptied of meaning because they have no use, they answer to no desire, they cannot be owned or moved or enjoyed . . . things too dangerous to see, charged with frightening emotional power.

These points that seeing is a matter of culture are atypical of how sight is understood by both sighted and blind people who ascribe to the medical model. Nevertheless, his work has made a significant contribution toward explaining the phenomenology of sight, vision, and blindness. Journalist Jim Knipfel studied phenomenology during his days at university and then applied it to his own experience of progressive blindness: "As the sight fades, every day really does become one ongoing phenomenological experiment" (personal communication, March 3, 2005). John Hull (1990, 2001a, 2001b) and Michalko (1998, 1999) stress that blindness should not be considered an incomplete form of sight; rather, it is a complete form of a different experience. Blindness is an alternate way of being in and knowing the world—not inferior to sight and not inherently tragic or pitiful. Antithetically, many blind people describe their phenomenological experience of blindness as one of the best things that happened to them. Knipfel (1999) refutes his home living skills rehabilitation worker's prediction that he would become depressed because he was blind. He writes:

> I tried to explain to him that I was depressed most days, and that it had little to do with blindness. If anything, going blind was giving me a boost. It's a fascinating thing, experiencing the complete collapse of one of your major sensory organ systems. (p. 201)

Spending a good part of her life as a sighted person, Lisa Fittipaldi (2004) took up art after becoming legally blind. She is most well known for her realist art and describes blindness as a new epistemology: "When the world no longer comes to you through your eyes, you have to go out and move through the world in order to understand it" (p. 32).

Fittipaldi has learned sight creates distance while touch requires intimacy. Sight and vision privilege the sighted to observe and surveil blind people from a socially comfortable, safe distance. Blindness prohibits opportunities for equidistant observation of those who gaze at them. From a distance, sighted people remain unobserved, while blind people are powerless to gaze back with any degree of accuracy, although borderland blind people can sometimes take on the observer role at shorter distances.

Simulating Blindness

"Simulation exercises" ostensibly mimic various conditions of blindness and are commonly used in disability awareness events. Everyone finds their own best ways to get from one place to the next; blind people rely on touch, hearing, residual vision, taste, imagination, and memory according to their own abilities, needs, and desires. Societal stereotypes about blindness, however, fail to recognize or respect the many alternative ways the blind can know the world around them. Instead, those who participate in simulation exercises often assume mistaken beliefs about what it is like to be blind, and so treat every blind person they meet as if they are carbon copies of the other. They might also have irrational beliefs that sight and blindness are static.

Simulation exercises also fail to evoke genuine understanding or the emotional intensity associated with new situations and an ever-changing environment. Kuusisto (1998, p. 19) describes how architecture, changing conditions, and lighting can reduce a borderland blind person to "helplessness, panic, self-consciousness, or awkwardness." Varying conditions make borderland blind people appear more blind or, at other times, more sighted, which often confuses observers. Knipfel (2004) explains that what might otherwise be perceived as discrepancies in his story are due to changing environments and vision: "These things help explain why, at some points in this book, I seem to be completely blind, while at others, I seem to be seeing reasonably well" (p. 4). All these factors are impossible to replicate in simulation exercises.

The merits and failings of simulation exercises are hotly debated topics in the field of blindness (and other disabilities). Like Kleege (1999), J. R. believes simulation exercises are helpful. During his work with the Boy Scouts, he noticed that the requirements for a "disability badge" addressed mobility impairments but contained no information about blindness, so he created blindness simulation exercises for the troop. J. R. thought the boys learned from participating in his activity. I have no doubt that J. R.'s exercises were informative and most certainly filled a gap in the boys' education. However, it is important to remember that simulation exercises cannot possibly reproduce social, cultural, and personal factors that all make up blindness.

"It's All How You Look at It"

Uniqueness of vision is a common denominator among borderland blind people. It is extremely difficult to measure or understand borderland blindness because, for one thing, environmental factors greatly affect how, what, where, and when they see. In her advice to teachers of blind children, Cheadle (2005) cautions them to keep in mind that the children's vision can change day by day and hour by hour, depending upon lighting, fatigue, weather conditions, and so on. Larry reports that his vision changes with even subtle differences in the weather—rainy days affect him differently than misty days, and cloudy days have a different impact than foggy conditions. Sunshine is his least favorite weather condition, especially in combination with snow, because laser treatment scars cause sensitivity to brightness and glare; he experiences "physical pain." Larry applies his photography background to describe various weather conditions as analogous to "f-stops in that you have to close down the f-stop because all the light coming in screws up the readings." The other three participants also described extreme light sensitivity (photophobia); their reports are consistent with both medical descriptions and personal accounts (see Kuusisto 1998).

Legally blind people experience the world around them in many different ways, and no one way fits all. No matter how much time I spend with legally blind friends and colleagues, I can neither assume nor accurately guess how they view and see. I have met only one other person with the same eye disease I have, and her description of what she sees is different from mine because the progression of her disease process is not at the same stage as mine. As nearly impossible as it is for legally blind people to know each other's sight and vision, it is impossible for sighted people to experience legal blindness merely by participating in a simulation exercise.

For instance, Hull (1990) describes blind people's reliance on sound to compensate for lack of sight by juxtaposing acoustics with silence, observing that the "silent world" is nonexistent to blind people. Sighted people doing simulation exercises could well miss this subtlety; it takes actual living as a blind person to understand what components make up the whole blindness experience. According to de Sena Martins (2004, no page no.):

> This imagination not only produces personal anxieties towards blindness but is also mobilized as a way of access to the reality of blind persons. The question is that such an imagination allows an apprehension of the eventual impact of a sudden loss of vision, but it fails to understand how someone's life can be reconstructed in other terms without vision.

Moreover, simulation exercises ignore what de Sena Martins (2004, no page no.) calls "the experiences of suffering and deprivation that can be directly associated to the physical fact of blindness." In response to criticisms of the social model of disability's avoidance of personal experiences of embodiment, de Sena Martins (2004) advocates for examination of aspects of embodiment he calls the "anguish of corporeal transgression"; that is, "the vulnerability in the existence given by a body that fails us, that transgresses references in the manner of being in the world." Hull (1990, pp. 109–110) points out the erroneousness of simulation exercises with regard to touch: "Deleting sight but leaving touch untouched gives a false impression, because touch is affected when sight is deleted. In other words, the blind person sees with his fingers."

Paradoxically, ocularcentric literature about blindness has been written not only by sighted people, but by blind people as well. For example, Kleege (1999, pp. 2–3) writes, "Though I see less than 10 percent of what a normal person does, I would have to describe myself as intensely visual. . . . Although my eyes are blind, my brain is still sighted." While she admits there is a stigma attached to blindness, she characterizes vision to be easily understood by sighted people through simulation exercises, which are individual, not social, experiences. She suggests that people simulate blindness merely by closing the eyes:

> Simply close your eyes. . . . So go ahead. Close your eyes. It is not an unfamiliar condition for you. You experience it every time you blink. You are the same person with your eyes closed. You can still think, remember, feel. See? It's not so bad. You discover not that you hear better but that you are better able to make sense of sounds. (1999, p. 32)

Kleege's suggestion to use simplistic simulation exercises (which fail to place the blindness experience within an everyday broader sociocultural context) is naïve in that blindness is complex and cannot be experienced or replicated with any degree of accuracy or totality. While a simulation exercise may momentarily demonstrate the embodied experience of reliance on all the senses, simulations occur in a social vacuum wherein no participant is stigmatized for closed or squinted eyes, groping, or stumbling. Therefore, simulation exercises can mistakenly leave participants with the impression they have truly experienced blindness, even if just for a minute. De Sena Martins (2004) believes the danger is that "corporeal imagining of blindness" leads sighted people to erroneous conclusions, and that simulation exercises result in sighted people perceiving blind people as not able and trapped in sensory deficit. Sighted participants mistakenly think they imagine the corporeal experience of blindness, which evokes strong negative emotions in the participants.

Neither can simulation exercises replicate photophobia, a physiological side effect of many eye diseases that cause legal blindness. Many legally blind people need strong light to see; yet, such light can be a source of excruciating pain (e.g., severe headaches accompanied by eye muscle tension). Additionally, legally blind people often become *more* blind when moving from one light setting to the next, for example, indoors into sunlight and vice versa. Those attempting to understand legal blindness through momentary simulation exercises do not endure chronic neck pain, which legally blind people experience from bending over to look closely at things, or severe eye strain and fatigue from using low vision aids. Nor do participants in simulation exercises gain mitigative skills acquired through time and practice.

Shared Stories of Blindness: Embodied Experiences

Personal accounts of whole-body experiences of legal blindness, including how and what legally blind people see, are more accurate and educational than brief, contrived simulation exercises. For example, Kuusisto (1998) provides brilliantly articulated descriptions of the way many legally blind people view the world around them: "The sensorium of the blind who possess some marginal vision is by turns magical and disturbing . . . it's a mad, holy vision, the repeated appearance and disappearance of the physical world" (p. 12). Such description can never be simulated by sighted people.

He further suggests that blind people know what it is like to be old: "The legally blind know what it is to be old. Even before the third grade I am hunched and shaking with effort, always on the verge of tears, seeing by approximation, craving a solid sentence" (1998, p. 29).

Derrida (1993) describes the uncertainty inherent in the approximation: "Standing on his own two feet, a blind man explores by feeling out an area that he must recognize without yet cognizing it—and what he apprehends, what he has apprehensions about, in truth, is the precipice, the fall. . . ." (p. 4). Not knowing on what your next step will land can be most unsettling; blindness requires attention to environmental minutia, and just when it seems an environment becomes known, it changes.

As might be anticipated with eye conditions or diseases that cause vision to qualify as legal blindness, each participant encountered phenomena unique to their particular eye condition and body; none of the participants had etiology in common with each other. Despite the unique features of each of their eye conditions, they describe some adjunct physical features in common. Again, while this study does not seek generalization, it is interesting to report and analyze how the participants interact with the built environment and social world in similar ways not only to each other but also with blindness memoirs and other personal narratives. This section examines similarities and differences in the participants' bodily experience of blindness with all it entails, including their inner-directed reasons for blindness-related behavior.

Sight and vision are indeterminate and unpredictable. As Elkins (1996, p. 11) asserts, "seeing is metamorphosis, not mechanism," which is an especially salient point when applied to the nebulous world of legal blindness. The participants' reports of ever-changing, unreliable, situationally dependent, and interpretable vision are highly congruent with Elkins's opinions. Larry's examples illustrate the point:

> Every single thing you do that is . . . it's like playing golf. No two shots are alike, all right? And, when you're blind, no two scenarios or situations are exactly alike. I mean, even if, even if the damned knife is five inches over to the right from where it was last time, and the lighting isn't as bright, and maybe you're cutting a carrot instead of a tomato.

Medicine might attempt to explain Larry's examples as containing predictable variables, and this may well be the case; nonetheless, phenomenology's emphasis on subjective interpretation is evident in Larry's golf analogy.

Michalko (1998, 1999, 2002) deconstructs the medically constructed sightedness/blindness binary that places blindness on the negative side of the equation. He perceives blindness as "difference" rather than "lack." Elkins's (1996) work also disputes medical model thinking, which perceives sight and vision as observable, measurable, and predictable—as merely mechanism rather than as a culturally embedded, subjective experience that is interpreted and acted upon inimitably by each individual. People who have no clear recollection of "normal" vision, such as children or people with congenital blindness, may not regard themselves as lacking vision because they have nothing with which to compare their own vision experience, or because they do not notice visual "lack," or because they do not know how to articulate what they do or do not see. Cheadle (2005) asserts that children with visual impairments neither know what they are missing nor are able to describe what their vision looks like from their side of the lens. Catherine's and my experiences with childhood-onset blindness are consistent with both Michalko's and Cheadle's arguments and raise an important point about the confusions of both the blind and the sighted around legal blindness—confusion that precipitates pressure, both inner and external, to choose where one belongs.

Larry and J. R. each became blind during adulthood; therefore, they were quite aware of what was happening to them and were able to succinctly articulate the experience of moving from the land of the sighted into blindness. Larry said the sudden onset of his blindness was "like walking down the street and having a two-by-four embedded in your head . . . something was up because I couldn't see for shit." Larry worked his way through an existential crisis and soon found a renewed dedication to life. He discovered his potential for deep meaning and a keen commitment to new experiences each day, and he continues to relearn familiar tasks in new ways. He said:

> I mean, there's a difference there. There are no constants . . . other than your own initiative to do things. That's the only constant. So, I mean, like, if that's the only constant you have, babe, you better keep that tank full.

Larry's personal philosophy is consistent with that of Jim Knipfel (personal communication, 2004), who describes progressive blindness as "an on-going phenomenological experiment" and with Fittipaldi's (2004) belief that it is incumbent upon newly blind people (as she was) to go out and find the world because the world will no longer come through the eyes to the person.

J. R. first discovered declining vision when he was driving because he no longer saw cars, especially those to his left, that his eyes used to see reliably. Like Larry, he used photography analogies to describe how he sees: "take a picture, cut it down the middle, and throw out the left half." J. R.'s memory makes up the rest of each scene, which is consistent not only with the other participant stories, but also with numerous blindness memoirs, such as that of Kuusisto (1998, p. 18), who stated he had a "capacious memory . . . every inch of terrain had to be acutely remembered."

I rely on memory to know family and friends' faces, where I am and where I am going in my own neighborhood, and phone numbers, to name a few invaluable applications. Memory is a primary requisite for successful orientation skills.

The following section examines how blind people learn and develop alternate ways of being and knowing their surroundings. Blind people often increasingly rely on memory and on their other corporeal senses; although, contrary to popular myth, their other senses are *not* "heightened" or made superhuman. First, I discuss the phenomenology of memory as it is intimately bound up in the phenomena of sight, vision, and blindness. Blind people use memory in place of sight (and in conjunction with sight) for multiple purposes. I then demonstrate how other corporeal senses come into play in the everyday existence of blind people.

Memory: An Integral Aspect of the Blindness Experience

Blind people rely on memory in several ways. They rely on memory to protect themselves from injury and to orient themselves to the physical environment by, for example, counting stairs; counting the number of steps it takes to move from one location and another; memorizing where bus stops, curbs, and furniture are; and memorizing street names and landmarks. Blind people must know where they are to know where they are going; if they lose position, they lose direction. Hull (1990, p. 110) writes, "This is such a profound lostness that most sighted people find it difficult to imagine." Kuusisto believes that blind people who move quickly "have exceptional memories and superior facial orientation" (1998, p. 23).

Because legally blind people find searching for lost objects time-consuming and frustrating, they use a combination of memory and organization. They remember where kitchen knives are stored and remember to put them back where they belong after each use. Blind people often memorize telephone numbers, credit card information, and membership identification numbers, for example, because it becomes easier to use the trained memory than to search for small print on bits of paper. Kuusisto (1998) describes how he used memory for a dual purpose—to know his environment and to pass as sighted:

> I was sharpening a sixth sense that fostered the impression in my parents and almost everyone else that I could see far better than I really could. Such acting requires a capacious memory; in the gauzy nets of pastel colors where I lived, every inch of terrain had to be acutely remembered. (p. 18)

Legally blind people use memory to fill in the blanks where their sight is missing. Along with navigational utility, people with degenerative or adult onset blindness may use memory to imagine their loved one's facial features, to know what a baseball field looks like as they listen to a game in play, or to know what a sighted person means when they speak of a particular color. Like the old joke, "I can't hear you. I lost my glasses," blind people do not "see" as well when memory eludes them.

Elkins (1996) asserts memory is integral to vision. As proof, he explains why small children do not remember their existence before memory is well-developed. Before his brain linked vision and memory, he was unaware of his existence; he did not really see his surroundings. He claims he has "blind spots" in his childhood, even up to adolescence, because his memory gives him only "spotty and random" visual images of his youth (p. 202). Actually, our entire lives are lived in memory: because each moment is so fleeting, we are able to exist in memory only. By the time we are aware of the present moment, it has passed us by and only memory returns it to us (Kotre 1995). Memory is a critical component of nearly every blindness skill: home organization, clothes labeling, knowing the placement of furniture in the home and office, and orientation and mobility. The white cane often works in tandem with orientation, which counts on memory to be effective.

Larry, Catherine, J. R., and I all rely on memory to fill in the blanks that sight and vision used to know. Memory works like an internal global positioning system that helps orient ourselves to where we are going in relation to where we are and how we will return. J. R. describes how memory assists him:

> When I go to the window and I can't tell if this curtain's open or closed because I can see; I look at that window there and I see curtains all the way across it. But I can see everything outside too. [Laughs].

He laughed because he knew he could not *really* see everything outside, because the curtains were closed; his memory painted the portions of the picture he could no longer see. J. R. describes the process: "imagination, um just a memory of what the picture looks like, and it just fills it in." Sometimes his "mind's-eye" leads him to believe that he sees something that he knows for certain he cannot see; for example, when he turns off a light, his mind's-eye sees the light switch as a visual reality. Memory is a blessing that can be used purposefully, but it is, indeed, an unreliable trickster. For instance, my recollection of an oft-traveled staircase might lull me into a false sense of safety as I head quickly down only to twist an ankle on a chunk of step broken off since the last time I was there.

Most blind people rely on orientation skills to make their way through the physical environment. Because bus stop and street signs typically hang high out of their range of vision, borderland blind people might use buildings or trees as landmarks, count steps on staircases, and memorize sequences of street locations, bus locations, where their favorite coffee shop or tavern is, exactly where their classrooms or offices are located—all accomplished by memorization. Of course, orientation works in familiar territory, but it is rendered useless in unknown places. Catherine illustrates: "If I was in a completely different city? I wouldn't know the [train] stops."

Larry began orientation and mobility training soon after we met and came to each subsequent interview with finely tuned descriptions about how to get around town using the direction of the sun on his face or neck, white cane travel, logic, imagination, and memory. His descriptions are reminiscent of Kuusisto's (1998, p. 23) report that he "understands destination by motion and light and temperature." Good orientation and mobility skills require many hours of training and practice—a point lost on sighted people who participate in simulation exercises with the goal of reliably experiencing blindness.

Organization Saves the Day

As James Baldwin (1974) notes, "the only coin time accepts is life." Despite my hesitancy to use a problematic medical model concept of "quality of life," it seemed appropriate when coming from self-reporting rather than outsiders' judgments based on "normality." All of the participants said when they organized their daily routines and physical environment, their quality of life improved. In an organized home, time is not wasted searching for items; therefore, excessive frustration is avoided. One of blindness rehabilitation's aims is to teach clients how to organize their stuff, their schedules, and their chores. Rehabilitation helps clients garner good organization techniques; they learn to return items to where they found them, and to have designated places for everything, including clothes, kitchen items, cleaning supplies, and so on. Catherine said, "You've got to know where everything is because you need your resources. This is your space. You know."

Larry said, "If you're blind, you can't, you can't allow yourself that luxury of 'mañana.'" Blind people organize their days by bus and train schedules, so misplacing something could delay departure from home, and that leaves the person running behind the rest of the day. If they use paratransit, a last-minute search for house keys might result in losing their ride altogether, because the rules allow (usually) only 5–10 minutes for waiting before the van leaves for its next pickup.

Larry, J. R., and I all experienced the loss of flexibility, ease, and spontaneity when we quit driving. We three probably drove longer than we should have. At first, Larry "was fighting, not wanting to give in." He started to self-monitor where and when he would drive. There was no public transportation in his area; he said. "God, without a car, you're dead. You're dead in the water."

Because Catherine was diagnosed as legally blind at age two (even though the impairment was congenital), she uses observation to form opinions about some differences between how she conducts her life compared with sighted people. She said:

> . . . people can just go, go, go, go, go. You're like. When they do their day their list of chores is twice as long as my list of chores because my list of chores takes me twice as long to do. [Laughs] It's like I can't go from the grocery store, to the pharmacist, to blah-blah-blah-blah because I have groceries. I don't have a car to put it in. I have school books from school. It's like I end up being a mule all day long, just schlepping here, and schlepping there.

Just Goes with the Territory: Physical Pain

The physical discomforts of legal blindness are not limited to the eyes alone. During the interviews, I asked the participants if they experience any discomfort in their bodies from seeing and looking. I felt comfortable asking this question because of my "insider" status, and I believe that the participants were more forthcoming than they would have been with a sighted researcher. All four participants experience what Kuusisto (1998) describes as "crushing headaches" and eye muscle strain, and Catherine and I both experience posture-related back and neck pain. As Kleege (1999) notes, blindness necessitates what society might consider "odd" postures. Monoculars, binoculars, magnifiers, low vision wide-angle and short-focus glasses all require exacting and uncomfortable body positions. The act of looking out of borderland blind eyes requires extraordinary strain, not just on the eyes, but on the neck and the shoulders. Catherine sums it up:

> chronic neck—yeah that's the reading, you know. It's like god damn it my back hurts so bad. It's like you want to read in the bathtub like this. With the lamp angled up [at] the book, and you're just like, why didn't I do this before? And it's like oh I know why because if you lean your head back for this amount of time you can't really lift it up after an hour.

When I hold a book or magazine two inches from my face for more than a few minutes, my forearms and hands go numb, and I have to shake them and shake them to get feeling back into them.

During my second visit to Catherine's home, as we talked, she worked on a school assignment. On the large paperboard spread across her dining room table, she created a "graphic novel" composed of a series of highly intricate sketches and tiny, neat print dialogue balloons. Catherine kept her back straight as she folded her body at the waist, leaning over to view the work at approximately a two-inch distance. I also have a two-inch focus when I use wide-angle microscope glasses (which are the only way I can access print at all), and

> my body can tolerate them for maybe 15 minutes before my neck spasms, I get a burning sensation in my shoulder muscles, eye muscle pain, and finally, my eyes just plain quit; they refuse to see what they saw half an hour before.

Catherine notes the upside of the awkward neck postures borderland blind people must use; she thinks that borderland blind people's necks are nice and attractive because they get an extra workout.

In summary, the embodied experience of legal blindness is not limited to the eyes. The entire body involves itself in seeing and looking, bending and craning, walking and lifting, pain and strain, and so on. Society's notions about blindness are shattered by existing blindness literature and participants' stories. The phenomenological experience of legal blindness is manifold. Every aspect of blind people's life experience is affected to some degree. The participants engage in advance organization and planning in order to interact successfully with the built environment and with sighted people. Societal shortcomings, such as inadequate public transit, affect blind people's embodied and social experience in that they must plan thoroughly and well in advance of travel through the built environment.

Personal Safety

Personal safety and crime prevention emerged as another sub-theme, especially for Catherine and me, perhaps because we are women and so are more likely than men to think about ourselves as potential targets of street crime. Such thoughts are not baseless: "It is actually quite common for blind victims to be assaulted and robbed" (*BBC News* 2007; *Europe Intelligence Wire* 2006). According to Sherry (2010), the Disability Rights Commission and Capability Scotland asserts that blind people are four times more likely to be assaulted or attacked than their sighted neighbors (p. 24).

Not being able to drive, or more to the point, not having access to a car trunk, coupled with not having enough vision to see oncoming people—to distinguish friend from foe—are critical factors in how blind people feel about themselves as potential crime victims. Catherine said:

> By the time I'm done I have a portfolio, three bags of groceries . . . something like cat litter . . . you have bags on every shoulder, bags on hands. Like what if someone's going to come up and mug you? You're not going to see them come up and mug you.

Catherine completed a one-day judo class for blind people to learn how to defend herself under attack. She and I both say "hello" to passing strangers even though we cannot see them, so they will know we are aware of their presence and that we are strong and unafraid even when we are fearful, or perhaps, especially when we are fearful. By acting assertively, we claim our rights as citizens in a sighted world.

Both Larry and J. R. have thought out the possibilities of using the white cane as a defensive weapon. J. R. said, "I usually take my cane and I fold it in half and I leave it on my lap. And I have a rule: you don't hurt me I don't hurt you." One time someone at a transit center grabbed J. R.'s arm to "help" him, so he pulled his arm up bringing the handle of his cane into the stranger's face. The white cane is not merely a stick to make up for lack of vision and sight; it is loaded with social meaning. It is essential to many borderland blind people's embodied experience, and it is a universal symbol of pity, clumsiness, helplessness, misery, and poverty.

For many legally blind people, the use of the white cane is a symbol of both identity and identification (positive and negative)—a fundamental instrument of essential sensory information, a basic method for alternate ways of knowing the world and, conversely, for the world knowing them as blind. Derrida (1993) observes that a blind man used the white cane as a "saving eye, his emergency eye, one might even say his optical prosthesis, more precious than his own pupils, than the apples of his eyes" (p. 9).

The Phenomenology of the White Cane User

Unlike totally blind people, many legally blind people have the choice to adopt a white cane or to navigate the environment on their own. The white cane is simultaneously a positive thing to those who use it, and a lightning rod for stigma, fear, avoidance, and rejection. Whichever way it is understood, it is, in fact, a powerful navigational instrument. Some of those living in the borderland resist using the white cane because of its negative connotations; some reject it because it is the ultimate symbol of blindness, forcing them out of denial as well as making a public proclamation of their blindness. Some believe the white cane marks them as potential crime victims, but others regard their cane as a weapon at hand against interlopers. The white cane sometimes is purposefully used as an instrument for flaunting blindness—for embracing "difference."

Some blind people have not reasoned out why they choose not to use the white cane. They may decide to have a guide dog instead (Michalko 1999). For those who do use white canes, conversation may turn to "shop talk"—which type of cane is best for particular purposes, which cane tip they use, and, at times, bragging about the dents, scratches, nicks, and paint chipping on their canes the way gunfighters of old might have spoken about notches on their Colt 45 gun. For example, at the National Federation of the Blind's training facility in Denver, Colorado, staff member Dirk's cane finally broke beyond the point of the possibility of duct tape repair. Dirk remarked, "I've put hundreds of miles on this baby, all kinds of weather, all kinds of streets. . . . Now the old duct tape won't even hold her" (Kudlick 2005, p. 1065). He then had his blind colleagues feel the "notches."

Knipfel (1999, pp. 195–196) describes how he shifted reliance from vision to touch when he took up the white cane: "My eyes had slid into the palm of my hand." Michalko (1998) describes the experience of a young girl coming to understand the powerful possibilities of the white cane: "My finger, my warm handle. Touch the sidewalk, touch the ground, keep touching. Touch the world" (p. 20).

When vision departs, touch steps in, serving as an epistemological alternative to seeing the world through the eyes. Like a well-crafted metaphor, the replacement of sight with touch offers blind people a rich synesthetic experience. For many legally blind people the white cane takes over where vision fails. Vibrations through the cane shaft carry detailed information to the user's hand, making the immediate environment readable. The white cane offers safety and independent travel. Although the white cane is an inanimate object, it is much more than that. The white cane extends the sense of touch; it acts as an explorer, pilot, and navigator in partnership with its user as together they survey terra firma. The sense of touch gains distance both in the use of a white cane and with a dog guide.

Conclusion

While I anticipated some mention of the white cane during participant interviews, I did not arrange the study to have its own separate sections. However, as I immersed myself in the existing body of blindness literature, I uncovered numerous descriptions and analyses of the white cane—its history, its social meaning, and its individual significance for users. As the interviews ensued, it quickly became evident that the white cane demanded noteworthy attention.

The embodied experience of borderland blindness begins with biology of the eye and of the brain, for without physical blindness there would be little reason for society to act against those diagnosed as legally blind in ocularcentric ways. The embodied experience of borderland blindness is ripe with diversity, uniqueness, and commonalities. The embodied experience entails more than the eyes alone. Borderland blind people use artifacts of the embodied experience, such as the white cane, to meet their own navigational needs and to greet the social world.

There is a good deal of overlap between the white cane as part of the phenomenology of blindness and as a marker of identity. The next chapter examines the ways in which many blind people use the white cane as a disability identity marker.

10
Identity

This chapter calls upon both postmodernism concepts of identity formation and social constructionism to examine how blindness identity shapes and adapts itself. Postmodernism perceives identity as amorphous and in play with time, place, and circumstance—continually deconstructing and reconstructing itself, resisting or defying definition (Moore 1994). Identity is not so much about categories as it is about "processes of identification and differentiation" (Moore 1994, p. 2). Social constructionism perceives identity as something created and expressed through all societal bodies and processes of social interaction, and it also understands identity to be a fluid process conferred upon marginalized groups, often without consent of its members (Rosenblum and Travis 2003; Goffman 1986; Gilman 1991).

Identity formation is created by means of an aggregate of individual and social processes, such as naming and being named; aligning oneself with a particular group, or, in the reverse direction, being unwittingly identified by society as a member of a group based on distinct personal attributes (Rosenblum and Travis 2003; Omansky Gordon and Rosenblum 2001; Thomas 1999; Goffman 1986).

In his landmark book, *Stigma: Notes on the Management of a Spoiled Identity*, Erving Goffman (1986) writes about people who do not fit society's criteria for "normalcy," and so have "spoiled" identities. Goffman (1986, p. 4) describes the many ways members of marginalized groups behave in reaction to a complex set of processes of social control, which he calls "stigmatization." He explains that stigma involves a "special kind of relationship between attribute [condition] and stereotype" (p. 4) and briefly includes physically disabled people among the groups that society stigmatizes. Blind people can be described as having a "spoiled identity" because blindness is perceived as something abnormal and out of the ordinarily anticipated condition.

As one consequence of social stigmatization, some people experience internalized oppression, accepting as truth the negative societal attitudes toward devalued personal characteristics or group membership. Yet others covertly and/or actively resist stigma and internally maintain a positive identity. Catherine opines:

> I'm being kind of mislabeled as a blind artist . . . and I think a lot of people get mislabeled. They don't know what the true labels are. Having identities like "this is who I am as an artist. This is what I work on." Family, I think, is where all identities come together and have not been accurately portrayed. They think of me more as blind, a little hippie, and . . . whereas in my arts community I seem a little stuck-up sometimes, and I try to stay away from the Blind Identity. I'm a little bit more conservative [laughs]. I love saying that.

Issues of identity for legally blind people are confounded by the borderland between sightedness and blindness, which can result in mixed internal reactions. Legally blind people live in the margins of the marginalized since they may be able to pass as sighted, as "normal."

I Can See Clearly Now: Passing as Sighted

"Passing" is an interactional social tool employed by all people, in one way or another, as they produce personal identities within (and influenced by) the cultural contexts in which they live. Some blind people employ premeditated strategies as they attempt to pass as sighted and/or to engage in social interaction in ways that are understood and unquestioned by sighted people. Michalko (1999) and Hull (1990) describe intricate ways they negotiate meeting and greeting oncoming people beyond their field of vision. Michalko

(1998) uses eye contact with sighted people. He stays aware not only of his seeing, but of how and where he directs his eyes so that sighted people assume he is making direct eye contact. If he gazes where he needs to in order to see them, he appears as though he is not looking at the other person at all. I have central vision loss, so when I look at a person's face, they often think I am looking behind them or looking at their hair instead of into their eyes:

> Depending on where I am and who I'm with, I might try to appear as if I'm making eye contact. Sometimes I will tell people that even though it appears I'm not looking at them, I really am, but I have to feel emotionally ready for an onslaught of nosy questions before I do that.

Catherine said she has problems with relationships because of her vision. She can't pick up signals such as body language or a "certain look" to know, for example, if someone is "getting pissed off." Catherine can't identify people approaching her. She has to learn the sound of their walk. She said, "I have to know them because you can feel people's energy in a way." But, when borderland blind people use familiar clues to identify people or things, sighted people disbelieve their blindness, and then they have to reassert that, yes, they really are blind, which is another social pitfall distinctive to the borderland. The struggle to be believed can be emotionally draining because such disbelief assaults their integrity and essential as well as social identity. Catherine said:

> It's like you're always having to confirm "I'm blind but I'm not too blind." It's like back and forth, and you're just like constantly pulling at them and you don't realize that; and they don't realize that you feel like you're manipulating the crap out of them and that they're invalidating you. And they're invalidating your blindness. You're just like, either way I go they hate me. [Laughs] It's like you just feel like you're hated even though you know yes, no it's not about you.

Borderland blind people might attempt to pass or, at the very least, to remain unnoticed, which keeps things simpler in social situations. Explaining one's blindness several times a day to several different strangers gets tiresome, distracting, and boring. Catherine

believes sighted people act like "little anthropologists" trying to figure out blindness culture, and "in the process they're destroying the
living hell out of it and objectifying your blindness, and objectifying you, and, oh. This is *huge*."

Sometimes borderland blind people deny themselves use of
access equipment such as white canes or low vision glasses; or they
might take unnecessary risks such as not asking a passerby what
color the traffic light is at an idle intersection—all to avoid the
attention that a "spoiled identity" attracts (Goffman 1986). *Passing*
is *acting*, that is, practicing in a creative, methodical way how to perform as something they are not—sighted. Larry said that his need
for perfectionism drives how he presents himself in public:

> Yeah, the challenge is greater; therefore the perfection has to be
> greater. . . . See, if people come up to you and say, "Gee I didn't
> know you were blind," I say I hit a home run.

Catherine hesitates to use her blindness as an excuse even
when it is a quite legitimate reason for a particular behavior,
explaining, "You don't want to blame it on you being blind though,
that's the problem." She describes her reticence to be judged by
sighted people:

> When a lot of things are caused by not seeing you don't want to
> keep saying it over and over again because people get kind of like,
> okay, you're going to blame everything on that, you know. . . . You
> have to be really self-sufficient sounding, even if you're kind of
> leaving out bits of the reason.

I understand Catherine's reasoning. I think long and hard
before invoking blindness as a reason for something I did or did not
do, because I am concerned that people will think I'm using my
blindness—as Sally French (1993) writes, "playing up"; they might
think I'm a complainer or not "adjusted." Multiple identities further confound the dilemma. For example, this is my perspective:

> I think people might misconstrue my holding money close up to
> my face to read the denominations on bills, or feel the edges of
> coins to tell quarters with their ridged edges apart from smooth-

edged pennies and nickels. I'm concerned that people will think I'm doing all this because I am Jewish; that is, inviting them to invoke stereotypes about Jews having an extreme attachment to money. I guess I'd rather be thought of as a pitiful blind person than a money-hungry Jew. So, I try to be inconspicuous when I look at bills or count change. I have a wallet with several pockets to help me keep it all organized . . . so I don't have to fumble as much.

Personal Costs of Passing or Coming Out

A lot of forethought, creativity, time, and energy gets spent carrying out strategies for passing as sighted, and the personal costs can be high. Catherine said that when she self-discloses her blindness, she feels vulnerable, and she does her best to resist falling prey to the negative societal stereotypes that blind people are "fools" (Monbeck 1973). She said:

> You don't see it. And so you're constantly dealing with these things that come at you and you don't know what it is . . . and you know it's like having to explain to people. It's like yeah I might not see but I'd; you *cannot* pull one over on me.

The white cane is not merely a tool or a blindness artifact—it is often a powerful symbol of the user's identity. Borderland blind people can make choices about when and where they use the cane to find their way and when to use it as an identifier to alert drivers and other pedestrians of their presence, or they can choose never to learn cane travel at all. The white cane can be a marker of "coming out" as a blind person, representing both inner self-identity as well as how the person wants the world around them to know who they are.

The Personal Is Political

The white cane is a highly charged cultural artifact and an essential access tool for many borderland blind people. The white cane intersects embodied experience, social aspects, and identity, at times working symbiotically, and other times at odds.

The bottom sections of white canes come in a variety of reflective tape color schemes from continent to continent, each signifying different impairments. For instance, the typical and accepted cane bottom in the United States is all red, but in the UK all red signifies deafness and blindness. Some European countries—Sweden, for instance—commonly recognize an all white cane with two red stripes near the bottom to signify blindness. When I purchased the cane I currently use, I chose an all white one. I like it for aesthetic reasons, but it has caused problems a few times when bus drivers questioned my eligibility for reduced disability fare (known in my hometown as "honored citizen" fare), asserting the cane was not a real blindness aid despite the fact that I used it to guide myself up the steps onto the bus and despite that other than the absence of red, it is an unmistakably typical long white cane.

In North America, white canes are primarily used as a mobility aid, and cane users select their cane length according to what is most tactilely efficient. In the UK, people sometimes employ two different cane lengths, one for tactile travel use and a shorter one known as a "symbol cane" or "identification cane" to alert others for safety purposes. This is not a common practice in the United States, and the term "symbol cane" is not familiar here. I use my mobility length cane as an identity indicator in particular situations, such as high traffic areas, and certainly as a marker of pride and affiliation at disability gatherings.

All of the participants have experience with the white cane. Michalko (1998) remarks on the cultural stigma the white cane generates; he observes that the white cane is a symbol of "pathos" and "gracelessness." No matter how much he attempted to resist such stigma, he nevertheless experienced it. The white cane calls for holding the elbow and wrist in an awkward and mostly fixed position, which can induce elbow, wrist, and hand cramping, as well as elbow tendonitis. If white cane users let their hold on the cane shift, causing the cane handle to move toward the center of the body, and the cane encounters an obstacle, such as a crooked sidewalk or a rock in the grass, the cane handle jabs into the hip or abdomen, which is a very painful and potentially embarrassing experience— graceless, indeed. Many is the time I hoped no one noticed my clumsiness, and I've caught myself joking my way out of awkward caning mistakes.

During her stay at a National Federation of the Blind (NFB) rehabilitation center, Kudlick (2005) came to understand that the stringent training was driven by the NFB's machismo-inspired desire to "reclaim masculinity for blindness via cane length"; she further asserts that the length of a person's cane makes it possible to discern a person's blindness politics. The white cane becomes more than a symbol of blindness identity; it becomes a symbol of identity politics. For those on the "inside" of the organized blindness community, the length of a white cane is an instantly recognizable yardstick by which the user's ideology about blindness is measured.

The National Federation of the Blind's long white cane is nearly eye high, while the traditional standard cane comes to the center of a person's chest. The NFB cane is rigid as opposed to folding into sections for ease of storage; the federation's philosophy promotes the idea that blind people who use folding canes use them to hide their blindness, while the rigid cane serves as a statement to the sighted world—an unmistakable identity marker. Despite countless blind people's successful use of dog guides, the NFB discourages their use, believing instead that "canes were about independence, confidence, assertiveness, and full social integration, while dogs were not" (Kudlick 2005). Kudlick (2005) uses the Harley motorcycle as metaphor to understand the long white cane as a representation and marker of American male gender identity, and as a tool for flaunting both blindness and American male gender identities. She describes some of the sexist attitudes, language, and rituals expressed by the "tough guys" (including one of the mobility instructors) at the NFB's Denver training center.

Kudlick describes how sighted people stigmatized her and candidly reveals how she confronted her own internalized oppression about blindness and its representative white cane. She also describes how the public treated her differently when she used the cane, speaking quietly, acting "solicitously," assuming that she was incapable and helpless, all because she held a piece of carbon fiber in her hand. She calls the cane her "stickmata" that draws the "wrath of human condescension raining down upon me . . . treating me like a dependent child or a delicate porcelain doll" (Kudlick 2005, pp. 1590–1591).

Catherine and Larry do not prefer the white cane for mobility, each for very different reasons. Catherine prefers not to use the cane whenever possible because she does not wish to appear in public as vulnerable or weak, although I recently gave her a cane I no longer use because she expressed a desire to use one to alert drivers when she crossed busy streets, and in a recent phone conversation, Catherine stated she "loves my cane," which she still uses as a marker of identity rather than a mobility aid. The white cane as a discretionary item for legally blind people is essentially not an option for totally blind people—it is yet another marker of life in the borderland. Larry learned white cane skills to fulfill the requirements for guide dog school. He made his goal clear from the outset; he wanted his "pooch." As Michalko (1998, p. 8) notes, a dog guide is more than a "piece of equipment." Larry now switches between his cane and his dog, but prefers the dog, for one thing, because of their interrelational bond. Michalko (1998, p. 6) did not want to use the white cane but did "not know why." When incidents made it evident to him that he required some sort of mobility aid, he immediately researched dog guide schools. Nevertheless, Michalko is proficient in cane skills, and since his treasured dog Smokie's death, he has once again become a full-time white cane user.

Analogous to members of car or dog breed clubs, white cane users have common interests, experiences, and emotional attachments. I "talked shop" with both Larry and J. R. about cane compositions, styles, lengths, tips, and how to efficiently maneuver this thing or that. J. R. uses his engineering skills to refine his cane handle and tips and has conducted classes in cane repair for lay white cane users. He finds pragmatic value in the cane; for instance, he appreciates that its reflective tape acts as an identifier for passing drivers. J. R., Larry, and I have all experienced problems when fellow pedestrians who are sighted tried to avoid the cane by jumping over it, which tends to trip up everyone involved. During the first several weeks of Larry's orientation and mobility training, he proudly showed me new nicks, paint chips, crooks, and dents in his cane, which reminded me of Kudlick's (2005) description of her experience with Dirk at the National Federation of the Blind training center.

The Superhero

Stories about blindness told within a medical model are stories of tragedy that can be "overcome" either through medical treatment, blindness service provision, supernatural miracle, or by sheer self-will, perseverance, and cheerfulness. These stories are sometimes couched in narratives of courage and heroism—triumph over adversity. Such are the stories told *by* blind people who have internalized medical constructions of blindness.

Narratives of heroism are often stories of athleticism, of heretofore never-been-done feats that find their way into biography, autobiography, and public media. Marla Runyan made headlines when she became the first legally blind person to compete in the Olympics as a track runner in the 2000 Sydney Olympics. In her memoir, Runyan (2001) does not personally characterize herself as heroic, stating, "the truth is, running is the easiest thing I do" (p. 7). Runyan is clear and matter-of-fact as she describes what she can and cannot see and when she explains the methods she uses to run at the highest competitive level. Unlike media portrayals of Runyan as a hero who triumphed over adversity, she presents the argument that societal attitudes are the problem, not her blindness. She writes:

> At times, people have not expected much from me, solely because I'm partially blind. I can feel them thinking, "Oh, you're visually impaired. Just go sit on the couch." When I'm about to run a race, I can hear people whispering, "There's this blind girl running. Isn't that great?" (Runyan 2001, p. 5)

Runyan prefers her primary identity to be as a runner rather than as a blind person, although she does not shrink from her blindness, either.

Prior to Runyan's fame, the life of George Mendoza, a legally blind Special Olympics runner, was told in *Running Toward the Light: A Blind Man's Incredible Triumph over Defeat and Despair* (Buchanan 1992). Because Mendoza was a Special Olympics athlete, he did not receive the same public attention as Runyan.

In order to advance the National Federation of the Blind's efforts to illustrate that blind people are as capable as the sighted, which can be proved if blind people are only given opportunities, the federation sponsored Erik Weihemeyer's trek to the top of Mount Everest in 2001. Weihemeyer (2001) wrote a memoir, *Touch the Top of the World: A Blind Man's Journey to Climb Higher than the Eye Can See*, about going blind as a young person, how society treated him because of his blindness, and about his climbing adventures. Although he is often portrayed as a hero who triumphs over blindness, Weihemeyer resists such stereotypical notions.

Conclusion

Identity formation is self-reflexive, contextual, ongoing, and multi-layered. Giddens (1991) asserts that while identity is expressed in both behavior and in reactions by others, the critical factor is "in the capacity to keep a particular narrative going. . . . It must continually integrate events which occur in the external world, and sort them into an ongoing 'story' about the self" (p. 52).

We have much to learn about ourselves by understanding that sight and vision are not merely sensory mechanisms, but are, in fact, creative, interactive devices that assist us in constructing and affirming our own identity, our own stories (Elkins 1996). Despite scientific and anecdotal evidence about the transformative relationship between emotion, sight and vision, and cultural identity, such deconstructions of sight and blindness fly in the face of accepted societal and medical beliefs. Blind people are taught to understand their blindness as solely a biological experience with unavoidable, painful psycho-emotional side effects.

PART 4

Conclusion

11

Intersections Along the Border

The way in which blindness is described depends upon who is doing the describing. Medicine describes blindness as pathology that needs to be acted upon either by treatment or by referral to "experts" who are bestowed with the authority to teach people how best to be blind. Medicine provides physiological descriptions of disease and its effects. When medicine discusses blindness as disability, it does not discuss its ontological significance to the person with the impairment. Hence, those who value sight as the only legitimate ontology impose these beliefs through cultural, economic, political, and social practices. French (1999) believes problems surface when sighted people impose their own notions about blindness onto blind people: "Conflicting discourses arise when sighted people define what 'acceptable' and 'normal' behavior is for a visually disabled person and use these definitions to contest that person's identity" (p. 21).

Ophthalmology, rehabilitation, and human service providers project their own negative beliefs that blindness is a tragic happenstance, and then project their emotions onto the blind person they are attempting to serve (Michalko 2002, p. 5). Thus, helping professionals are trained to believe that new skills are the only solution required for successfully coping with blindness; consequently, they rarely, if ever, directly educate blind people about constructing a self-empowering blindness identity. While alternative living skills are immensely important factors in the success or failure of adaptation to blindness, the parallel message is that by learning new living skills, they will *overcome* blindness, when the point actually is that blindness is to be lived with rather than overcome. Service provision is designed to have blind people achieve a social identity as close to "normal" (sighted) as possible.

The traditional medical establishment—indeed, society on the whole—expects disabled people to act like everyone else if they hope to lead successful lives; they have to act "normal," which requires them to "overcome" their impairments. But as Linton (1998), Michalko (2002), and others note, people do not "overcome," as that is impossible; people live with their impairments. As Linton (1998) observes,

> "overcoming" disability assumes that there is something inferior about their group membership, and the responsibility is left on the individual to work harder to be successful and to triumph over what otherwise would be a tragic life. (p. 17)

Another message in the concept of "overcoming" is that the person has gone beyond societal expectations of what people with impairments can achieve; the person has overcome the "social stigma of having a disability" (Linton 1998, p. 17).

Everyday Life in the Borderland

Sometimes people choose not to disclose their blindness, which results in exclusion from activities not because of sighted people leaving them out, but because they have left themselves out. On the other hand, they might disclose their impairments and ask for what they need despite feeling awkward and running the risk of being treated as different. Either way, there is a trade-off.

When blind people opt to disclose their visual impairment, they necessarily draw attention to themselves, so it becomes more difficult to be perceived as being like everyone else. They lose their anonymity and may be treated as "special." When Catherine wanted to participate fully in art school classes, she had to disclose her blindness so her teachers and colleagues could accommodate her need to shrink the space between them, their art, and herself.

She said, "I have to go up and look at things or else I absolutely cannot participate." In order to receive feedback from her classmates, she sat in front of her work and asked them to come up and point at what they are critiquing. When she had to sit close to something, she would do so and explain, "I can't see so I'm going to sit here." Catherine curbs her urge to explain herself, her life, to anyone, and wants to stop concerning herself with potential judgments about her and her blindness. When Catherine attends a sex party and goes into the "snuggle room," she asks the people to turn up the lights:

> You kind of like to know what they look like if you have that tool of sight, I mean, [with emphasis] come on! I organize my experience around where the lighting is. It's hard to get an organization that small to serve, um, individual needs.

Just because people ask for what they need does not guarantee their requests will be fulfilled. J. R. talked about people who think they know what blind people are going through and say something like, "Oh gee, my brother knew a friend who was; had a friend who was blind, or something like that," and then proceed to give unwanted or the wrong kind of assistance. Blind people tell stories about sighted people grabbing them by the arm at street corners, and then tugging them all the way across the street even though they had not asked for assistance or had not even wanted to head in that direction in the first place. One evening, a woman grabbed me as I made my way through a theater aisle and literally pulled me to where she thought I wanted to go without ever asking if I needed assistance (Omansky Gordon 2003, p. 224). Apparently, my white cane drafted her into do-gooder duty. Rod Michalko (1998) relates a story about someone pressing a dollar into his hand as he and his dog guide stood at a traffic light together. He told the man he did not need it and asked him to take it back. The man insisted Rod take it. So, he did and then gave it to a panhandler.

Legal blindness raises complex identity issues that those with total blindness cannot experience. Michalko (1999) explains that legal blindness has a "mixed nature" (p. 131); thus, legal blindness is neither complete deficit nor complete wholeness. When he was initially diagnosed with an eye disease, he understood blindness as a binary phenomenon; he believed he was required to make a choice between blindness and sightedness, since they were presented by the medical model as "antithetical to each other" (p. 131).

When he was initially going blind, Jim Knipfel worked hard to construct and maintain an identity as "sighted" in order to avoid asking for help. Preserving a sighted identity required him to do such things as getting his snacks before movies started so he wouldn't have to find his way back to his seat in the dark. Attempts to pass as sighted require forethought, advance planning, and a lot of energy, which, most likely, cause performance anxiety. Knipfel (1999) describes his strategy: "Mostly I resorted to semantic interference. I gave people nonsense mixed with solid information in order to confuse and disarm them, and get them quickly away from me" (p. 122). The author candidly reveals his increasingly self-imposed isolation because he was afraid of getting lost or injured, or "looking like the fool I was" (Knipfel 1999, p. 173).

These anecdotes reveal the difficulties of openly assuming a blindness identity. Legally blind people move back and forth across the unique border between the sighted and blind worlds, treated like illegal immigrants on both sides of the border. They constantly make choices about when and where to "pass" or "come out," and there are personal costs paid for each decision. When a blind person openly uses visual or mobility aids or asks for help, the public will more than likely project their own anxieties about blindness onto the person, and this creates tension and awkwardness. On the other hand, when legally blind people choose not to identify as blind, they might not have their social and safety needs met. Their identity is in flux, both internally and to the world around them.

Theoretical Framework

This book called upon an interdisciplinary disability studies approach to discover what it is like to be legally blind in a world built by and for sighted people; it further sought to know what meaning the research participants made of their experience living across and between the sightedness/blindness divide. The book challenges ocularcentric assumptions that position sight as superior of all the senses, which is especially significant considering that blindness research and praxis are powerfully entrenched in the medical model. Consequently, education, rehabilitation, and other social and civic policies and procedures are geared to ignore idiosyncratic phenomenological and sociocultural differences between legally blind and totally blind people's lived experience. This study intends to be one way to redress the issue.

Moreover, I strayed from orthodox disability studies research because I wanted to learn and record the embodied experience of legal blindness as well as issues of blindness identity formation. By using postmodern methods of analysis, I was able to avoid framing these aspects within a medical model even though they are about impairment; instead, they were analyzed within a social model of disability.

Another innovative aspect of this study is the application of a postmodern concept of the "borderland" to create an overarching tool of analysis to help make sense of the medically constructed blindness/sightedness binary.

The Borderland and Ocularcentrism

This research authenticated that some legally blind people do reside in a borderland between medically and socially constructed categories of sightedness and blindness. The participants' stories challenge societal stereotypes about what blindness is and is not. Society generally disregards the unique phenomenological or social experiences of borderland blindness. As the participants' reports revealed, society often presses borderland blind people into lands that may not be of their own choosing and may, in fact, not be where they can pursue their full human potential.

The research data revealed that education and human services policies emanate from ocularcentric beliefs. Participants affirmed that programs and services are often problematic from the outset. Education is confused and confusing, which rendered Catherine and me unprepared for a workable future. We were left to fend for ourselves in classrooms geared for the sighted, where knowledge is presented through visual modes such as blackboards, whiteboards, video, and print formats—all inaccessible to most borderland blind students. Borderland blind students are likely taught to rely on their residual vision instead of learning blindness skills, even when using the eyes becomes physically painful and inefficient—all because sight is the more socially valued method of acquiring information and because educational institutions are in denial about the needs of legally blind children. Oftentimes borderland blind students are judged on unequal standards compared to their sighted peers; they are not provided equal access to information and knowledge.

On the other hand, education and rehabilitation sometimes push borderland blind people all the way into the blindness side, where they are not allowed to use residual vision; instead, they are taught to "act" blind, such as being required to don blindfolds during orientation and mobility training. Despite its best intentions, education and rehabilitation do not adequately acknowledge distinctive aspects of the participants' borderland blindness.

The study's findings show that education and rehabilitation policies and procedures may be institutionally predetermined—cookie-cutter style, which limits options for blind people to make their own decisions about when to use their residual vision and when to acquire and use blindness skills. Despite federal guidelines that instruct counselors to involve clients to jointly develop individual education and rehabilitation plans, objectives, and goals, this critical step is sometimes sidestepped or altogether ignored. I could not count the number of times I've been requested to sign a rehabilitation plan—a legal, binding document—without having contributed anything to its creation or even been told I had a legal right to write my own plan. Other legally blind friends and colleagues have complained about similar treatment by their rehabilitation counselors.

In the classroom, teachers make assumptions about accommodations that might not be useful for every borderland blind person. For example, some of my graduate school professors insisted I use large print materials even though I could not comfortably or efficiently access them; this costs education time and money, which could have been better used had the teacher consulted me beforehand.

Considering the approximately 81 percent unemployment rate of blind people in the United States, it seems fair to conclude that the rehabilitation industry is severely impaired. Rehabilitation institutions do not always offer blind clients print materials in accessible formats, resulting in clients agreeing to plans and situations without being properly informed about their legal rights. Blindness rehabilitation agencies often make exclusive or discount contracts with access technology companies. Often the agencies' employees are trained in only a few technologies, resulting in limitations on their clients' choices. For example, because she is pursuing a career that is nontraditional for blind people, Catherine had an unsuccessful dispute with her local agency to get equipment that was better suited for her intended purpose, that is, creating and viewing art. This particular policy problem could be remedied through a direct payments system, which would allow clients to act as "consumers"—a term often used by the rehabilitation industry but seldom implemented in any real way.

Unfortunately, rehabilitation funding is inadequate, which forces it to make decisions about who most needs services; legally blind people fall to the bottom of the Order of Selection because they are not the most severely disabled—they are not blind enough. Funding for sheltered workshops and other outmoded programs that maintain an underclass of low-wage workers might be better used to create innovative policies that would support blind people's efforts to achieve economic independence and social equality. For blindness rehabilitation to serve clients truly effectively, it will have to discard outdated ocularcentric paradigms and pay attention to clients' aspirations. Rehabilitation would involve clients actively, positively, and sincerely in decisionmaking processes, and it would stop encouraging blind people to settle for low-income jobs. If it would encourage and support clients to achieve their highest potential, rehabilitation might be able to do so for itself as well.

In social situations, borderland blind people face different treatment than either the sighted or totally blind. The sighted world does not cope well with the ambiguities of borderland blindness. Both the literature and participants' stories exposed that, sometimes, strangers, acquaintances, and even friends and family accuse this population of fraudulence (faking blindness), which is an assault on their integrity and sense of honesty, and which often leaves the borderland blind feeling misunderstood. At times, some of the participants assume a sighted identity to avoid repetition of ill treatment they have endured in the past.

The data reveal that some borderland blind people make choices totally blind people cannot readily make, such as refraining from using a white cane in order to pass as sighted. While choosing to pass has its own social rewards, the data revealed that there are exquisite personal consequences for engaging in transgressive migrations. Unlike fully sighted people, who do not have to think about their majority status, or totally blind people, who by the nature of their impairments can not pretend to be sighted, the participants' stories told of spending a good deal of time thinking about and planning how they will present themselves in the everyday world as well as how they engaged with their own shifting internal identity formation.

This research has consistently shown the value of a detailed investigation of a specific impairment, situating it within a context of current educational, rehabilitation, and social practices. The stories revealed barriers, identities, and challenges uniquely experienced by people diagnosed and categorized as "legally blind." It is not yet known whether the concept of the "borderland" would be useful for examination of the lived experience of marginalization of people with other impairments, such as those who are hearing impaired but not totally deaf or those who use wheelchairs and also stand and walk. Nevertheless, the richness of the study's data analyzed within such a framework makes apparent that more research is needed on the appropriateness of theoretical concepts of the borderland and of postmodern ideas about ever-shifting identity formation among disabled people. Furthermore, public education efforts could help dispel stereotypes about blindness as a world of darkness, depression, helplessness, and despair. When family and friends do not labor under societal stereotypes, they are freer to ask their blind loved ones what they need, which might help all of them stay out of denial.

Acceptance of blindness by everyone involved is a key to successful integration of the borderland blind into both sighted and blind worlds. Comments such as, "I never think of you as blind" are not helpful to borderland blind people in pursuit of their own identity formation, because these remarks carry an underlying message that the borderland blind identity is a flawed identity. Moreover, such comments preclude blind people from asking for assistance because such asking disrupts the sighted person's concept of what blindness is supposed to "look like." Nevertheless, the fact is that blind people sometimes *need* sighted people's assistance. As Larry's daughter's annual gift of a bright yellow parka demonstrates, fore-thought, awareness, and common sense on the part of the sighted might help avoid awkward situations for borderland blind people. For instance, give your blind loved ones tactile, audio, or fragrant gifts instead of inaccessible print books, or better yet, ask them what they might like best. When observing a blind person moving toward an obstacle, simply say, "There's a curb right there," or "Can I help you?" Just because one blind person might have reacted neg-atively to an offer of assistance does not mean all blind people would do so. It is better to ask than to assume, but one does not have to take it personally if the offer is refused.

The next section addresses how the social models of disability in the United States and the UK may both be utilized in the same study to gain knowledge about various aspects of the lives of bor-derland blind people.

Building Bridges Across Social Models of Disability in the United States and UK

This research sought to facilitate a bridge between the traditional UK social model with its materialist bent and the US social model, which is largely housed in the humanities and emphasizes cultural constructs of disability as well as a minority model of civil rights advocacy. One need only peruse lists of references in both UK and US publications to discover that scholars are not, for the most part, making use of each other's work across the ocean, believing (per-haps stubbornly) that the two models have inherent unsolvable the-oretical conflicts.

Border Crossings in the Academy

Over the years, I immersed myself in disability studies literature from both the United States and UK and found innovative thinking and a great deal of merit within both materialist and cultural/minority models of disability, although, because of my background as a social democrat, I gravitate toward material analysis. Nonethe-less, after calling upon both models during this research, I was unable to find significant conflict between the two models, despite vociferous protestations to the contrary by protagonists on both sides of the pond. Materialist theory could not adequately address the everyday embodied experience of people with impairments and intricate matters of identity formation. Likewise, the cultural or minority model did not sufficiently analyze market forces at work against people disabled by a capitalist economy.

How It Worked

Based upon the review of existing literature about blindness as well as calling upon my education and training as a mental health professional interested in each participant's self-contemplative life, I organized the book along seven general themes: education, rehabilitation, work, social aspects, religion, embodiment, and identity. Education, rehabilitation, and work were natural categories for materialist analysis because education and rehabilitation—a form of education specifically designed for people with impairments—have as their end goals preparedness of their students or clients for entry or reentry into the labor force. Materialist analysis aptly developed the connections between quality of education, rehabilitation services, and opportunities for employment of legally blind people. I applied social constructionist theory (a sociological tool used by scholars in the United States, UK, and elsewhere) to explore social aspects concerning borderland blind people living in a world built by and for sighted people. The everyday embodied experience of the participants was best suited for phenomenological examination, a theoretical and methodological standpoint developed in the field of philosophy. Phenomenology enabled me to explain what the impairment of blindness is like from the inside looking out as well as how the body interacts with the environment. Additionally, phenomenology addressed my interest in what meaning borderland blind people make of their embodied experience. It must be said that the UK model strongly advocates for environmental access, and therefore does address embodiment in relation to the built environment, but it is not particularly interested in how the person introspectively experiences impairment.

I am aware that this study sometimes framed the UK and the US social models of disability as opposites in conflict with each other; nevertheless, the situation is more complex than can be addressed in one study and could, indeed, be a research topic in itself. Both models have admirable primary commonalities, such as passionate challenges to a hegemonic medical model and a commitment to the betterment of the lives of disabled people around the world. While it would be imprudent to conclude that a union between the UK and US models of disability was (or could be) achieved, this research demonstrated that it is possible to commingle both perspectives and that by doing so, it was able to present and analyze the participants' lived experience of impairment, disablement, and disability within a postmodern milieu. During the entire research process, I experienced no dissonance between the traditional UK model and the US concept of a social model of disability. Each model responds to different aspects of the human experience, and each model can develop analyses that do not clash with each other. For the purposes of this study, the two models acted synergistically quite successfully, which produced a deeper understanding of many life areas—to know what it is to live with an impairment; to know how society disables people with impairments and how disabled people respond to such treatment; to know how market forces are at work on disabled people and how these factors affect socioeconomic status; and finally, to know what meaning disabled people make of all these experiences.

Methodological Understandings

From the first seed of inspiration for this study, I knew I would use a qualitative life story approach to examine legal blindness as a marginalized, medically constructed category of impairment, disablement, and disability. This study fills a gap in existing literature in that, to the best of my knowledge, this approach has not been used before. Another original aspect is the use of the postmodern metaphor "borderland" to carve out a geographical space unique to legal blindness—a territory between sightedness and blindness where residents are pressed to migrate back and forth across its borders from situation to situation. In addition, these life stories contribute to the growing collection of disability history, but with an added postmodern analysis of the blindness experience.

Doing Emancipatory Research

As one means of redress for the historically unequal power relations between researchers and disabled "subjects," this study employed emancipatory disability research principles and objectives. Participants told their stories in their own words, they chose what was important for us to know about them, and they maintained control over their stories throughout the research and writing processes.

Emancipatory research was not easy, and it took much more time than a traditional model would use. It took a lot of time to conduct the interviews because the participants directed the rhythm and flow of the data collection process and of its content, which required me to adjust the design of the research as we went along. For instance, I had not set out to include religion in the data analysis, but then three of the participants revealed that religion is an important factor in how they perceive their blindness. Doing emancipatory research took more time than would working a paradigm that kept the power in the hands of the researcher because every phase of the research was collaborative. It took time to sort through the data with the participants, and we encountered access difficulties specific to this print-disabled population. Finally, it took a lot of time and coordination of schedules to engage with the participants in the last part of their involvement with the write-up. Nonetheless, the rewards far outweighed the complications because the participants' final edits and corrections of their portions of the study, and their enthusiastic agreement with the analyses provided validity to the study, and gave me confidence that the stories were presented exactly as the participants desired. All the participants reported that they better understand societal treatment of them as borderland blind people and respond in more self-empowering ways to their everyday contact with the sighted world. Moreover, because they read and edited the data chapters, they learned about the other participants and remarked that they were struck by the commonalities, which gave them a sense of not being alone in the borderland, an important knowledge since many blind people are not acquainted with other blind people.

The use of an emancipatory disability research model revealed that its collaborative nature drew the participants closer to the researcher than a traditional model of unequal power relations would have done; the more open the relationship is, the richer the data collected. Participants knew they had full control over their stories, and so felt at ease during the interviews, knowing that they would read and edit their stories near the conclusion of the study. They made only minor adjustments, mainly to clarify concrete facts such as numbers or timelines.

It is too soon to know if research such as this can actually influence social policy and research; yet this study showed that the participants felt self-empowered, which is worth pursuing as a research goal in itself. Overall, the model's benefits outweighed its complexities, and I would certainly attempt emancipatory research again. The data provided fertile contextual portrayals of the lived experience of borderland blindness, which was more easily accessed by employing this collaborative model of equal power relations and participants' sense of control over the destiny of their stories.

Insider Research

In the initial call for participation, I positioned myself as an insider. During the course of the research, each of the participants spontaneously self-disclosed they would not have responded to the posting if I had not self-identified as blind. Therefore, the first benefit of insider research was easier access to the population. The second benefit was evident as early as in the initial telephone calls, during which an almost instantaneous sense of camaraderie materialized. There was a certain familiarity between us based solely on our shared identity as legally blind. I knew to discuss transportation challenges such as which bus lines they lived near, whether they wanted me to travel to them or them to me. We shared very specific identifying information about where we would meet: "I'll meet you in front of the Broadway entrance to Starbuck's, not the side door, and I'll have my white cane with me. But if it's raining, I'll meet you inside right where you go to pick up your drink."

When we were together, the participants and I talked shop about white canes, transit barriers, magnifiers, and so on, which provided the type of bond between us that can be found only within community. We lived in the same neighborhood, that is, in the borderland.

At times during the interviews, I would relate an anecdote about an experience in common with what they had just described. I made decisions along the way about when and how much to share as I did not want to interrupt their flow and I also wanted to avoid coloring their opinions by injecting my own. It is incumbent upon insider researchers to be rigorously self-reflective so as not to lead participants where they might otherwise not go, or to become too emotionally involved. In summary, being an insider researcher opened doors to the participants that would have been closed to sighted researchers. Camaraderie helped establish trust, openness, and mutual empathy, which made for rich disclosure, hence important data.

Conclusion

This book offers up new knowledge about the lived experience of what it is like for people who do not entirely fit into either the land of the sighted or the land of the totally blind. The innovative commingling of UK and US social models demonstrated that there is genuine potential for researchers working within one paradigm or the other to enhance their work by utilizing aspects of both models. This book honors the common goals of both models—to help improve the social, economic, and cultural lives of disabled people everywhere, and it is my hope this might help make the way for a more unified disabled people's movement internationally.

Moreover, this book provides new knowledge about some advantages of using social constructivist, phenomenological, and postmodern identity theories in conjunction with each other to help make sense of embodied and sociological aspects of legal blindness. The overarching theme of the borderland provides a new framework for understanding the challenges, barriers, and richness of people traversing the lands of sightedness and blindness.

Additionally, the use of data not necessarily germane to the primary locus of inquiry added color and depth to the telling of the participants' stories in ways that would traditionally have been ignored by researchers. Hence, this creative scheme is a contribution to how research can be written up in original, interesting ways that engage the reader more intimately with research participants.

The inimitable findings in this life story research have both broad and explicit implications for disability researchers (medical and social model alike), ophthalmology, education, rehabilitation, policymaking, and blindness service provision because it offers innovative ways to learn about the experience of those labeled "legally blind." The data also reveal profound information for family, friends, and anyone who meets blind people anywhere, for it is in their stories that participants teach people how they wish to be treated.

I explicated from the outset that this qualitative research design did not seek a positivistic generalizability; for that reason, this book does not claim to represent the lived experience of all borderland blind people. Nonetheless, the study succeeded in the goal of finding commonalities between the participants' stories, which were noteworthy, especially their reports about interfacing with the rehabilitation industry, the workplace, and the general public. As part of the emancipatory process, the participants read (and approved) the data chapters, and we each reported being moved by the familiarity of each other's experiences. I hope that further research will be done, more stories will be told, more stories disseminated, and, most of all, that one day, borderland blind people will easily journey—at their own choosing—back and forth across the sightedness/blindness border and be accepted with full citizenship in both territories.

12

Epilogue

Near the end of preparing this book, I e-mailed the partici-pants to ask them if they would be willing to write something about what they have been doing since our last interviews. They all willingly agreed to do so, and each responded via e-mail. In keeping with the original methodology, I asked them only to tell me what they would like people to know about them now. So, without further comment or scholarly postanalysis, here is what we each wish to leave with the reader as we—Catherine, Larry, J. R., and I—continue our diverse journeys inside, outside, and along the margins of the lived experience of legal blindness.

Larry

The first thing I want to share is my guide dogs—both of them. Delmar was my first. He was my Zen warrior, my best friend, the holder of all my secrets, wishes, and fears. He was such a great person. He showed me what unconditional love was all about, my constant companion, my protector, my guardian angel in fur. He was a joy, and at times, a royal pain in the ass. He sat next to me whether we were traveling across country, or gambling in Vegas, or camping in alpine settings with snow 500 feet above us in August.

I never let him sleep with me in bed but I would sleep with him on the floor, and at times, welcome his additional warmth on cold nights in December. We had 42,000 air miles together, and when [he got cancer and] I had to put him down, I cried like a baby. He taught me about everything, and I am a better person for having him in my life. I will always be grateful to him, his puppy raiser, and GDFB [Guide Dogs for the Blind] for gifting him to me. He was a three-piece suit with wing tips.

Now Sly, my present guide, is well, kind of different. Sly is jeans, sandals, and a T-shirt. Whereas Del would avoid water, Sly will take me through it. If there is mud, Sly will find it. BUT, what a pal! Sly is teaching me things Del couldn't, and Del taught me things Sly can't. How blessed can a man be! I haven't had the opportunity to travel with Sly as I did with Del. Sly and I have only traveled about 20 to 30,000 miles together and we have places and miles to go before we hang it up.

But, to make the point—both my guides have given me the opportunity to truly experience life. Sometimes I call Sly, "Del"—he looks at me as if he understands and accepts. So, my guides have been an integral part of both my blindness and learning experience.

I feel everything in my life has been important—every situation, experience, person, tear, and joy has helped me get and be the person I am. There are people who have been influential, some not so positive but still important in the scheme of things. Each has, and still do help me know myself better. Hell, I am still very good friends with my "ex." When I go to New York she might be the one picking me up at the airport; still sends me recipes when I ask for them.

Yes I still love to cook; it is a creative outlet for me . . . nothing like a bowl of homemade soup on a cold rainy day in PDX [Portland].

The hardest thing about a relationship is the relationship. Being blind and an artist doesn't make it any easier, but I keep getting better at it. The thing all of these women have in common is good looks and intelligence.

I moved to Mexico with my "ex-lesbian" girlfriend. We went to study art, and get away from the rain and PDX. We lived there about eight months—mostly out of a suitcase—studying art, painting and drawing. I had five different residences, and it was difficult to keep track of which end was up. I was in my zone artistically. It was the best of times and the worst of times. I wouldn't trade a minute of it. I met my mentor in Mexico, and he taught me so much.

When I returned to the States I immediately opened a studio . . . very little studio. In fact, it was so small I had to step outside to turn my canvas around. But, it was my artistic womb. I was very prolific in that studio, producing well over fifty pieces of good art. I am now a regular exhibitor in a local gallery with work on shows most of the year.

I had another partner, another artist. I had to break off the relationship—I told her I had a mistress my easel and one mistress was all I could handle. I never pissed off another person as much as I did her, which is sad, that wasn't my intention. I have not seen her since. I met another lady who also modeled for my first sculpting. We are still good friends; we moved in together and had a great relationship. She was stronger than me, and decided to end our time together, but like they say, shit happens, and usually for the best. I had a little dry spell but came back with a vengeance.

You see, I feel at times more than others like a piece of driftwood. These are examples of my bouncing around, doing my thing, getting energy from the women that I'm cohabitating with—just doing my art, letting the river flow so to speak. Maybe I have been beating around the bush, so to speak, but everything I have mentioned is what I have felt and experienced.

I have been thinking how to explain this last piece. The only title I can give it that would come close to what I feel is "My Blindness, My Double-Edged Sword." There are times that I am angry about being blind—anger here is frustration. I don't get embarrassed spilling over a glass of water or wine. Shit happens. I feel comfortable when it happens in front of my blind friends—to them, it is a part of daily life. . . .

It bothers me that I can't see the soft skin of my grandchildren's faces, but only touch it. It annoys me when I can't find my credit card or an important piece of paper, although I know I put it in a specific place. It bothers me when I shop and items are not where they were the last time I was in the store. To a sighted person this might seem trivial, but it all impacts on my psyche, and not in an always nice or positive way. It upsets me when I can't distinguish between specific tones and hues of a color, especially when doing art.

I have always felt alienated—an alien life form in a human body. I think it has helped greatly with my blindness. My blindness has been, for all the frustration it causes, a blessing. I know and feel for certain, that my art could never have progressed to the point it is now if I did not lose my eyesight. My eyesight, not my vision—to me, they are different. It is my physical eyesight but it is my creative vision.

My present girlfriend, and hopefully, my girlfriend for a very, very long time to come, introduced me to her paddleboat team [dragon boat racing], "Blind Ambition." It is the first and longest running blind paddle team in the nation. When I first met my teammates, I knew without a doubt that I had come home. I was surrounded by other blind individuals that would not settle for being a victim. I finally found an arena where I could compete on a level playing field with sighted people. [The team works] to educate society that we are not victims, and have a place in the world, and not [in] some back room snapping boxes together.

There is more. Another joy of blindness is working hard at being significant. I volunteer and assist one-on-one other visually impaired people to become more independent. These joys don't come without paying painful dues. I believe in many things, and when it comes to disabilities, whether they be visual or physical, this is what I know. The old joke around my drug-induced friends is Rehab is for Quitters. HOW TRUE, but here I don't mean the visually impaired. I mean the people charged with helping the impaired. Now I don't mean all, but those that aren't quitters or more specifically, losers should do something about those that are.

Here is an example of what is totally wrong. I detest [disability] organizations that are self-serving, self-centered, and only care for their betterment, not [for] all disabilities. There are a number of organizations that pay lip service . . . and by their actions haven't given an ounce of thought to what is best; they take it upon themselves to decide what works. I just spoke about the problem and the solution, the quitters are behind the desk not the one sitting in front of the desk. I want to share with you an experience to have you better understand the cancer that exists. A few months ago I was asked to volunteer my time and teach visually impaired clients at an independent living organization. Of course, I agreed. After my phone calls never being returned by the director as well as e-mails . . . offering to volunteer my time, services, and even materials, if needed. Nothing was ever returned. When he was asked by a subordinate why he hadn't responded, his answer was, "I don't read e-mails." Well what the fuck does he do and get paid for? I can accept his inability to act if he was the only one being given a disservice, but he isn't. What he is doing is morally and ethically inappropriate—no, it's wrong, so very wrong. But, that's the situation. These people have the substance of a wet fart in a hot skillet. CHRIST! DOES IT PISS ME OFF!

I would like to mention how MW [current lover] has motivated new art, and how her presence in my life has made me resurrect a dream that started two years ago. MW loves my sculpting because she can touch and feel the line and texture. In a dark room she can barely make out some of my black and white prints. That is where I got the idea to do art on opaque plastic sheets running them through a printing press. I then put them on a light box. The most beautiful eight words I ever heard was when MW looked at my idea, and said, "I CAN SEE. I can see your art!" MW has been the most important driving force because I want her and other blind people to experience art. [She] has no concept of color and talking color theory is a chore, but we do it. She understands the color wheel not in terms of color, but in varying temperature and shades of gray. I finally found someone who appreciates space, solitude, a slow dance, the blues, a good glass of wine, and a smoke.

[Okay], I am leaving for studio in a little while, and must consume some dark roast and a smoke.

Catherine

Today, on the eve of my twenty-fifth birthday, I feel like it is a good day to respond to your question. I feel that I'm not only writing this to you, who have become a dear friend to me, but to my future self.

[Since our last interview] I view that time of my life as a time when anything and all things could and did happen. I had open relationships and I cared less about stability. Now my life is much different.

During the last of my undergraduate years, I became an adult with a clearer identity. It seems that I had to, as a teenager, undertake the role of an adult, but those school years allowed me to be a kid. I had a lot of fun, made a lot of mistakes, and I would not change any of my choices.

School became harder for me when my father's kidney disease caused all the veins in his body to calcify, which caused his heart to fail. The treatment was surgery. He spent twelve hours or more on the surgeon's table, and then a month nearly to the day in a coma inside the ICU.

I lived a few blocks away from the hospital. I was unstable in those days; "emotion" would not be an accurate description. It was the semester from hell. I spent every minute in that waiting room working on my homework. I was unable to do what I normally did with school, which was to do everything like every other student, and *that* [emphasis added] took me, it seemed, twice as long as every other student. I would not say that it was a particularly good thing that this happened to my family, but I would say it did give me the opportunity to learn something that I was too obstinate to learn any other way. Because of all the time I spent next to his bed and outside that ICU door, I was forced into the best choice I ever made while in school. I asked for [blindness access] accommodations.

At first, I was not so good at directing a reader and still a bit resistant to the idea. It took about a year to learn how to transform my use of a reader from something that was awfully awkward to use into a useful tool. I had a system by the end of it.

I have always been playing catch-up with everything in life and this was no different. I learned to get readings early, and send them by e-mail, if possible. I had a schedule of when a reader should email MP3s to me. I even developed a procedure for my readers for reading footnotes, page numbers, and words in other languages. This may seem small to the average blind person, and I know it is odd for the sighted because my friend thought it was odd, but this really was the beginning to a new self-accepting me.

By the time I had a grip on college it was just about over. At PNCA students are to develop a thesis during the senior year. I took as my advisor Ann Marie Oliver who helped me to see my full potential as an intellectual. My thesis was on the subject of devotional art and the contemporary art gallery. I painted a triptych depicting, what one could describe as, the nervous system of my faith.

After I gave my oral, my advisor said to me that I had made her prouder about a student than she had been for a long time. I will carry those words in my heart for the rest of my life. It really was an amazing day. I invited to attend my oral, Barbra, who was the saintly woman that taught me to read and write. As soon as I saw her face, I started to cry. At that moment, I knew how far I had come. I don't think I really acknowledged much, while in school were all the reasons to quit and give up until [after] it was over.

At one point not so long ago, I was a frightened angry child, learning to read far too late in life. I stood there and knew that I just gave one of the best thesis orals that I had ever seen. I am extremely proud of my accomplishments in regard to school. I graduated from PNCA with a Bachelor of Fine Arts.

The speaker, on behalf of the board of directors at my graduation, said something, which has stuck with me like a splinter wedged under a fingernail that is too short to pull out. His statement was to the effect of "I graduated in 1981 during the worst recession that Oregon had for a long time. And now, kids, you're going into something far worse! Better pull up your boot laces and hold on tight to those relationships that you have made here, because you are really going to need them." I can't say that I thought it was a nice thing to declare. However, the speaker was right. Only four or so months after I graduated the banks really started to fail. I grew up poor under Bush-economics and well, that was hard but nothing the likes of this. A lot of teaching jobs I have applied for I did not get—not because I was underqualified or not a good fit. It has been the case that the enrollment has been so low for non-accredited children and teen art programs. By the time interviews were finished there was no need for the position. It is more than a bum deal.

I trained to be an art teacher. And, with my eyes on Yale for graduate school, I need some work experience before attempting to apply. And more than that, just like everyone else, I need to have an income. Most people say jokingly that English degrees and art degrees are credentials to be a waiter, but in my case that is not an option because there are no jobs, and well, I do not know how to do that . . . and well, the mood lighting in most places would not work well for me.

I guess now it might be helpful to explain why my motivations have changed over the last year. No one really enters the adulthood until his or her parents have passed. I lost my best friend and my best ally in life—my father. Each day I feel emptiness without him. I would say to him that I was so impressed and delighted that he, by example, showed me how people change all throughout their lives, and that strength and determination are all you need to get the important things in life. I actually dedicated my thesis to him about seven months before he passed. There is a long shadow marking this year. But in the darkness, that aloneness, I was able to find myself. It is only when your parents are gone that you really feel all at once, a helpless baby and a responsible adult. I wrote in a journal a month after his death that I felt like a strong mountain standing alone, cold but proud, strong but vulnerable. Once I accepted that, then I really started to mourn.

I can say that in a year that has brought me the deepest pain, this year has brought the greatest joy. I know that after my father's death I will never see anything the same way again. . . .

I currently am in a loving, monogamous relationship with the most amazing man. He makes my world stop. After my father's death, I chose to put graduate school on hold and live life for a moment. My goal still is to go to school so that I can teach but moreso my goal is to build up my family, and to find a comfortable place to be. I know to savor love and life just that much more after my father's death. I think that in his death this is his last gift to me.

I still am a life drawing model [and] I do clothing modeling and photo from time to time. [One summer], I moonlighted as a pinup girl—but the kind you could show your mother, of course.

Currently, I work for three art schools on a routine basis as a model. The joy of being immortalized in student artwork aside, the job does not pay the bills, nor does it in its self further my goals of being a successful artist and an art teacher.

I have to admit it, that I had a little postgraduate, father passed away, I am turning twenty-five freak-out a few months ago. It was a long road of asking everyone I know about possible ways to stay here in Portland and get some work experience. Recently things started to look up. I am busier than I have ever been, but I feel like I know myself. I am proud of what I am doing. Twenty-five really would look a lot different to me if not for my two internships. I have an unpaid internship with PNCA as a Youth Program Volunteer Intern. I work under a teacher teaching teens to paint. I also have an internship with Disability Arts and Culture Project, interning under the arts director. I am totally unqualified to do the job, but I am learning a lot and I think for the most part, landing gracefully or okay on my feet. In truth, this job is the first job that I have had where I know what I am doing is helping people, and I know it is important. It forces me to own my identity, and it helps me to recognize the importance disability art is to the broader culture.

People with disability have to collaborate to survive and make art. Unlike mainstream art culture where usually collaboration is an "everyone has a say" kind of thing, but really I have not seen that so far. Mostly it seems that people help each other then get help back. Maybe a better word to describe this phenomenon is a collaborative-symbiosis.

I just want to say one thing about how the climate has changed for the visually impaired in the past few years. . . . There is no longer a state school for the blind. Although personally I did not fit in well with the institution during my one summer there, I still feel that it is important that there are places for children to grow in that kind of environment. The beginnings of disability culture started in those kinds of places. I felt the only revision I would have made to the school would have been a few more teachers with disabilities, and more advanced education programs to challenge the gifted, and, more importantly, stimulate the mediocre. It seemed to me that the closing of the school meant that students that would not want to be mainstreamed would not be able to grow up into productive adults.

Everything is stacked not in favor of people with disabilities. In no way was closing the school a help to the future of our society. I am a very driven person, but I know that I am discriminated against and at a disadvantage. This last year, the Oregon Commission for the Blind was almost shut down. I have had issues in the past working with them, but the bottom line is that I need them to get started in life. It seems to me that during this economic disaster, no one is really taking in consideration the long term cost of SSI and state health care that would have to be paid to every person with a disability for the duration of their lives compared to the short-term cost of rehabilitation, which creates jobs and produces productive happier citizens.

I feel like the government is full of idiots. I guess I really have grown up then. I think Dad said something about becoming more pessimistic as one grows older.

J. R.

I think that I have had more than my share of mishaps since we last talked. Thankfully, I have a membership in AMR (American Medical Response) so, ambulance rides are free. I fell down the stairs at Camera World breaking three ribs. [I] fell backwards off a curb, landing head first for four stitches. Then, I fell across the bathtub, landing head first on a soap dish; that got me three more stiches in my forehead. If that wasn't enough I had a stroke that affected my coordination and now I get around on my BMW (Blind Man's Walker).

Overall, things aren't so bad; the addition over the garage finally got finished. I even got the 2,500 outdoor Christmas lights up and working this year. Like I often have said, "Living on a fixed income isn't too bad as long as you get it fixed high enough."

I should bring you up to date on family additions. We lost Coco to cancer, so we went to the Humane Society and got Lucky. He is a very playful two-year-old gold and white male cat. He likes to sit on my computer and watch the birds and squirrels. Yes, we now have a Squirrel family. Billy, the biggest, Millie, the middle-sized one, [and] Willy and Nilly, the little ones.

Beth

The last time I went to the ophthalmologist he told me two new things. First, he said my eye disease started up again and it involved more of my retinas and it would continue to degenerate. I had noticed for a while the vision in my left eye seemed worse, and was convinced I needed a new prescription in my glasses. My eyesight had been stable for many years and it never dawned on me the problem was internal. That was a bit of a shock. The doctor went on to say they were beginning a new study next year, and asked me if I would like to participate. Without a second thought I said, "That would totally mess with my identity." He laughed. I was serious. He assured me this would not be a cure, and, if successful, my vision would not significantly improve—I would still be legally blind. But, it could slow down or stop the degeneration. I've thought about it now and then but haven't called the doctor back so guess that's my answer. I'm not that interested in anything resembling "cure."

I was to a city disability advisory committee. The majority of people on the committee are disabled. During the first few months, I noticed the city's website is out of compliance with disability law and is inaccessible to access tech users and some people with learning and motor impairments. When I raised the issue, most of the people didn't seem that interested but we formed a subcommittee. After much frustration with the committee and the city's computer technology department, our subcommittee drafted a letter to the mayor and city council. We believed they had never been apprised of the problem and we wanted to inform them and get their support. The larger committee not only balked at this, they actually disbanded our subcommittee and took all our power away. The three of us resigned from the city committee in protest. It's just so awful when disabled people in power don't care about anything but retaining their power.

During that time, one of my subcommittee members, Michael, and I became close friends and we considered each other our best advocacy partners. Shortly after we resigned from that committee, we were asked to participate in a joint city/county committee to address an issue we had raised for over a year—an emergency registry website for disabled people was inaccessible to access technology users and some people with cognitive or motor impairments. I'm not going to go into the whole story here. One afternoon Michael and I attended a meeting with three county representatives and a city rep who called into the meeting. The meeting was moderated and "ground rules" established, which to me, Michael and I were being silenced by those in power and authority. Michael and I were the only disabled advocates in the room. As the meeting progressed, it became more evident that promises to Michael were broken, and that we were involved in the same old useless song and dance. The county guy spoke. I responded. Then Michael began to speak, and partway into his first sentence, he said, "I don't feel good" stood up, took a few steps, collapsed against a chair onto the floor, and within a few moments, he died.

We lose so many disabled activists way too soon. There's such a huge personal cost to advocacy. We lost a brilliant, talented young man—42 years old. I miss him terribly, and not a day goes by that I don't remember something about Michael— his passion, humor, intelligence, gift for strategy, kindness, and artistic talent. I believe with all my heart that the system killed him. There are a few people I will neither forgive nor forget because of how they mistreated Michael. They disgust me.

Right around the same time, the blindness agency assigned me to a new counselor. I didn't know this until several months after she was assigned to me when she called to say she was closing my case out. But, I didn't have a job yet, which meant I hadn't reached my rehabilitation goal. During that conversation she said she disliked statistics about blind people's unemployment rates because they didn't take into account "all the blind people who just wanted to stay home." After that I refused to talk with her by phone, instead, I corresponded with her by e-mail so I'd have a record of everything she said. She wanted me to sign an IPE (Individualized Plan for Employment, which is a binding, legal document between a rehabilitation agency and a client) that I never agreed to or even participated in creating. When I refused, she said I was uncooperative and closed [my case] based on her contention. Two days before she was going to close the case, Michael died. I wrote to her, explained that my friend died right in front of me, and asked her please to wait until the next week so I could respond to her. Two days later, the notification letter closing my case arrived in the mail. She claimed I was too late with my request because my e-mail arrived twenty minutes past the close of her business day. I filed an appeal. I took all the e-mail exchanges with me to the appointment with my attorney and the agency manager. I didn't want anything from the agency except to be assigned to my old counselor, and to receive technical support in case I ran into computer problems. The agency knew full well I rely on my computer for writing, networking, advocacy efforts—pretty much everything. I won the appeal, and got reassigned to my old counselor. I never did need technical assistance, after all, but got some good advice from him about possible career choices.

Anyway, the manager of the agency started closing cases left and right, including all my blind friends who were clients. My counselor suggested I be closed as a successfully rehabilitated consultant but the manager refused and closed my case as "unsuccessful." She did this so that if or when I got a job, they would not have to assist me in any way. I would have to get in the back of the line and start a new application all over again, which means I would be subject to that Order of Selection— long wait. Of course, they—the agency people—they all have their jobs despite the fact they keep cutting service provision to blind people. Oh, yeah, every one of them I've met is sighted.

I joined a synagogue that is devoted to social action and social justice. Their activities are consistent with my political beliefs. I have made some nice friends there. But, it's been a tough couple of years. My first and closest friend here in town, Peggy, died. So did one of my childhood friends, and Michael, of course. And our rabbi drowned in Mexico. Recently, my sister died suddenly, and my stepbrother died exactly one week later. So, the older I get, the more I work on thinking not in terms of "good" or "bad" events. I learn the most from the so-called "bad" things. These are the character builders. I am not a very patient person, and I think blindness requires a lot of patience because it takes so much longer to do everything. Blindness is my teacher. I'm also not good at asking for help. This ongoing struggle really has nothing to do with my blindness. Like I said when I was a little girl, "I'll do it all my by self." I know it's better to ask for help when I need it but I still go through a lot of mental gymnastics before I finally ask. Blindness has taught me the more I ask for help, the more independent I become. Borderland blindness is full of paradox. All in all, it's like Leonard Cohen sings, "There is a crack, a crack in everything— that's how the light gets in" (1992).

Bibliography

Abberley, Paul. 1999. [Review of books by Tom Shakespeare]. *The Disability Reader: Social Science Perspectives* and *The Disability Studies Reader*. In *Disability and Society*, 14, no. 5, pp. 693–697.

Abrams, Judith Z. 1998. *Judaism and Disability: Portrayals in Ancient Texts from the Tanach Through the Bavli.* Washington, DC: Gallaudet University Press.

Adams, Rachel. 2001. *U.S.A.: Freaks and the American Cultural Imagination.* Chicago: University of Chicago Press.

Aguinaldo, Jeffrey P. 2004. Rethinking validity in qualitative research from a social constructionist perspective: From "Is this valid research? *to* what is this research valid for?" *The Qualitative Report*, 9, no. 1 (August 30, 2005), pp. 127–136. Retrieved on October 29, 2005, from http://www.nova.edu/ssss/QR/QR9-1/aguinaldo.pdf.

American Council of the Blind. 2004. *Randolph-Sheppard Vendors of America.* Retrieved December 19, 2004, from www.acb.org/rsva.

American Foundation for the Blind. 2001. Retrieved on December 20, 2005, from www.afb.org.

Anzaldúa, Gloria. 1987. *Borderlands/La Frontera: The New Mestiza.* San Francisco: Spinsters/Aunt Lute.

Arendt, Hannah. 1978. *The Life of the Mind.* New York: Harcourt Brace Jovanovich.

Artman, William N., and Hall, L. V. 1872. *Beauties and Achievements of the Blind.* Rochester, NY: B. R. Andrews Book and Job Printer.

Asch, Adrienne. 2004. Critical race theory, feminism, and disability: reflections on social justice and personal identity. In Bonnie G. Smith and Beth Hutchison, eds. *Gendering Disability.* New Brunswick, NJ: Rutgers University Press, pp. 9–44.

Ausubel, Nathan. 1948. *A Treasury of Jewish Folklore.* New York: Crown.

Baldwin, James. 1974. *If Beale Street Could Talk.* New York: Dell.

Barasch, Moshe. 2001. *Blindness: The History of a Mental Image in Western Thought.* New York: Routledge.

Barnes, Colin. 1992. Qualitative research: Valuable or irrelevant? *Disability, Handicap and Society,* 2, pp. 115–124.

———. 1996. Theories of disability and the origins of the oppression of disabled people in western society. In Len Barton, ed. *Disability and Society: Emerging Issues and Insights.* London: Longman.

———. 1999a. Disability studies: New or not so new directions? *Disability and Society,* 14, no. 4, pp. 577–580.

———. 1999b. Visual impairment and disability. In G. Hales, ed. *Beyond Disability: Towards an Enabling Society.* London: Sage Publications.

———. 2004. Reflections on doing emancipatory disability research. In John Swain, Sally French, Colin Barnes, and Carol Thomas, eds. *Disabling Barriers–Enabling Environments,* 2nd ed. London: Sage.

Barnes, Colin, and Geof Mercer, eds. 1997. *Doing Disability Research.* Leeds, UK: The Disability Press.

———. 2003. *Disability.* Cambridge, UK: Polity Press,

———. 2004. *Implementing the Social Model of Disability: Theory and Practice.* Leeds, UK: The Disability Press.

Barnes, Colin, Geof Mercer, and Tom Shakespeare. 1999. *Exploring Disability: A Sociological Introduction.* Malden, MA: Blackwell.

BBC News. 2007. Blind man robbed in street attack. July 13. Cited in Mark Sherry, 2010. *Disability Hate Crimes: Does Anyone Really Hate Disabled People?* Surrey, UK: Ashgate Publishing.

Bertaux, Daniel, ed. 1981. *Biography and Society: The Life History Approach in the Social Sciences.* Beverly Hills, CA: Sage.

Blind Citizens Australia. 2004. *Blind Citizens Australia.* Retrieved on April 19, 2004, from www.bca.org.au.

Bogdan, Robert. 1988. *Freak Show: Presenting Human Oddities for Amusement and Profit.* Chicago: University of Chicago Press.

Bothamley, Jennifer. 1993. *Dictionary of Theories.* Hants, UK: Gales Research International.

Bowen, B. B. 1847. *Blind Man's Offerings.* Boston: printed by author.

Bruner, J. 1986. *Actual Minds, Possible Worlds.* Cambridge, MA: Harvard University Press.

Bryant, M. Darrol. 1993. Religion and disability: Some notes on religious attitudes and views. In Mark Nagler, ed. *Perspectives on Disability.* Palo Alto, CA: Health Markets Research.

Buber, Martin. 1970. *I and Thou.* Translated by Walter Kaufman. New York: Charles Scribner's Sons.

Buchanan, William. 1992. *Running Toward the Light: A Blind Man's Incredible Triumph Over Defeat and Despair.* Leicester, UK: Ulverscroft Large Print.

Butler, Grant. 2010. Portland's Blind Cafe dinner in utter darkness offers perspective on world without sight. *Oregonian.* Retrieved on November 17, 2010, from http://www.oregonlive.com/dining/index.ssf/2010/08/portland_blind_cafes_dinner_in.html.

Cauvin, Henri E. 2010. In study, half of D.C. cab drivers pass by blind people with guide dogs. *The Washington Post.* September 1. Retrieved on September 1, 2010, from http://www.washingtonpost.com/wp-dyn/content/article/2010/09/01/AR2010090102344.html?nav=hc module tmv.

Center for Advanced Research in Phenomenology (CARP). 2006. What is phenomenology? March 16. Retrieved June 2007 from http://www.phenomenologycenter.org.

Cheadle, Barbara. 2005. Twelve tips for classroom teachers. *Future Reflections: The National Federation of the Blind Magazine for Parents and Teachers of Blind Children, Special Issue: Low Vision and Blindness,* 24, no. 3.

Cheung, Chan-Fai, Ivan Chvatik, Ion Copoeru, Lester Embree, Julia Iribarne, and Hans Rainer Sepp. 2003. *Essays in Celebration of the Founding of the Organization of Phenomenological Organizations.* Retrieved June 2008 from www.o-p-o.net [cited July 4, 2004].

Coffey, Amanda Jane, and Paul A. Atkinson. 1996. *Making Sense of Qualitative Data: Complementary Research Strategies.* New York: Sage.

Cohen, Leonard. 1992. Anthem. *The Future.* Sony Music Entertainment.

Cohler, B. J., and Cole, T. R. 1994. Studying older lives: Reciprocal acts of telling and listening. Paper presented at the meeting of the Society of Personology, Ann Arbor, MI.

Conference of Education Systems Chief Executive Officers. 2000. *The Stolen Generations Fact Sheet.* Australia Government. Retrieved January 13, 2006, from www.education.gov.au/goved/classroom/factsheets/52.html.

Corey, Gerald. 2000. *Theory and Practice of Counseling and Psychotherapy.* Pacific Grove, CA: Brooks/Cole.

Corker, Mairian. 2000. Review of *The Two-in-One: Walking with Smokie, Walking with Blindness,* by Rod Michalko. *Canadian Journal of Sociology Online,* September-October. Retrieved on October 17, 2001, from http://www.ualberta.ca/~cjscopy/reviews/twoinone.html.

Corker, Mairian, and Sally French, eds. 1999. *Disability Discourse.* Buckingham: Open University Press Buckingham.

Cowman, A. G. 1957. *The War Blind in American Social Structure.* New York: American Foundation for the Blind.

Criddle, Russell. 1953. *Love Is Not Blind.* New York: W. W. Norton.

Davis, F. James. 1991. Who is black? One nation's definition (originally entitled The nation's rule). In *Who is Black? One Nation's Definition.* University Park: Pennsylvania State University Press.

Davis, K. 1986. *Developing Our Own Definitions—Draft for Discussion.* London: British Council of Organisations of Disabled People.

de Beauvoir, Simone. 1948. *The Politics of Ambiguity.* New York: Philosophical Library.

D'Emilio, John. 2004. *Lost Prophet: The Life and Times of Bayard Rustin.* Chicago: The University of Chicago Press.

Denzin, Norman K. 1989. *Interpretive Biography.* Newbury Park, CA: Sage.

Derrida, Jacques. 1993. *Memoirs of the Blind: The Self-Portrait and Other Ruins.* Chicago: University of Chicago Press.

de Sena Martins, B. D. G. 2004. Blindness: Cultural and corporeal productions of a condition. Paper presented to Disability Studies Association Conference, Lancaster, England.

Diderot, Denis. 1966a. Letter on the blind for the use of those who see. In Lester Crocker, ed. *Selected Writings.* New York: Macmillan.

———. 1966b. Letter on the deaf and dumb for the use of those who hear and speak. In Lester Crocker, ed. *Selected Writings.* New York: Macmillan.

Duckitt, J. H. 1992. Psychology and prejudice: A historical analysis and integrative framework. *American Psychologist,* 47, pp. 1182–1193.

Dylan, Bob. 1965 (copyright renewed 1993). Subterranean homesick blues. *Bringing It All Back Home.* Special Rider Music.

———. 1979. Precious angel. *Slow Train Coming.* Special Rider Music.

Elkins, James. 1996. *The Object Stares Back.* New York: Simon & Schuster.

Embree, Lester. 1997. *What Is Phenomenology?* Center for Advanced Research in Phenomenology. Retrieved on January 13, 2006, from www.phenomenologycenter.org.

Europe Intelligence Wire. 2006. Blind man robbed in street attack. March 30.

Fanon, Frantz. 1967. *Black Skins, White Masks.* New York: Grove Press.

Filene, Benjamin. 2000. *Romancing the Folk: Public Memory and American Roots Music.* Chapel Hill, NC: University of North Carolina Press.

Finlay, Linda, and Brendan Gough. 2003. *Reflexivity: A Practical Guide for Researchers in Health and Social Sciences.* Oxford, UK: Blackwell Science.

Fittipaldi, Lisa. 2004. *A Brush with Darkness: Learning to Paint After Losing My Sight.* Kansas City, MO: Andrews McMeel.

Foucault, Michel. 1979. *Discipline and Punish: The Birth of the Prison.* Translated by A. Sheridan. New York: Vintage Books.

Frank, Arthur W. 1991. *At the Will of the Body: Reflections on Illness.* New York: Houghton Mifflin.

Frankenberg, Ruth. 1993. *White Women, Race Matters: The Social Construction of Whiteness.* Minneapolis: University of Minnesota Press.

Freedman, H., and Maurice Simon, eds. 1961. *Midrash Rabbah.* London: Soncino Press.

French, Sally. 1993. Can you see the rainbow? The roots of denial. In John Swain, Vic Finkelstein, Sally French, and Michael Oliver, eds. *Disabling Barriers, Enabling Environments.* London: Open University Press.

———. 1999. The wind gets in my way. In Mairian Corker and Sally French, eds. *Disability Discourse.* Buckingham, UK: Open University Press Buckingham.

————. 2001. *Disabled People and Employment: A Study of the Working Lives of Visually Impaired Physiotherapists.* Aldershot, UK: Ashgate.

————. 2002. Review of *Sight Unseen,* by Georgina Kleege. *Disability and Society,* 17, no. 7, pp. 857–859.

————. 2006. *An Oral History of the Education of Visually Impaired People: Telling Stories for Inclusive Futures.* Lampeter, Ceredigion, UK: Edwin Mellen Press.

Friel, Brian. 1994. *Molly Sweeney.* Loughcrew, County Meath, Ireland: Gallery Press.

Fry, Marilyn, ed. 1983. *Politic of Reality: Essays in Feminist Theory.* Freedom, CA: The Crossing Press.

Giddens, Anthony. 1991. *Modernity and Self-Identity.* Cambridge, UK: Polity Press.

Gilman, Sander L. 1986. *Jewish Self-Hatred: Anti-Semitism and the Hidden Language of Jews.* Baltimore, MD: The Johns Hopkins University Press.

————. 1991. *Inscribing the Other.* Lincoln: University of Nebraska Press.

Gitter, Elizabeth. 2001. *The Imprisoned Guest: Samuel Howe and Laura Bridgman, the Original Deaf-Blind Girl.* New York: Farrar, Straus, Giroux.

Goffman, Erving. 1961. *Asylums: Essays on the Social Situation of Mental Patients and Other Inmates.* New York: Anchor.

————. 1986. *Stigma: Notes on the Management of a Spoiled Identity.* Englewood Cliffs, NJ: Prentice-Hall.

Gonzales, R. C., J. L. Biever, and G. T. Fall Gardner. 1994. The multicultural perspective in therapy: A social constructionist approach. *Psychology,* 31, no. 3.

Goode, David. 1994. *A World Without Words: The Social Construction of Children Born Deaf and Blind.* Philadelphia: Temple University Press.

Goodley, Dan, Rebecca Lawthom, Peter Clough, and Michele Moore. 2004. *Researching Life Stories: Method, Theory, and Analyses in a Biographical Age.* London: Routledge Falmer.

Goodman, Lenn E. 1976. *Rambam: Readings in the Philosophy of Maimonides.* Translated with commentary. New York: Viking.

Gordon, Beth. 1994. Of human blindness: I wanted to learn. They taught me the dark side of charity. *Washington Post,* April 10, pp. C-1, C-4.

————. 1996. I am legally blind. In Karen E. Rosenblum and Toni-Michele C. Travis, eds. *The Meaning of Difference: American Constructions of Race, Sex and Gender, Social Class, and Sexual Orientation.* New York: McGraw-Hill.

Gregory, Stephen R. 2004. *Disability, Federal Survey Definition, Measurements, and Estimates.* American Association of Retired Persons. November 3. Retrieved from http://research/aarp.org/il/dd98_disability.pdf.

Hayhoe, Simon. 2008. *God, Money, and Politics: English Attitudes to Blindness and Touch, from the Enlightenment to Integration.* Charlotte, NC: Information Age Publishing.

Hertz, Rosanna, ed. 1997. *Reflexivity and Voice.* Thousand Oaks, CA: Sage.

Hollins, Mark. 1989. *Understanding Blindness: An Integrative Approach.* Hillsdale, NJ: Lawrence Erlbaum Associates.

Hughes, Bill, and Kevin Paterson. 1999. Disability studies and phenomenology: The carnal politic of everyday life. *Disability and Society*, 14, no. 5, pp. 597–610.

Hull, John. 1990. *Touching the Rock: An Experience of Blindness.* New York: Pantheon Books.

———. 2001a. *In the Beginning There Was Darkness: A Blind Person's Conversations with the Bible.* Harrisburg, PA: Trinity Press International.

———. 2001b. *On Sight and Insight.* Oxford: Oneworld Publications.

Husserl, Edmund. 1900–1901. *Logical Investigations: First Part. Prolegomena to Pure Logic.* 1st and 2nd ed. Edited by Elmar Holstein. Retrieved from http://www.husserl.net/books/title.php?opt=1&source=20.

Husson, Therese-Adele. 2001. *Reflections: The Life and Writings of a Young Blind Woman in Post-Revolutionary France.* Translated and with commentary by Catherine Kudlick and Zina Weygand. New York: New York University Press.

Ingstad, Benedicte, and Susan Reynolds Whyte, eds. 1995. *Disability and Culture.* Berkeley: University of California Press.

Javits-Wagner-O'Day Act. 1994. Pub.L. 103–355.

Jay, Martin. 1993. *Downcast Eyes: The Denigration of Vision in Twentieth-Century French Thought.* Berkeley: University of California Press.

Kirchner, Corinne. 2003. Yes, people with disabilities probably *are* in your sample: Methodological issues and strategies for including them effectively. Paper presented to American Association for Public Opinion Research, Nashville, TN, May 17.

Kleege, Georgina. 1999. *Sight Unseen.* New Haven: Yale University Press.

———. 2006. *Blind Rage: Letters to Helen Keller.* Washington, DC: Galludet University.

Knipfel, Jim, 1999. *Slackjaw.* New York: Penguin Putnam.

———. 2004. *Ruining It for Everybody.* New York: Jeremy P. Tarcher–Penguin.

Kocur, I., and S. Resnikoff. 2002. Blindness and visual impairment in Europe and their prevention. In *British Journal of Ophthalmology*, 86, no. 7 (July).

Koester, Frances J. 1976. *The Unseen Minority: A Social History of Blindness in the United States.* New York: David McKay.

Koosed, Jennifer L., and Darla Schumm. 2005. Out of the darkness: Examining the rhetoric of blindness in the Gospel of John. *Disability Studies Quarterly*, 25, no. 1 (Winter). Retrieved on December 25, 2005, from http://www.dsq-sds.org.

Kotre, John. 1995. *White Gloves: How We Create Ourselves Through Memory.* New York: The Free Press.

Krieger, Susan. 2005a. Losing my vision. *Qualitative Inquiry*, 11, no. 2 (April), pp. 1–7.

———. 2005b. *Things No Longer There: A Memoir of Losing Sight and Finding Vision.* Madison: University of Wisconsin Press.

Kubler-Ross, Elisabeth. 1970. *On Death and Dying.* New York: Macmillan.

Kudlick, Catherine J. 2001. The Outlook of *The Problem* and the problem with the *Outlook:* Two advocacy journals reinvent blind people in turn-of-the-century America. In Paul K. Longmore and Laurie Umansky, eds. *The New Disability History: American Perspectives.* New York: New York University Press.

———. 2005. The blind man's Harley: White canes and gender identity in America. *Signs: Journal of Women and Culture in Society*, 30, no. 2, pp. 1589–1606.

Kudlick, Catherine J., and Zina Weygand. 2001. *Reflections: The Life and Writings of a Young Blind Woman in Post-Revolutionary France.* New York: New York University Press.

Kugelmass, J. Alvin. 1951. *Louis Braille.* New York: Julian Messner.

Kuusisto, Stephen. 1998. *Planet of the Blind: A Memoir.* New York: G. K. Hall.

———. 2005. Blind Pew walks across Columbus, Ohio. *The Ragged Edge.* Retrieved on January 29, 2006, from http://www.raggededgemagazine.com/life/blindpew0604.html.

———. 2006. *Eavesdropping: A Life by Ear.* New York: W. W. Norton.

Lakoff, George, and Mark Johnson. 1980. *Metaphors We Live By.* Chicago: University of Chicago Press.

Lather, P. A. 1993. Fertile obsession—Validity after poststructuralism. *Sociological Quarterly*, 34, no. 4, pp. 673–693.

Levin, David M. 1993. *Modernity and the Hegemony of Vision.* Berkeley: University of California Press.

Lincoln, Y. S., and E. G. Guba. 1985. *Naturalistic Inquiry.* Beverly Hills, CA: Sage.

Linton, Simi. 1998. *Claiming Disability: Knowledge and Identity.* New York: New York University Press.

Lomawaima, K. Tsianina, 1995. Domesticity in the federal Indian schools: The power of authority over mind and body. In Jennifer Terry and Jacqueline Urla, eds. *Deviant Bodies.* Bloomington: Indiana University Press.

Lowenfeld, Berthold, ed. 1973. *The Visually Handicapped Child in School.* New York: John Day.

Lukoff, Irving Faber. 1960. A sociological appraisal of blindness. In Samuel Finestone, ed. *Social Casework and Blindness.* New York: American Foundation for the Blind.

Lunsford, Thomas R., and Brenda Rae Lunsford. 1995. Research forum—
The research sample, Part 1: Sampling. *Journal of Prosthetics and Orthotics*, 7, no. 3, pp. 105–112.

Mannheim, Karl. 1953. *Essays on Sociology and Social Psychology*. London: Routledge.

Marks, Deborah. 1999. *Disability: Controversial Debates and Psychosocial Issues*. London: Routledge.

Marshall, C., and G. B. Rossman. 1989. *Designing Qualitative Research*. Newbury Park, CA: Sage.

Mason, Micheline. 1990. Internalized oppression. In R. Reiser and M. Mason, eds. *Disability Equality in Education*. London: HEA.

McAdams, D. P. 1996. Personality, modernity, and the storied self: A contemporary framework for studying persons. *Psychological Inquiry*, 7, no. 4, pp. 295–321.

Mearns, Dave, and J. McLeod. 1984. A person-centered approach to research. In R. F. Levant and J. Shlien, eds. *Client-Centered Therapy and the Person-Centered Approach: New Directions in Theory, Research, and Practice*. New York: Praeger.

Mercer, Geof. 2004. From critique to practice: Emancipatory disability research. In Colin Barnes and Geof Mercer, eds. *Implementing the Social Model of Disability: Theory and Research*. Leeds, UK: The Disability Press.

Merleau-Ponty, Maurice. 1962. *The Phenomenology of Perception*. London: Routledge.

Michalko, Rod. 1998. *Mystery of the Eye and the Shadow of Blindness*. Toronto: University of Toronto Press.

———. 1999. *The Two in One: Walking with Smokie, Walking with Blindness*. Philadelphia: Temple University Press.

———. 2002. *The Difference That Disability Makes*. Philadelphia: Temple University Press.

Mitchell, David, and Sharon Snyder. 1997. *The Body and Physical Difference*. Ann Arbor: University of Michigan Press.

Mitchell, H. 1998. The insider researcher. In M. Allott and M. Robb, eds. *Understanding Health and Social Care: An Introductory Reader*. London: Sage.

Monbeck, Michael. 1973. *The Meaning of Blindness: Attitudes Toward Blindness and Blind People*. Bloomington: Indiana University Press.

Moore, Henrietta L. 1994. *A Passion for Difference*. Bloomington: Indiana University Press (in association with Polity Press, UK).

Moore, Michele, Sarah Beazley, and June Maelzer. 1998. *Researching Disability Issues*. Buckingham, UK: Open University Press.

Morris, Jenny. 1992. Personal and political: A feminist perspective on researching physical disability. *Disability, Handicap and Society*, 7, no. 2, pp. 157–166.

———. 1993. *Independent Lives? Community Care and Disabled People*. Basingstoke, UK: Macmillan.

Morrow, Susan L. 2005. Quality and trustworthiness in qualitative research. *Journal of Counseling Psychology*, 52, no. 2, pp. 250–260.

Moss, Glenda. 2004. Provisions of trustworthiness in critical narrative research: Bridging intersubjectivity and fidelity. *The Qualitative Report*, 9, no. 2 (June), pp. 359–374. Retrieved on February 2, 2006, from http://www.nova.edu/ssss/QR/QR9-2/moss.pdf.

Murphy, Robert. 1987. *The Body Silent.* London: Phoenix House.

Myers, Michael D. 1997. Qualitative research in information systems. *MIS Quarterly*, 21, no. 2, pp. 241–242. (*MISQ Discovery*, archival version). Retrieved on June 26, 2006, from http://www.misq.org/discovery/MISQDisworld.

Naples, Nancy A. 1997. A feminist revisiting of the insider/outsider debate: The "outsider phenomenon" in rural Iowa. In Rosanna Hertz, ed. *Reflexivity & Voice.* Thousand Oaks, CA: Sage. Originally published in *Qualitative Sociology*, vol. 19, no. 1 (1996).

National Eye Institute (NEI). 2001. *PAB 2001.* National Institute of Health. Retrieved on January 14, 2006, from www.nih.gov.

Norden, Martin F. 1994. *The Cinema of Isolation: A History of Physical Disability in the Movies.* New Brunswick, NJ: Rutgers University Press.

Oakley, Ann. 2000. *Experiments in Knowing: Gender and Method in the Social Sciences.* Cambridge: Polity.

Ochberg, R. L. 1994. Life stories and storied lives. In A. Lieblich and R. Josselson, eds. *Exploring Identity and Gender: The Narrative Study of Lives.* Thousand Oaks, CA: Sage.

Oliver, Michael. 1987. Re-defining disability: Some implications for research. *Research, Policy and Planning*, 5 (Spring).

———. 1990. *The Politics of Disablement.* London: Macmillan.

———. 1992. Changing the social relations of research production? *Disability, Handicap and Society*, 7, no. 2, pp. 101–114.

———. 1996a. A sociology of disability or a disablist sociology. In Len Barton, ed. *Disability and Society: Emerging Issues and Insights.* London: Harrow Longman.

———. 1996b. *Understanding Disability: From Theory to Practice.* New York: St. Martin's Press.

———. 2002. Emancipatory research: A methodology for social transformation. Unpublished paper presented to National Disability Authority Conference, Dublin, December 3. Retrieved on February 17, 2004, from http://www.leeds.ac.uk/disability-studies/archiveuk/index.html.

———. 2004. The social model in action: If I had a hammer. In Colin Barnes and Geof Mercer, eds. *Implementing the Social Model of Disability: Theory and Practice.* Leeds, UK: The Disability Press.

———. 2009. *Understanding Disability: From Theory to Practice.* Basingstoke, UK: Palgrave Macmillan.

Omansky Gordon, Beth. 2003. I am legally blind. In Karen E. Rosenblum and Toni-Michelle C. Travis, eds. *The Meaning of Difference: American*

Constructions of Race, Sex and Gender, Social Class, and Sexual Orientation. New York: McGraw-Hill.

Omansky Gordon, Beth, and Michael Oliver. 2003. How long must we wait? Unmet promises of disability law and policy. In Karen Rosenblum and Toni-Michelle C. Travis, eds. *The Meaning of Difference: American Constructions of Race, Sex and Gender, Social Class, and Sexual Orientation.* New York: McGraw-Hill.

———. 2009. Unmet promises of disability law and policy. In *Understanding Disability: From Theory to Practice.* Basingstoke, UK: Palgrave Macmillan.

Omansky Gordon, Beth, and Karen E. Rosenblum. 2001. Bringing disability into the sociological frame: A comparison of disability with race, sex, and sexual orientation statuses. *Disability and Society,* 16, no. 12 (January), pp. 5–19.

Oplatka, Izhar. 2001. Building a typology of self-renewal: Reflection upon life story research. *The Qualitative Report,* 6, no. 4 (December). Retrieved on June 13, 2005, from http://www.nova.edu/ssss/QR/QR6-4/oplatka.html.

Oyserman, Daphna, and Janet Swim. 2001. Stigma: An insider's view. *Journal of Social Issues,* 57, no. 1 (Spring), p. 1–14. Retrieved on October 22, 2004, from http://www.findarticles.com/p/articles/mi_m0341/is_1_57/ai_75140958#.

Pickett, J. P., ed. 2002. *The American Heritage Dictionary of the English Language,* 4th ed. New York: Houghton Mifflin.

Pierce, Barbara. 2005. Low vision, blindness, and federation philosophy. In *Future Reflections: The National Federation of the Blind Magazine for Parents and Teachers of Blind Children, Special Issue: Low Vision and Blindness,* 24, no. 3.

Pobursky, Adam. 2005. Reflections on the history of white cane safety. *The Braille Forum,* 44, no. 3, pp. 18–21.

Potter, J., and Wetherell, M. 1987. *Discourse and Social Psychology: Beyond Attitudes and Behaviour.* London: Sage.

Priestley, Mark. 1997. Whose research? A personal audit. In Colin Barnes and Geof Mercer, eds. *Doing Disability Research.* Leeds, UK: The Disability Press.

Riddell, Sheila, and Nick Watson. 2003. *Disability, Culture, and Identity.* Edinborough Gate, Scotland: Pearson Education.

Roberts, Ed V. 1989. A history of the independent living movement: A founder's perspective. In Bruce W. Heller, Louis M. Flohr, and Leonard S. Zegans, eds. *Psychosocial Interventions with Physically Disabled Persons.* New Brunswick, NJ: Rutgers University Press.

Roget's New Millennium Thesaurus, 1st ed. 2006. Lexico Publishing Group. Retrieved March 3, 2006, from http://www.thesaurus.reference.com.

Rosenau, Pauline Marie. 1992. *Post-modernism and the Social Sciences: Insights, Inroads, and Intrusions.* Princeton, NJ: Princeton University Press.

Rosenblum, Karen, and Toni-Michele C. Travis, eds. 1996. *The Meaning of Difference: American Constructions of Race, Sex and Gender, Social Class, and Sexual Orientation.* New York: McGraw-Hill.

———. 2003. *The Meaning of Difference: American Constructions of Race, Sex and Gender, Social Class, and Sexual Orientation.* New York: McGraw-Hill.

Ross, Ishbel. 1951. *Journey into Light.* New York: Appleton-Century-Crofts.

Royal National Institute for the Blind. 2003. *Royal National Institute for the Blind.* Retrieved on December 12, 2005, from www.rnib.org.

Rubin, Allen, and Earl R. Babbie. 2000. *Research Methods for Social Work,* 4th ed. Pacific Grove, CA: Brookes.

Rubin, Stanford E., and Richard T. Roessler. 1995 (1987). *Foundations of the Vocational Rehabilitation Process.* Austin, TX: Pro-Ed.

Runyan, Marla (with Sally Jenkins). 2001. *No Finish Line: My Life as I See It.* New York: Berkley Books.

Scheurich, James J. 1996. The masks of validity: A deconstructive investigation. In *Qualitative Studies in Education,* 9, no. 1, pp. 46–60.

Schweik, Susan M. 2009. *The Ugly Laws: Disability in Public.* New York: New York University Press.

Scott, Robert A. 1969. *The Making of Blind Men: A Study of Adult Socialization.* New York: Russell Sage Foundation.

Shakespeare, Tom. 1994. Cultural representation of disabled people: Dustbins for disavowal? *Disability and Society,* 9, no. 3, pp. 283–301.

———, ed. 1998. *The Disability Reader: Social Science Perspectives.* London: Castle.

Shapiro, Joseph. 1993. *No Pity: People with Disabilities Forging a New Civil Rights Movement.* New York: New York Times Books.

Sherry, Mark. 2002. If I only had a brain. Unpublished doctoral thesis, University of Queensland.

———. 2010. *Disability Hate Crimes.* Farnham, Surrey, UK: Ashgate.

Siller, Jerome, Linda Ferguson, Donald H. Vann, and Bert Holland. 1967. Structure of attitudes toward the physically disabled: Disability factor scales—amputation, blindness, cosmetic conditions. In *Studies in Reactions to Disability,* no. 12. New York: New York University School of Education.

Stone, Emma, and Mark Priestley. 1996. Parasites, pawns, and partners: Disability research and the role of non-disabled researchers. *British Journal of Sociology,* 47, no. 4, pp. 699–716.

Taeckens, Geri. 2007. *Blind Man's Bluff.* Sault Ste. Marie, MI: Accessibilities.

Thomas, Carol. 1999. *Female Forms: Experiencing and Understanding Disability.* Buckingham, UK: Open University Press.

Titchkosky, Tanya. 2003. *Disability, Self, and Society.* Toronto: University of Toronto Press.

Titon, Jeff Todd. 1980. The life story. *Journal of American Folklore*, 93, pp. 276–292.

Tomm, Karl. 1987. Interventive interviewing: Part II, Reflexive questioning as a means to enable self-healing. *Family Process*, 26, pp. 167–184.

Toombs, S. Kay. 1995. The lived experience of disability. *Human Studies*, 18, pp. 9–23.

UK. 1995. *Disability Discrimination Act*.

UPIAS. 1976. *Fundamental Principles of Disability*. London: Union of the Physically Impaired Against Segregation.

US Bureau of the Census. 1996. *National Health Interview Survey on Disability 1994–95*. Washington, DC: US Bureau of the Census.

———. 2004. *Current Population Survey 2004 Annual Social and Economic Supplement*. Retrieved on March 13, 2006, from http://www.census .gov/hhes/poverty/threshld/thresh03.html.

US Department of Education. 1995. *OSEP Memorandum 96-4*. November 3. Retrieved on December 4, 2005, from http://www2.ed.gov/ legislation/FedRegister/other/2000-2/060800a.html.

US Federal Government. 1936. *Randolph-Sheppard Act*. Pub.L.74-732 As Amended By Pub. L. 83-565, and Pub. L. 93-516 (20 U.S.C. 107 et seq.).

US Federal Government. 1938. *Wagner-O'Day Act*, 25 June, 1938, c. 697, § 5, as added 23 June, 1971, Pub.L. 92-28, § 1, 85 Stat. 81, and amended 25 July, 1974, Pub.L. 93-358, § 1(3), 88 Stat. 393; 21 April, 1976, Pub.L. 94-273, § 3(22), 90 Stat. 377.).

US Federal Government. 1977 *Code of Federal Regulations 34*, CFR PART 107a., 1977.

US Federal Government. 1990. *The Americans with Disabilities Act*. US Pub. L. 1990, 101-36.

US Federal Government. 2005. Testimony of James Gashel before the US Senate Hearing on issues related to oversight of federal programs for persons with disabilities, including the *Randolph-Sheppard* and *Javits-Wagner-O'Day* programs. Washington, DC.

US National Eye Institute. 2001. *PBA*. Retrieved on January 6, 2006, from www.nih.gov.

Vance, Marguerite. 1956. *Windows for Rosemary*. New York: E. P. Dutton.

Van Manen, Max. 1990. *Researching Lived Experience: Human Science for an Action Sensitive Pedagogy*. London, Ontario, Canada: University of Western Ontario.

Vickers, Margaret H. 2001. *Work and Unseen Chronic Illness: Silent Voices*. London: Routledge.

Virginia Department for the Blind and Visually Impaired. 2005. Brochure on Virginia Rehabilitation Center for the Blind. Retrieved on November 26, 2005, from www.vdbvi.org.

Walker, Betsy. 1997–2002. *V.I. Guide*. Retrieved on January 20, 2006, from http://www.viguide.com/vsnschools.html.

Wallace, J. B. 1994. Life stories. In J. F. Gubrium and A. Jankar, eds. *Qualitative Methods in Aging Research*. Thousand Oaks, CA: Sage.

Ward, Linda, and Margaret Flynn. 1994. What matters most: Disability, research, and empowerment. In Marcia Rioux and Michael Bach, eds. *Disability Is Not Measles: New Research Paradigms in Disability*. North York, Ontario, Canada: L'Institut Roehr Institute.

Watson, Nick. 2004. The dialectics of disability: A social model for the 21st century. In Colin Barnes and Geof Mercer, eds. *Implementing the Social Model of Disability: Theory and Research*. Leeds, UK: The Disability Press.

Weihemeyer, Eric. 2001. *Touch the Top of the World: A Blind Man's Journey to Climb Higher Than the Eye Can See*. New York: Dutton Adult.

White, Michael, and David Epston. 1990. *Narrative Means to Therapeutic Ends*. New York: W. W. Norton.

White, Patrick. 2003. Sex education; Or, how the blind became heterosexual. *Journal of Lesbian and Gay Studies*, 9, pp. 1–2.

Whiteman, Martin. 1960. A psychological appraisal of blindness. In Samuel Finestone, ed. *Social Casework and Blindness*. New York: American Foundation for the Blind.

Williams, James M. 1998. Lowering the handicaps for golfers with disabilities. *Business Week Online*. August 24. Retrieved on August 9, 2005, from http://www.businessweek.com.

Wilson, James. 1895. *Biography of the Blind: Including the Lives of All Who Have Distinguished Themselves as Poets, Philosophers, Artists, etc.* Washington, DC: Friends of Libraries for Blind and Physically Handicapped Individuals in North America, and the National Library Service for the Blind and Physically Handicapped, The Library of Congress.

World Bank. 1994. *Overcoming Vitamin and Mineral Malnutrition in Developing Countries*. Retrieved on January 4, 2011, from http://web.world bank.org.

World Health Organization (WHO). 2004. *International Statistical Classification of Diseases, and Related Health Problems (ICD)*. Retrieved March 14, 2004, from www.who.int/whosis/icd10.

Yin, R. K. 2002. *Case Study Research, Design, and Methods*, 3rd ed. Newbury Park, CA: Sage.

Zuckerman, Diana M. 2004. *Blind Adults in America: Their Lives and Challenges*. Washington, DC: National Center for Policy Research for Women & Families.

Index

About the Book

A person may be legally blind, yet not "blind enough" to qualify for social services. Beth Omansky explores the lives of people with legal blindness to show how society responds to those who don't fit neatly into the disabled/nondisabled binary. Probing the experiences of education, rehabilitation, and work, as well as the more intimate spheres of religion, family, and romantic relationships, her frank and theoretically sophisticated portrait of the legally blind experience offers an original insight into our understanding of the social construction of disability.

Beth Omansky is an independent scholar and activist in Portland, Oregon.